RAVENSBRÜCK

Germaine Tillion

RAVENSBRÜCK

Translated by Gerald Satterwhite

ANCHOR BOOKS

Anchor Press/Doubleday · Garden City, New York

1975

Ravensbrück was originally published
by Éditions du Seuil, Paris, France.
Copyright © Éditions du Seuil, 1973

Anchor Books Edition

Library of Congress Cataloging in Publication Data

Tillion, Germaine.
  Ravensbrück.

  Includes bibliographical references and index.
  1. Ravensbrück (Concentration camp) 2. World
War, 1939–1945–Prisoners and prisons, German.
D805.G3T5413   940.54'72'430943155
ISBN 0-385-00927-5
Library of Congress Catalog Card Number 74-25135

TRANSLATION COPYRIGHT © 1975 BY
DOUBLEDAY & COMPANY, INC.
ALL RIGHTS RESERVED
PRINTED IN THE UNITED STATES OF AMERICA
FIRST EDITION

CONTENTS

INTRODUCTION

We are almost thirty years past the end of World War II; the eyewitnesses have not completely disappeared, but they are becoming fewer and fewer, while for some years the tribe of historians, memorialists, and collectors has increased.

Finding myself somewhere in the middle of these two trends, I have attempted to evaluate what each has brought to the surface—or let slide into obscurity. And there have been mistakes on both sides.

Those who were eyewitnesses often took considerable risks to save from almost certain destruction the bits of information they had compiled from personal experience; in many cases, the more authentic the information, the less complete it was. As for the secondhand, second-person accounts, they demand of their authors a great deal of time, patience, and ability. Simply to avoid getting lost in the deadly confusion of history they have had to decipher innumerable and incredibly tedious official documents—some of the most important of which had been falsified. First of all, these documents had to be found, but there were special problems in the case of the Ravensbrück concentration camp: the memoranda, the lists, the orders, the letters—most had disappeared. Were they intentionally destroyed? It is quite possible.

Of those that do exist, the errors in some and the vagueness of others have an inevitable result: the destruction of the historical certainty of what was all too real and cruel to those who knew it. But this destruction is a premise I cannot accept.

This book, then, is devoted basically to the Ravensbrück concentration camp (located 20–30 miles north of Berlin), but it is also a refraction of an entire body of recent history into three distinct levels.

The first part is an eyewitness account, the writing of which, going back to 1945, was based on notes taken secretly beginning in 1942.[1] The second part, written between 1947 and 1953, might be classified as a historical study, as it calls upon historical documents—evaluated and closely scrutinized—interspersed with the recollections of living witnesses and the notes they had taken.[2] In a third part, recently written and heretofore unpublished, I have sought to point to some questions which even today remain unanswered—and they are very serious questions indeed.

The first part has both the virtues and the faults involved in all eyewitness accounts. Concerning the Ravensbrück camp as a whole, I wrote in 1945 what I had seen and learned at Ravensbrück itself. This study was then entitled "In Search of the Truth," a fitting title, since it was indeed this anguished quest for the truth about Ravensbrück, which from the very first gave me the courage to make all the necessary inquiries despite obvious risks and hardship and then, immediately after my release, to record all I knew.

In the first part will be found only the information that could be brought together by the captives; even so, one will see that it is extensive and important. On the whole—and often even down to the details—what has slowly become known over the past twenty-seven years has served only to confirm the accuracy of what we knew then. On certain points, however, I have come to believe that I was in error; these have

[1] Published in 1946, along with other shorter accounts, under the general title *Ravensbrück* in a collection edited by Albert Béguin, "La Baconnière." Out of print.

[2] Published in the *Revue d'histoire de la Deuxième Guerre Mondiale* under the title "Réflexions sur l'étude de la déportation," nos. 15–16 (July–September 1954), pp. 3–38. This issue has long since become unavailable.

been corrected in passing, and I have noted the date of the correction.

The things which affected me most deeply and directly were not in this account, perhaps because I didn't have the strength to speak of them. My only excuse is that I wanted to show over-all conditions and the fate of everyone, and that I believed I could do so in almost abstract terms.

I realize, however, the inherent incompleteness and obscurity of an eyewitness account which does not include the personal interpretations about the witness. I am also aware of the interdependence of our thoughts, actions, and the events of one's life with the private vision of the world one always maintains. Even today I find these memories overwhelming, and I will speak of them later in this introduction.

The second part, "One Convoy of Frenchwomen," was written between 1947 and 1953. It is not a personal eyewitness account but an attempt to use, simultaneously and comparatively, both eyewitness accounts and official documents and to evaluate the one with the other. Unlike the first part, this section does not address the entire monstrous world of Ravensbrück but isolates one of its fragments: a single convoy of French prisoners who were known in camp argot as the *twenty-seven thousands* because their registration numbers fell between 27,300 and 27,988.

This study is based on a number of documents drawn up by the SS for their own use, and particularly on an original list which was hidden away during the period of wholesale destruction preceding the liberation of the camp. The Czech prisoner who kept it safe eventually gave it to me. As an official document, it possesses a degree of accuracy a personal account could not claim. Not only could I then compare the information in it with that in others of similar origin, but I examined it line by line with the witnesses involved—those who survived. I was given additional clarification by the prisoner-secretaries who, under SS supervision, kept such lists up to date.

In this second part I have also hoped to demonstrate the general absurdity in basing judgments on "statistical averages," an unfortunate tendency which today so dangerously promotes bureaucratic "massification," an overreliance on computers, generalized studies of the "masses," and public opinion polls—all techniques which encourage laziness of mind and spirit and which have consequently proved to be totally inefficient for forecasting.

I began writing the third part a few years ago when I realized that some aspects of what I considered to be basic truths about this period of history might be subject to dispute, and I decided to do what I could to support these conclusions. I then undertook a new review and examination of all the documents at my disposal, and to the first two parts I have added the details, explanations, and even refutations which seemed necessary: these are interpolated into the text, but indented on the page to indicate their date (1972). I have also done away with a stylistic convention whose pedantic archaism I have never cared for, and whose ambiguity I have disliked even more: the "royal We." Who are "We?" "We French, we historians, we prisoners, we transient passengers in an uncertain world?" What can one really know about this indefinite plural?

To me, there are two approaches to history that one can truly rely upon: the witness can say "I was there; I saw something happen," or even "Someone told me this story." The historian has a right to say "I believe this to be true for these reasons." These are reliable enough; others are questionable.

Among the three parts there are, inevitably, similarities, even repetitions, simply because the same events are being considered. But they are observed on three distinct levels: a very individual vision—personal, intense, total, but vague; then, a rediscovery through myriad and amorphous notes and documents, often stripped of all context but accurate nonetheless; finally, a re-examination in the light of the many questions that have remained unanswered. It would be best, of course, to avoid unnecessary repetitions; in any case, I have reduced them to a minimum.

In order to avoid disturbing the continuity of the central narrative about Ravensbrück I have waited until the end of the book to recount the methods used to carry out the inquiry into the convoy of the "twenty-seven thousands." Also included as appendices are several other accounts which I hope might serve as a point of departure for a wider examination of the Nazi concentration-camp system and the incredible accommodation it managed to maintain between practical, cleverly contrived mutual accords and some very fundamental disparities among the operations of various camps. These accounts deal especially with the measures taken for the "final" extermination in three camps in the same "category" as Ravensbrück: Buchenwald, Mauthausen, and Dachau.

On the subject of Buchenwald, I have summarized the excellent study by Eugen Kogon and received the kind assistance of Professor Balachowsky (one of the Resistance leaders in the camp) in the completion of an account of the last days there. On Mauthausen, Serge Choumoff, an engineer and deportee to that camp who had compiled a documentation[3] of events there, authorized me to reprint his letter to the newspaper le Monde on extermination and the gas chambers. As for Dachau, there is only a summary of a report prepared in 1945 for the American Army by a French chemist, Captain Fribourg, who was kind enough to send me the report and review the summary I prepared. (This unpublished report concerns a gas chamber which had just been installed. Captain Fribourg describes it in great detail.)

These brief glimpses are meant to complement another proposition expounded elsewhere: according to Olga Wormser-Migot, these gas chambers were purely mythical. I must say here that such an assertion, in a historical work, astounded me.[4]

I also thought it fitting to include as an appendix an account of certain aspects of the Algerian war, in which legionnaires who had been in the SS took part. This addendum

[3] Serge Choumoff, Les chambres à gaz de Mauthausen, Amicale de Mauthausen, 1972.

[4] Olga Wormser-Migot, Le Système concentrationnaire nazi (Presses universitaires de France, 1968), pp. 12, 13, 541.

might seem a bit strange, but I think others might agree that it has its place.

All the details I could gather are condensed within this triple perspective, and in all cases I sought to determine their origin and the sources of information used by those who supplied them. I deeply regret that I was not always successful, since such background information seems quite necessary to determine the degree of accuracy of the data I have used.

The data on prisoners, in fact, sometimes originated from a furtive observation by one prisoner of another group being taken from one place to another, or being treated in a certain way. But at least these actions were *seen*—and recorded immediately. These figures might also be simple approximations: certain prisoners or SS, for example, might *know* that 150 prisoners were destined for the gas chamber, and might *believe* that the gas chamber was functioning on certain days; whenever asked about the number of exterminations, they might give a figure which seemed plausible, but which they had not verified. Other figures appear in my documents: the so-called "Mittwerda" lists, ostensibly related to a camp by that name (fictional) but actually a list of women sent to the gas chambers. But even if we had all of these lists (and most of them were never recovered), we would still be unsure that their figures corresponded with the actual number of exterminations, since we can never really know whether the idea of using a special list based on the name of a mythical prison camp to account for those killed by gas came from the commandant of Ravensbrück before this type of killing was begun or while it was taking place.

In following this reconstruction of one fragment of the German concentration-camp system (Ravensbrück)—then of a fragment of this fragment (a transport of Frenchwomen)—it should always be kept in mind that, whatever the quality of the information collected, there could never be a perfect reconstruction of what actually happened, but only a compilation of what one learned—bit by bit—of the real events.

At Ravensbrück itself I had tried to keep a running account of the workings of that monstrous machine, to understand how it fit together, but for a while I only noted certain landmark events. Then, when I began to think I had little chance of survival, I began taking more explicit notes which, after my liberation, I did my best to complete and verify.

I also gathered data on the identities of the deported Frenchwomen, which I completed after my return home. The information was machine-processed by the National Institute of Statistics and Economic Studies—an excellent job for which I must again express my gratitude. Beginning in 1947 I submitted copies of this information to the registry section of the Veterans Ministry, where the lists, in addition to their usefulness to the ministry and various ex-prisoners' associations, served as a basis for the necessary verification of other information: there were, in fact, those who falsely called themselves deportees, as well as true deportees who later gave false testimony.[5]

As early as 1945 I had begun a chronological census of deported Frenchwomen: the trains from France and lists of those in the various work Kommandos which left Ravensbrück. When I suspended my research into German war crimes in 1954, I turned this part of my documentation over to my friends in two organizations—ADIR: the Association of Former Resistance Prisoners and Deportees, and the Ravensbrück Amicale; they completed the research and used it in a jointly produced book, les Françaises à Ravensbrück (Gallimard, 1965, pp. 339–44).

The invasion of France in 1940, the dangers it brought and the duties which became unavoidable—and afterward the task of documentation I have just mentioned—interrupted for fourteen years my studies of North African civilization, while forcing me, somewhat against my will, to devote myself to an examination of the "decivilization" in Europe. Identical reasons led me to abandon this pursuit in 1954, when the war in

---

[5] In February 1950, Geneviève de Gaulle-Anthonioz and I went to Rastadt as defense witnesses for two German Aufseherinnen (the female prison supervisors). We did not know one of them; the other we knew as a brute. But both had been accused of totally imaginary crimes by authentic deportees.

Algeria broke out. Once again, I should say, because of un-avoidable duties.

I was aided in the verification of my information by two friends—comrades from Ravensbrück—Denise Vernay and Anise Postel-Vinay. Without them it would have been im-possible. Together we discussed at great length all the hypoth-eses and reviewed and sifted all the details. I also consulted an international trio of friends: Nina Iwanska (Polish), Grete Buber-Neumann (German), and Zdenka Nedvedova (Czech).

On August 13, 1942, I was arrested at the Gare de Lyon in Paris, where a traitor who had penetrated our "Musée de l'Homme" resistance network had arranged a meeting with two of us. He was a priest and the vicar of La Varenne, the parish adjoining mine. His name was Father Robert Alesch.

At Alesch's trial in May 1948, his German superior Com-mandant Schaffer—the former deputy to Colonel Reile of the Abwehr—was a witness. Schaffer testified that Alesch had signed on with the Gestapo as early as 1941, on his own initia-tive, and that he had been used by the Abwehr beginning in 1942. He sent scores of people to their deaths, including some very young ones from his parish youth organization, whom he incited to acts of resistance simply to be able to betray them. For this he was paid, in addition to certain "head bo-nuses," a fee of 12,000 old francs, plus 3,000 francs for his mistress and another 2,000 for someone named Claude; with his expenses, it all came to about 25,000 francs a month.

After my arrest, I was confined in the Santé prison in Paris (Division I, Cell 96), then—along with the entire section con-trolled by the Germans—I was transferred on October 13 to the Fresnes prison just outside Paris (Division III, Cell 326). I was interrogated seven times during August and October; not knowing at the time who had betrayed us, and fearful of telling too much to our enemies, I denied everything.

On Friday, October 23, 1942, a uniformed captain read to me the offenses I had been charged with; the officer who had usually questioned me—named Weinberger—provided a running translation. After each paragraph I was even allowed to make "corrections," which I did. Their attitude as they listened to me seemed sarcastic, but they recorded what I said; I listened to them attentively, politely, but rather gloomily. . . . The process was a long one and, except for the absence of an attorney, rather like the final interrogation in the presence of a "real" magistrate. Every now and then the captain stopped for a moment, looked at me thoughtfully, searching for words. When he had finished detailing the charges, he took on a solicitous air: "We are not like the French police, or the English. We are lenient with women. Very lenient. And, if we get a little help, we might even release a woman who has committed espionage. . . ." He broke off the sentence hesitantly, seeming unconvinced of what he was saying, while Weinberger translated. I made an effort to appear suddenly full of interest, and my reply literally made them gasp for an instant: "And those who have not committed espionage— what do you do with them?" Then they both laughed, nothing more.

My bill of accusations included five acts carrying a death sentence, one of which—"harboring English agents"—directly endangered my mother. Hearing the charges gave me some idea of the Germans' information about me—much of what they knew but, unfortunately, not everything. I still did not know how they had gotten whatever information they had, since I had not yet learned that Alesch was a traitor. Nor did I know that several of his accusations had been confirmed by an IS agent arrested along with me. Isolated in a cell later, he had denounced everyone he knew. My mother, arrested the same day, was kept in prison because of his confessions; she had denied everything, as I had.

I was not completely certain of my mother's arrest until January 12, 1943, when I was told by the German chaplain at Fresnes—who also gave me a small volume of *Imitation of Christ*. I still have the book today; in it I had recorded landmark dates of my imprisonment, which until then I had written with a nail on the walls of my cell.

My mother was imprisoned on the second floor, on the courtyard side; my cell was opposite hers, on the fifth floor.

Every day, when the soup was passed around and my door was opened, I tried to catch a glimpse of her cell. On April 11 our two doors were opened at the same time, and I saw her for the first time since our arrest. She waved at me and tried to smile; I waved back and tried to smile. The German guard (a woman) did not hurry me, allowing us a very long moment of reunion, and weeping as she watched us. We were still far from Ravensbrück.

On August 18, 1943, I learned that she was no longer at Fresnes, and for four days I foolishly hoped that she had been released. But my German floor officer told me on the twenty-second that she was at Romainville. Since I was no longer in solitary confinement at the time, I could receive parcels and send my clothes for laundering on the outside, so we managed to communicate in various clandestine ways.

When I was deported on October 21, 1943, my mother was not on the train carrying about twenty of the "NN" prisoners,[6] a group which included other women accused of "offenses" similar to mine. One week later, our convoy was joined by a second NN group at the Aix-la-Chapelle prison; we were sent together to Ravensbrück. I became hopeful again that my mother might have been released, and that hope made my own deportation easier to endure.

Our convoy was placed in quarantine as soon as we arrived at Ravensbrück, and almost all of us became very ill. In my case there were, in quick succession, diphtheria, double otitis, a serious incidence of bronchitis, complicated by an attack of scurvy. Two Czech deportees who did not know me—Zdenka and Hilda—saved my life. I have no idea how long I was kept in the Revier (the infirmary), since during those first few months at Ravensbrück it was impossible to maintain anything near an accurate diary.

Then, on February 3, 1944, a convoy of 958 women arrived from France—the transport known as the "twenty-seven thousands"—and my mother was among them. The second part of this study will examine this group in detail.

[6] Beginning on p. 91 is an explanation of this ominous designation, which was an abbreviation for *"Nacht und Nebel"* (Night and Fog).

Soon afterward, during a roll call, I learned of her presence in the camp. The message was passed along in whispers along the almost silent rows as 18,000 or 19,000 women stood immobile. I think it was during a morning roll call, but I am no longer certain; I remember being almost paralyzed with grief, and I could see only darkness.

When we finally were able to have a reunion—and it was an emotional one—she did not seem to feel any sadness. Her convoy was lodged in Block 15, and, if I had not been an NN prisoner, I almost certainly could have moved in there unnoticed by the authorities, since no one in that block ever betrayed me. But the Blockova of the NN block—Kate Knoll, a German prisoner—was vicious and untrustworthy, and I was NN.

The NN prisoners were not allowed to be placed in work Kommandos assigned to stations far from the camp, and for that reason were selected in sufficiently large numbers to form their own work column, known as Bekleidung (clothing supply), where the duties included unloading the trucks and rail cars crammed with some of the bizarre spoils accumulated by the German police in their pillages throughout Europe. Because of the Bekleidung—and despite the regular searches of the prisoners who worked there—a goodly number of useful articles filtered down to the prisoners, especially medicines. As for me, I managed to set aside by the handful enough odd bits of cloth to put together a pillow for my mother; she also received linens and warm underclothing.

From day to day my mother and I managed to learn almost everything the best-informed prisoners could find out about what was really happening behind the scenes at Ravensbrück. First—and throughout 1944—there were the executions and the *"transports noirs."*[7] Then, in January 1945, they created a sort of "annex" to Ravensbrück, where they exterminated selected prisoners. This "annex" was the small Uckermarck camp, which was more often known as "Jugendlager."[8]

[7] See pp. 40 and 131.
[8] See pp. 94 and 141.

Throughout January and February, the terror became more tangible day by day: there were increasingly frequent disappearances of prisoners not only from Uckermarck, but also from the infirmary of the main camp—the Revier.

Nevertheless, on March 1, 1945, I took the risk of going to the Revier because of an extremely painful abcess in my jaw, which for several days had kept me from opening my mouth. (I fed myself with scraps of stale bread soaked in water.) While I was in the Revier, the camp police moved in on several blocks, including the NN block, preventing any escape. All those caught inside were transferred to the Strafblock (the punishment section), my mother among them. I managed to get into the Strafblock that evening; I do not remember exactly how, but probably by saying—truthfully—that I was an NN returning from the Revier. Because of the police roundup, a majority of the Frenchwomen and most of the surviving Hungarian gypsies were, from that point on, isolated in the smaller confines of the Strafblock. The overcrowding was such that there was no possibility for normal sleep. My mother was very distressed and very tired, but did not complain; I too said nothing. And she wanted to remain sitting up throughout the first night.

The next day, two friends who "enjoyed" considerable seniority in the camp—Anicka (Czech) and Grete (German)—arranged with the police[9] for me to return to the Revier for treatment. I was thinking that I would be away for an hour at the most, but before leaving I embraced my mother, and—because of our distress and all that we knew but would not say—I held her in my arms for a long time, as if it might be the last. And it was the last time.

While I was in the Revier, these same friends decided it was imperative that they get as many as possible out of the Strafblock, and they took out my mother and two NN comrades.

[9] The policewomen of the camp were always chosen from the most senior German-speaking prisoners; they wore red armbands, as did the bosses of the work columns. Our police force included many prisoners who had been arrested for common crimes, and some of them were truly brutal scoundrels, but even they might go easy with compatriots they had known for a few years.

They did the best they could for my mother, putting her in a "normal" block, number 27, "on a bed, near the door."

About one o'clock that afternoon, we learned at the Revier that there would be a new general roll call, lasting the rest of the day. I was taken under the potective wing of Grete Buber-Neumann, a German prisoner at Ravensbrück since 1940. She was well-educated and had been a Blockova at one time. After removal from that post and a stay in the Straf-block, she became a secretary, working in a series of different offices in the camp. That day, she occupied a small cell—with a real bed. She took an enormous risk, hiding me at her feet, under the bedclothes. When Pflaum came in for the roll check, he noticed nothing and closed the door.

At five, when movement around the camp became possible again, my friend Danielle came to tell Grete in German that my mother had been taken away during the roll call.

I can no longer remember how I managed to rejoin my block and relocate, one by one, my very efficient friends. But the next day I had one of them, an Austrian, take a final word of warning to my mother, to tell her to "hold out" as best she could. My friend also took a package no larger than a deck of cards—two or three sulfamide pills, a slice of bread, and the three sugar cubes and the biscuit my Czech friends had given me. On Monday (March 5) and on Tuesday, I persuaded an-other secretary to transmit a second and third letter, a second and third tiny package. . . . On Thursday, Miki returned the three packages and the three letters. It was foolish to hope any longer; I knew this, but I could not believe it.

On Sunday the eleventh, hiding in Anicka's block, I was able to have a rather long conversation with Irma, one of the secretaries who had been shuttling between the main camp and Uckermarck for the roll calls. I was trying to maintain a record of landmark dates; I wrote down the following: *Mother's name is on a list of 700 who left on Tuesday the sixth—with a false number, 27,993, which belonged to a Rus-sian prisoner (Ochewska). . . . There are still 700 women up there, including 50 who went yesterday. . . . I run into J. d'A., who tries to tell me she has heard good news from "up there," that . . . etc. I do not listen. I am running every-*

where, trying to find the secretaries. At noon I find two of them who, horrified, refuse to take the little parcel I still want to send despite all I've heard (some biscuits, a bit of sugar, medicine). . . .

During this period, at all hours, the "hunts" were carried out throughout the camp to fill the ominous trucks which—quite openly by this time—shuttled among the various blocks, the Revier and the crematorium. The Revier nurses saw their patients taken away in hospital gowns, saw the trucks leave, and kept listening until they heard the trucks stop at the ovens. Then they saw the trucks return empty for a new load. One nurse clocked the time needed for a trip from the Revier to the crematorium, unloading and return: seven minutes. And —day and night—we could see the smoke pouring from the crematorium chimneys.

Even when I had lost almost all hope, I continued to search desperately for some trace, someone who might have seen my mother—just one woman from among the many penned up in the Jugendlager but still alive. I knew there were many who had not yet been killed, since from time to time groups came back down for work details, to make room for others, for any number of reasons.

Then, on Monday, March 19, I wrote: *France Odoul and Marguerite Solal, in Block 7,*[10] *noticed Mother passing by on Friday evening. They did not even remember who was with her.*

On Monday the fifth I had undergone surgery by someone completely unknown to me—a pleasant woman, very young, and visibly terrified by the instruments in her hands. While she hesitated, Hellinger had passed through the room. This only worsened the distraction of my young surgeon, since I was there fraudulently to begin with, and Hellinger's only known function was to extract gold teeth from the dead—a task which insured that the living kept a respectful distance from him, as one would from a hyena or vulture. He stopped,

---

[10] See the camp diagram on p. 238. Block 7 was located directly on the Lagerstrasse, the main street of the camp which led to our "industrial park." Beyond that was the Jugendlager.

came to look at me, even leaning over a bit to get a better view. I recall showing very little concern at the time; otherwise, he might have been more interested. . . . During the next several days, the nurses often dressed my wounds in such a way that I could be taken out quickly, since the Revier was then one of the most dangerous places in the camp. On March 15, I felt that I should try to walk, but my legs would not support me; my comrades took my temperature: 104°. The physical suffering was still intense, but at times it seemed almost a comfort, to the extent that it kept me from thinking.

Two weeks later, on April 2, 1945, 300 Frenchwomen were liberated through the intervention of the International Red Cross of Geneva, but the NN prisoners were not among them. On April 23, however, the NN were included in the liberation organized by the Swedish Red Cross and the negotiations of Count Folke Bernadotte.

The prisoners left with little more than the clothing they were wearing. Before the leave-taking there were, of course, innumerable searches by the Germans, but it was fruitless: the prisoners managed to pass from hand to hand those precious articles they wanted to keep. Thus two hidden "objects" somewhat more remarkable than the rest escaped the final inspection—the last two surviving French babies.[11] My friends divided up some of my papers: the *Imitation of Christ,* full of important notes, left the camp in one of Danielle's (Anise Postel-Vinay's) pockets, an operetta—entitled *Verfügbar in the Underworld*—which I had written the previous summer and hidden in a box in the Bekleidung Kommando, was taken care of by Jacqueline d'Alincourt. For my part, I took out the notes I had taken during the last days,[12] as well as the identities of the principal SS figures of the camp, vaguely coded and disguised as recipes. I also managed to hide a roll of undeveloped film showing the gangrenous legs of the schoolchildren who had been the subjects of Dr. Karl Geb-

---

[11] There were also two other infant boys, one French and one Polish, who survived in an outside work Kommando.

[12] The entire chapter titled "The Final Days" (p. 99) was written from this documentation.

hardt's experimental operations.[13] I had kept the film in my pocket since January 21, 1944—always wrapped in scraps of filthy cloth to avoid its attracting attention during the searches.

The fact that I survived Ravensbrück I owe first—and most definitely—to chance, then to anger and the motivation to reveal the crimes I had witnessed, and finally to a union of friendship, since I had lost the instinctive and physical desire to live.

This tenuous web of friendship was, in a way, almost submerged by the stark brutality of selfishness and the struggle for survival, but somehow everyone in the camp was invisibly woven into it. It bound together surrogate "families": two, three, or four women from the same town who had been arrested in the same "affair," or perhaps a group formed within a prison cell or in a railroad car at the time of their deportation—all of them later clinging to one another to keep from being engulfed in the horrors of the prison camps. The major dividing line—more than nationality, political party, or religion —was language. But there were networks of mutual aid which functioned above these sometimes artificial divisions.

These invisible chains of communal aid among prisoners had a formidable counterpart: the organized networks of our captor-murderers. Systematic slaughter was not too easy outside of the organizations established specifically for that purpose—the "death factories" of Auschwitz and Lublin-Maïdaneck. While the extermination of prisoners at Ravensbrück was carried out by means one might call "inventive," our workshops continued to function, fed by a work force decimated by chronic famine, which was sufficient to do away with a certain number of prisoners without creating panic. And, while the number of cremations that could be accommodated by the ovens was not increased significantly, it is now known that a gas chamber with a capacity of about 150 persons was set up nearby. Why 150, and not 50 or 300? Was the number proportioned to the capacity of the ovens? Was the gas chamber installed in an existing structure? But the

[13] See p. 79 for the chapter on "Les Lapins" (The Rabbits).

fact remains that it always functioned at the same time the other forms of organized murder were following their usual course—the more "personal" form, perhaps, of the terrifying "tête-à-tête" between the assassin and his victim. "Proper murder," like "proper torture," is a wild illusion.

There were, of course, thousands of individual journeys to a personal Calvary, but for only one of them was I able to mark every "station of the cross" with witnesses. That one terrible journey, which concluded in a merciful death, might help in finding the meaning behind the mere words of history.

Claire, a sweet and shy young woman, was held in great affection by her comrades, partly because of her knowledge of poetry; I think she was a professor of literature. My mother liked her and often spoke to me about her. In March 1947 I sent an account of what I had learned about her death to the others who had known her: *Do you remember Claire? First of all she was cruelly bitten and mangled by a dog. Who set the dog on her? We do not know, but he was Claire's first assassin. She went then to the Revier, where she was denied treatment. Who refused her? We don't know for sure, probably Marschal. The second murderer. Her wounds did not heal, and she was sent to the Jugendlager. Who sent her? We don't know—probably Pflaum or Winkelman. The third murderer. Now that she was among the ranks of the condemned, who kept her from fleeing? An Aufseherin, or one of the police? Possibly both, possibly von Skine or Boesel. The fourth murderer. At Jugendlager, Claire refused to swallow the poison Salveguart had given her, and Salveguart, with the help of Rapp and Köhler, beat her senseless with a club and finally killed her.*

Claire was only one woman among 123,000—one solitary agony. For this one victim, five bands of murderers. And for all the others there were the same assassins, or some like them; every victim was killed and rekilled. We were all caught in a terrifying cycle, with an assassin waiting at every turn.

Part One

THE RAVENSBRÜCK
CONCENTRATION CAMP

(Indented sections embody corrections and additions made in 1972.)

1

Realities of the System:
Pre-Ravensbrück and Later

Before my arrest on August 13, 1942, I was aware of certain isolated information on the criminal substructure of German society, all of which should have been sufficient to make me give the matter serious thought, but I had no proof that the information was correct. And since it was also easy to believe that certain events were almost accidental—or at least not part of some grand design—I had not given them the serious consideration they deserved. As it was, my information, whatever its merits, was typical of a body of knowledge that was quite accessible in France at the time, provided one maintained an interest in events which were calamitous by any standard, but which seemed to have no immediate effect on a Frenchman.

By 1942, I had heard that:

1. The Germans had been killing the insane and feeble-minded, the supposedly incurably ill, the destitute aged; they were executed by gas or injections.

2. They often finished off their military wounded (soldiers, not officers) whenever the wounds threatened to cause permanent disability.[1]

3. I also had somewhat vague and uncertain information that they had gassed entire trainloads of Jews; I did not know the exact circumstances of these events, and I could not imagine any motive for such crimes. In general, I believed that

---

[1] In a decree predated September 1, 1939 (but actually drawn up in October, after the Polish campaign), Hitler had ordered that all "mentally ill" and "incurably ill" be put to death. Those who had lost an arm or leg were considered incurable. (1972)

the anti-Jewish measures were a means of intimidating an enslaved populace as a whole, without threatening most of them directly—fear paralyzes, while a threat incites action. It was altogether a quite cunning attempt to provoke general fear while diverting the real threat onto a defenseless and unprotected minority.

4. I knew that concentration camps existed; in particular (and quite by chance), I had read a book on the subject by a German actor who had been imprisoned on charges of Communist activity: *Under the Nazi Whip*. This rather restrained book, along with other accounts by German refugees, gave me some idea of life in these camps—an idea which, I'm afraid, only scratched the surface.[2]

On the other hand, I had considerably greater, and more precise, knowledge of German activities in France: the executions, Gestapo torture, the treatment of prisoners—especially beginning in the spring of 1941, the time of the first arrests in my resistance group. Until then, the simple fact that there were Germans on French soil seemed sufficient justification for anti-German activities. . . . It was only then, when I began to know the cruelty of the Gestapo—and even more so after the executions of hostages and French patriots (particularly in August 1941 and February 1942)—that I felt violent indignation on top of my natural hostility. To me, the Germans became not only personal enemies but criminals in an absolute sense. . . . But I realize today that despite this I did not know how to draw decisive conclusions from the diverse items of information I already possessed (such as those men-

[2] The evolution of the German concentration camp system—both in size and in the increasingly murderous treatment of its victims—was almost uninterrupted, as described very competently by Eugen Kogon in his treatise on Buchenwald (published in English as *The Theory and Practice of Hell*, Farrar, Straus, 1950; Octagon Books, 1973). A summary is included here as an appendix beginning on p. 223. I believe today that descriptions of these camps appearing before 1940 were neither more nor less than the truth, but that what I experienced between 1943 and 1945 was quite different. There is no doubt that any organized system of repression, whose principles openly and avowedly sanction simple cruelty, will eventually evolve into true atrocity. (1972)

tioned above). I realize as well that my actions were based on what I saw or learned myself, not upon broader and less tangible ideas. I am ashamed to admit this, and my only excuse is that in the depths of my heart I could not completely believe all I had heard, much as I did not, at first, believe the treason of Vichy. In order to completely comprehend their reality, I had to see with my own eyes how far cruelty, on one hand, and cowardice, on the other, could go.

I therefore had an unconscious tendency to think that the facts mentioned above were more or less isolated or exaggerated and did not reflect fundamental truths about the German system. And, at the beginning, my opposition to Germany was based more upon nationalism than on justice.

My fourteen months in prison at Santé, then at Fresnes, only confirmed what I already knew about the procedures of investigation and arrest by the German police. I had known about, tried to evaluate, and struggled for months against their immense network of *agents provocateurs* and traitors. The questioning (with its tortures, blackmail, and traps) and the executions (especially of hostages) I knew about before I saw them, and I detested them. But to me, none of this represented any particularly new historical phenomenon: all tyrannies are established and maintained through the murder of their enemies; the German police only expanded upon a system they had not invented. These were not the absolutely new collective crimes, or the original outrage against humanity.

We arrived at Ravensbrück on a Sunday evening around the end of October 1943.[3] Within a few hours we became brutally aware of reality: the forced labor, the experimental operations on young girls (we soon saw for ourselves their miserable, martyred limbs), the transports noirs, individual and mass executions, the ill being "put out of their misery," the dogs, the beatings, the gas chambers. . . . And all of this assaulted our consciousness almost simultaneously, through

[3] Two works describing this arrival have been published: *Trois Bagnes,* by Jacqueline Richet (J. Ferenczi et Fils, 1945), and *Nuit et Brouillard,* by Odette Amery and G. Martin-Champier (Berger-Levrault, 1945).

our own eyes or in countless, irrefutable personal accounts by others.

We all brought with us from France some of the small comforts of civilized life, which had been slowly collected from the packages sent by our families—decent clothing, toothpaste, soap; we still believed in certain rights—in any case the rights which in our country were recognized even for those condemned to death: the right to a fair trial and an attorney, and the rights to have a doctor, a priest, and two meals a day. . . . Before the end of the first day we had been stripped of everything: those minor little articles we had brought, our rights, and our hope. All we had now were a few filthy rags which didn't belong to us—and a number.

A group of Czechs who had returned from Auschwitz were lodged in the block with us. They had horrible tales to recount —in whispers: the systematic annihilation of Jews by gas, the burned bodies and mountains of human ashes. With them were several Jews awaiting their departure for Auschwitz. They knew their fate.

Before I began dealing with explanations, details, and statistics, a terrifying reality assaulted us from all sides: the almost total dissipation of a majority of the prisoners—haggard, dressed in tatters, mere skeletons covered with suppurating sores, and, in their eyes, a dead, vacant stare. And we were still human beings, retaining from a more civilized world some bases of comparison for measuring the depths of misery here, in which we would, of course, soon be engulfed.

The prevailing state of mind among the Frenchwomen was, more than real fear, a rather dazed sense of alarm. During the first encounter, it was our somewhat empty-headed optimists who received the most severe shock. Almost all of us were in the Resistance and accustomed to danger, and none would flinch before the Germans. But at night, in the solitude of the barracks, there were tears and fits of hysteria among the weakest. They would recover very quickly—within two or three days—and would try afterward to deny the reality around them, to fight it pathetically with jokes, lies, fantasies, talk of food and recipes. Many would become angry when some new horror was revealed: "Even if it's true, I don't want to know about it" was the reply of quite a few comrades I tried to enlighten.

One example of this phenomenon occurred late in the war, after the "little paratroopers" were executed (in late January or early February 1945). We managed to reconstruct, step by step, the circumstances of their deaths. There were nine of them, all women: four French, three English, one Czech, and one Russian. They had to leave behind their shoes and part of their clothing, and then left the camp accompanied by an Aufseherin, Ruth Neudecker (born in Breslau, 1913), later an Aufseherin at Jugendlager, and always a volunteer for executions. On the way out, their route, which led past the crematorium toward the Siemens factory, was barred by the SS. A few days later their numbered dresses were found in the clothing-storage depot.

The other Frenchwomen, for the most part, refused to believe that the paratroopers had been killed, preferring to think they had been sent to another camp.

> When the SS had come to the block, ostensibly to search for our parachutist comrades, the "old" prisoners (those at Ravensbrück for more than three years) knew they were going to be executed. There had already been numerous executions at Ravensbrück, always shrouded in mystery, but preceded by the same "signs" noticed on this occasion: unusual meetings and movements, special messages—the arrival of which caused considerable anxiety, but to which the prisoner-secretaries had no access; then there was something special about the men who came to take the young women away. And even more significant, the preparation of an extra ration of alcohol for the SS in the canteen (where some of the prisoners worked).

> The executions had always taken place within the enclosure where the cremation ovens were located, and where, for example, at least two hundred Polish women had been shot (the number given by Oberaufseherin Binz in one of her interrogatories). Although this perilous area was not one of general circulation, prisoners were

often sent there on labor details to perform almost any kind of work. They, in turn, passed along intelligence to other prisoners employed in the administrative offices. The latest information, relayed with understandable terror, was that the SS had ordered gallows built.

The sure sign that executions had occurred—or so the prisoners thought—was the return of clothing to the laundry; after our nine comrades were taken away, we kept watch; the clothes came back. To our small group at least, the executions could no longer be questioned; we were right, unfortunately, and our conclusions seemed to be supported by the presence of the new gallows. One thought was obvious at the time: our comrades had been hanged. There is little doubt that they were executed, but probably by firearms, or so I believe today.

One year later, in fact, the deputy commandant of Ravensbrück, under questioning by an English judge, gave an account of the executions and declared they had been shot. His statements, to the extent that I could check them, I found to be true.

We were unaware at the time, of course, that a group of German officers implicated in a plot against Hitler had been sentenced to death and confined in the bunker at Ravensbrück. And, in the Third Reich, the method of execution was determined by the tribunal handing down the death sentence. These circumstances offer the most likely explanation for the Ravensbrück gallows.

I should add that any other prisoner, equipped with some knowledge of German law and the same information I possessed, would probably reach the same conclusion, since the daily experience of the camp had convinced everyone that death for the ordinary prisoner was not a matter of ceremony or prescribed methods: one could be routinely killed at any time, by anyone, in any manner. But the forms of death were not mutually exclusive; there were still those who had to die "by the rules," and, in a way, more "personally"—provided with a formal judgment and even a death certificate. The others, killed systematically or randomly, were numbers among the camp's death statistics, no more. If necessary, death could be attributed to "cardiac arrest."

Executions at Ravensbrück were not public affairs; the ill in the transports noirs were "officially" being sent away to convalescent camps; and, if a prisoner was dispatched on the spot, it was done discreetly, away from the crowds. Anyone who wanted to remain unaware that such things were happening could, if necessary, accomplish exactly that, at least partially. These were in the majority.

At Auschwitz, where reality was more obvious (and to those least capable of enduring it), where executions and mass annihilations took place before the eyes of everyone, the psychic shock was so violent as to be fatal in itself. A friend, who was a doctor at the Auschwitz infirmary, told me that at a roll call women would often collapse from the shock of what was happening. They would be taken to the infirmary, and my friend would do all she could for them (which was quite limited; no medication was necessary, since there was nothing physically wrong with them). After a few days they died, without having had any discernible illness, nor had they reached the point of physical exhaustion.[4]

When a courageous and intelligent woman finally came to the end of her strength, there were two symptoms which presaged death: she stopped fighting the lice, and she began to believe the wild stories circulating through the camp, which until then she had been able to dismiss. This condition usually did not last long—no more than a few days. Did she die because she had stopped struggling? Or did she cease struggling because she was dying? But she died.

Others, as I have said, were settled into unreality and ready to believe anything: that the Russians or the Americans had

[4] Observers of so-called archaic societies have often pointed to deaths, occurring either very suddenly or after a few days of prostration, among young and otherwise healthy persons after a curse or violation of a taboo. I think it would not be inappropriate to coin a word to fit such cases, which are not all that rare. I would propose "anxiocution"; one can die of anxiety or horror without having the usual "heart attack." (1972)

arrived, that there would be an exchange of prisoners at the Swiss border—anything meaning the end of their misery. And they still refused to accept the truth—the executions, poisonings, the gas chambers . . .

At that final limit of exhaustion, the period just before death, there were no more elaborate tales to believe, only a solitary image in an unanchored brain—some merciful transport away from the misery, an impossible departure. During her final hours, our friend Colette P. (whose husband, a colonel in the air corps, had just been killed in Libya) talked of "the white airplane" that would come to take her away. Those were her last words. Annie de M. called to an imaginary chauffeur. As for myself, I remember being first haunted —during a siege of diphtheria and delirium—by poetic visions of ghostly ships, then by the bare image of a hospital train with a white bed, an image which I bled dry of all the solace it could provide. And yet, at the same time, I experienced the occasional realization that it was all a game, and the physical pain (I was suffering simultaneously from a serious case of diphtheria, double otitis, primary bronchitis which became chronic, scurvy, and bedbugs), the total neglect (I was the only Frenchwoman among a number of diphtheriaques, and I was not given so much as a glass of water until I was adopted by a ward neighbor who looked after me and actually saved my life[5]), and the prospect of imminent death— all seemed to be endurable and compatible evils. There are ills which are unendurable and incompatible with human strength: the suffering and death of a loved one; for someone totally immersed in action and responsibilities, the shock of being forced to stop, the torturous impotence of being in prison, the knowledge of dangers faced by compatriots one can no longer save, the constant thoughts of the thousand precautions one could have taken . . . but that it is now too late. These are crushing trials. . . . But solitary death, physical suffering, and neglect come from general human experience, on a level with the living. Given a private conversation with the Creator, I would compromise and accept them all

[5] Hilda Synkova.

(except the bedbugs, which I consider an abuse of authority on His part).

Such are the "hallucinations of death," so similar to the hallucinations of hunger and thirst: first the romantic fables —well-arranged, almost believable—in which you spar with your obsessions; then the obsessions which dominate every other thought.

We had to fight them, but carefully, for they were as necessary as they were dangerous, necessary because they kept us from wishing too strongly for death, dangerous because they could break down our distrust of the traps of Ravensbrück.

2

The Truth Within Reach

Fantasies aside, the truth about Ravensbrück was near at hand and not difficult to seek out:

One guiding principle of the camp was to have the prisoners do everything: drain the bogs, build the roads, install windows and plumbing—but also to fill out the medical- and political-information cards, type correspondence, keep the accounts and statistics, and even police the camp and administer the blocks (tasks which fell to the Blockovas and Stubovas).[1] To be sure, the most important positions were usually (but not always) assigned to the most reliable prisoners, many of whom had attained the perfect accommodation with their masters—based partly on the satisfaction of these prisoners' worst instincts of domination and cruelty, partly on attendant "privileges": the extra ration of sausage or margarine which could mean survival. Most of them were more than willing to talk to their friends about the work, and, with a little effort, one could acertain some of the basic truths about the operation of Ravensbrück.

A shortage of free time was not the greatest obstacle to this effort. Since I came to know the camp rather well (and the failings in its administration), but more importantly because I had many friends of all professions and nationalities, I managed to almost completely avoid working in the factories and workshops. Only "almost": there were eleven days

---

[1] The official German titles were Blockälteste and Stubälteste; the words Blockova and Stubova were part of the Germano-Slavic slang which developed in the camp.

in April 1944 when I was a fur seamstress, three weeks as a dockworker in the Bekleidung (summer of 1944), and two weeks as a woodcutter. Otherwise my status was that of *"Verfügbar"*—"available." The SS used us for their digging operations.

While I was writing this account, it seemed most essential to break down the system and derive some over-all sense from it. This was indeed the most important goal, but because of it I neglected, to some extent, the precise details of daily life in the camp.

To understand, for example, the Verfügbar status, one must know that every morning, long before dawn, there were two roll calls in quick succession.

The first and longest was numerical. The prisoners, lined up by tens in front of their respective blocks, were counted and recounted interminably, since the total for all blocks had to correspond to the official aggregate list for the camp. If there was a discrepancy of even one number, we had to remain in place until they came up with an explanation. Even for the dying there was no question of being excused from that roll call. Immediately afterward there was a second—the "work call." Lined up along the Lagerstrasse, the prisoners had to fall in with their assigned work columns as they marched past.

All prisoners not assigned to a workshop, in quarantine, confined to the Revier, or scheduled for some sort of garrison duty were required to fall in with the Verfügbar column, and it was there that the SS in charge of the various workshops "recruited" (always without warning) the personnel for whom they had work. The rest of the Verfügbar were left to the digging detail.

If one wanted to remain Verfügbar, it was necessary to take occasional diversionary measures such as hiding temporarily in another work column, in the quarantine block, or among the Narchiste[2] (night shift); or trying

---

[2] The proper German term was *Nachtschichte,* from which the French prisoners derived *"Narchiste,"* as in "anarchist."

to take on the appearance of a "Schmuckstück," an informal appellation for some of the most decrepit and forlorn prisoners.[3] This latter technique was designed to make one totally repugnant to the SS responsible for recruitment for work. All of this was very difficult and very dangerous, since the least violation of camp regulations was punishable by a sentence to the Strafblock. Perhaps worse, when the transport noir (which carried the sick to an extermination camp and always accommodated a fixed number of victims) had taken all the prisoners it could from the Revier, they collected the balance from the "Innendienst,"[4] or those deemed incapable of serving in a work column, sometimes simply because of a sore on the hand.

One day in January 1944, looking out a window in Block 27, I saw a woman—whose nationality I did not know—seized and forcibly taken away from Block 28. Why her instead of others? Had she been assigned to the Revier? Had she displeased someone? I do not know, but I saw it happen: carried away, with her arms entwined above her head, like the mourners on a Greek vase. I know nothing else about the incident except that it took place a few hours after the major "selection" for the month[5]—that is, during a period when the camp was more or less "normal" and a full year before the exterminations. Under similar circumstances, and probably on the same day, Anise Postel-Vinay saw a very young Russian girl dragged away by the SS, her body literally contorted in despair.

The status of "missing" Verfügbar, which was my constant goal, required a repertoire of ruses, subterfuges, and conspiracies large enough to rule some oriental kingdom. But the situation allowed me a fair amount of free time, provided I was able to hide in the quarantine block, where I ran little risk of being exposed. The greatest obstacles were the enervation

[3] See p. 23.
[4] Garrison duty—those left to internal services in the blocks.
[5] See p. 18 and the tabular chronology on pp. 244–45.

caused by the diphtheria I had contracted as soon as I arrived in the camp and the crushing fatigue caused by chronic hunger. Despite all this, I did not experience any perceptible diminution of mental activity except perhaps in the area of memory, but my physical condition reached the point where I did not even have the strength to speak, and this feeling of total exhaustion remained with me until the liberation. And I was forced, as a precaution, to record potentially damaging information in a form of shorthand code, which was a tremendous hindrance to later evaluation of what I had gathered. How many times I must have dreamed, during those worst years, of a time when I could finally resume and freely pursue this search for facts and causes. But when that time came, it took an enormous effort to avoid trying to forget this world of horror.

There were several comrades who, like me, considered it a duty to know all we could; so we observed—closely. . . . We also believed it a duty to compel others to know, in spite of themselves. One principal motive was, simply, self-protection. Whenever prisoners were taken away to be killed, there was always the possibility that a few could have escaped if they had tried. But, alas, most—especially at the beginning—preferred to believe they were being led to safety and went to their deaths like lambs to the slaughter. And besides, we always had to consider the possibility of a general extermination—or at least an attempt at it—during the last days of the war. And that, indeed, is what the Germans tried whenever they could.

Here, in any case, is the information that I—under the limitations of being a prisoner—was able to gather on the spot:

Ravensbrück as a concentration camp lasted about six years, from 1939 to April 1945.[6] Since each new arrival had a printed number sewn onto her sleeve, it was easy to learn, day by day, how many prisoners had passed through the camp. Shortly before the liberation, a figure of 115,000 was

[6] The camp was opened in the spring of 1939 with several hundred prisoners from Lichtenburg and a group of biblical scholars from Mohringen. (See the chronology on p. 240.)

reported to me, but during the very last hours a prisoner told me of having seen the number 123,000.[7]

German prisoners were sometimes released along the way, but in small numbers, and only rarely.[8] On the other hand, some prisoners—considerably more numerous—were numbered twice.[9]

A simple chronology will give some idea of the movement of prisoners [pp. 240–43].[10] As noted there, during the three years from May 1939 to May 1942, the camp received about 10,000 prisoners. Then from August 1942 to August 1943, there were about 9,000 arrivals—the rate had almost tripled; from August 1943 to August 1944 there were 36,000 —more than ten times the rate of the first three years. At that point, the rate of arrivals leaped to about 10,000 a month.

The camp could hold about 10,000 prisoners in its sixteen small blocks and eleven larger ones. Living conditions in 1943 were very harsh; one could, with some difficulty, escape the obligatory labor duty of twelve hours a day, but there was no escape from the four interminable roll calls: two in the morning (a general call and a work call), one at noon (a work call), and one in the evening (a general call). Windows and doors had to remain open day and night in temperatures often falling below zero. One had to eat standing, since there were no stools, and rise before the official reveille to be able to wash, etc. The death rate was high, of course, but the "of-

[7] Questioned later on this point, the Ravensbrück commandant replied: "I have given the figure of 110,000–115,000. But I repeat that this is purely an estimate; I do not deny that the camp register went as high as 123,000." (Interrogation of December 5, 1949, Rastadt.) (1972)

[8] The prisoner-secretaries estimated that these releases totaled about 3 per cent for the first four years, after which they were completely halted. A few French prisoners were also freed.

[9] This double numbering affected about 3,000 women (counted by the labor office) or 2,000 (counted by the political office), but these figures seem a bit low. Perhaps certain numbers were restored to the rolls just before the very last days, since it was during this period that changes were most numerous.

[10] See also the tabular chronology for 1944–45, which I put together after my return. I completed it for this edition with information gathered during the Hamburg trials.

ficial" rate was reduced by the use of transports noirs:[11] from time to time groups of insane (or those declared to be), infirm, and tuberculars simply disappeared. They were, in fact, sent to another camp—an extermination camp.

Toward the end of January 1944 an enormous transport noir preceded by a few days the arrival of the French convoy known as *the twenty-seven thousands;* I was told at the time that the transport was made up of 900 women. The "selection" of them involved a veritable animal hunt throughout the camp.[12]

Of the 115,000 (123,000?) women who passed through Ravensbrück, a portion came directly from the arrests and roundups conducted by the Germans throughout Europe, but many others came from other camps and had been moving about for months—some for years—from fortress to prison, from concentration camp to fortress. One could put together at Ravensbrück itself a sort of documentation on almost all the concentration camps, jails, and penitentiaries—on the system as a whole. So it was then only necessary to ask questions and record the information, which is precisely what I did beginning in 1943. Some of the conclusions:

There were two principal types of concentration camps in Germany, labor and extermination, and it seemed immediately apparent to me that the two were complementary, governed by the same principles and differing only in the rate of extermination.

The guiding principle was, of course, the extermination of

[11] What I was able to learn later about the relationship between the transports noirs and the death rate will be found on pp. 131 and 173.

[12] It was said around the camp that the SS had rounded up about 900 women; some secretaries later recorded the number 800; and Wanda Kiedrzynska spoke of 1,000 (including 300 Poles and forty Jewish children).

The transport went to Maïdaneck (Lublin), and the prisoners were not killed immediately. Meanwhile, the Polish women had managed to get a message out; London radio later reported the existence of this transport. Eventually the women involved were dispersed among various camps, most of them dying at Auschwitz. Nonetheless, I later heard of three survivors. (1972)

enemies and/or undesirables—a goal unfortunately all too commonplace. But the innovation of this system was to organize the extermination in such a way that instead of being costly to the exterminators, it produced substantial profits.

These two "principles," profit and extermination, evolved as the same in both types of camps; that is, those condemned to an extermination camp were nonetheless expected to produce a profit, and those assigned to a labor camp could expect to be killed eventually. The two ideas, although contradictory to an extent, help explain certain inconsistencies in the German system.

For example, when transports of Jews arrived at Auschwitz, an immediate "selection" was made at the train station: most (80–90 per cent) went directly to the gas chambers; the remainder (the percentages varied from day to day) went into the camp to meet a fate worse than immediate death. *But since the Germans wanted to kill them, why not do it right away? Why separate mothers from children only for a few extra days; why the added suffering and suspense? Why were there always, in all the convoys, a few temporary survivors?* My comrades who despairingly asked these questions invariably reached the same conclusions: *The sadism, disorder, madness, inconsistency . . . of the Germans.*

Sadism, to be sure, had a part in all this, but only as a sort of accidental addition to the bargain; as for the rest, it was not a matter of inconsistency, but the most complete consistency; not madness, but method—the German Order. . . .

Although they jammed eighty or one hundred of these wretched souls into a single railroad car, without food or water for days, there was still the cost of coal for the locomotive, the costs of outfitting the train, the workers, the soldiers. Even the gas used for killing cost something, and one Auschwitz commandant had the idea of economizing in this regard on the children less than eight years old—or at least so I was told at Ravensbrück by a Czech prisoner who came from Auschwitz[13]—an adult could attempt to resist more strongly than a small child. Of course they retrieved the bag-

[13] Dr. Miklos Nyiszli (p. 150) also describes methods of extermination at Auschwitz worse than gas. (1972)

gage and personal effects of the dead—and their gold teeth, their hair, and their ashes (to make soap). But this was still not enough; this 10–20 per cent "survival" rate had to be followed for Auschwitz to be at the same time an efficient extermination camp and a non-deficit commercial enterprise.

From everywhere—Mauthausen, Bergen-Belsen, Lublin, Struthof—we heard of the same principles and the calculated "disorder" in the extermination system.

At Struthof, for example, there were work Kommandos of twenty men under the orders of a "kapo"—a duly chosen prisoner who had "proved himself." The Kommando left for work in the morning with its force of twenty, but was expected to return in the evening with only seventeen. The kapo had the freedom to achieve this reduction by whatever means he cared to use: a blow of a club or shovel, strangling, or perhaps burying some of his charges alive. If he managed to do so by noon, he would have three extra soups to eat—his personal profit. "And during the afternoon, one felt a little more at ease," one of the few survivors told me. Theoretically, the Kommando would be wiped out within a week, but since there were continuous arrivals of more or less exhausted men, some of the new ones died the first day, while some of the veterans managed to last several weeks, during which they might be transferred to another Kommando, then from there perhaps sent to another camp needing manpower.

While the extermination cycle lasted about a week at Struthof (for the Kommando I was told about, and for a necessarily brief period),[14] the rate at Ravensbrück, at least in 1943—the least deadly period—and in early 1944, was theoretically about five years if all nationalities are considered as a whole.

Suhren estimated at 8,000 the number of women at Ravensbrück in December 1942, shortly after he took

---

[14] I do not know whether this period, covering one or more cycles, lasted a week, a month or more. But in any case, Struthof was not a "death factory" like Auschwitz, but something more like a "death workshop"—more terrifying for the individual, perhaps, but less efficient.

command. We know that a prisoner who arrived on December 5, 1942, received the number 15,518, and that three and a half months later the number 19,244 was recorded; so, in the first three and a half years, about 16,000 prisoners were registered. As of the end of 1942 the work transports had not yet begun (the first left the camp the following March), so it was the transports noirs, more than actual executions on the spot, that accounted for a "population loss" of about 50 per cent in three and a half years. But from the moment Ravensbrück became a working enterprise (early 1943) until the wholesale exterminations began (December 1944), the "population losses" were considerably lower.

3

Resisting Death:
Some National Characteristics

In 1943 and 1944, the survival rate seemed to vary among the various nationalities represented at Ravensbrück: during that period, Frenchwomen died at a faster rate than both the Poles[1] and Czechs, and around mid-1944 I had calculated—based on figures supplied by comrades assigned to the Revier—that the average life of a Frenchwoman in the camp was approximately three years, much lower than the over-all average. Only the Hungarian Jews and the true social outcasts from Germany showed a resistance to death weaker than ours. The lack of defenses on the part of the Hungarian Jews was explained somewhat by the state of extreme misery to which they had been reduced before they arrived, as well as the particularly trying living conditions imposed upon them. As for the German outcasts, a long period of captivity in some form or another, and a lack of cohesion in their group, accounted for their problems; most of them, in fact, already belonged to that very special category known derisively as *"Schmuckstück."*[2]

A Schmuckstück was a seemingly human creature, the likes of whom I had never seen anywhere but at Ravensbrück, far past what is usually called emaciation and almost at a

[1] The mortality rate among the Poles had been high during the camp's first year, but by 1943, four years later, those who had survived were, evidently, especially robust; most received packages from outside and had had the time to get themselves assigned to the least dangerous Kommandos.

[2] A "little gem" or "precious little thing." In some other camps they were known as "the Moslems."

fatal stage of malnutrition (autopsies found all organs greatly reduced in size—a liver the size of a rabbit's); incapable of personal or social discipline, unwashed, resigned to the lice, clothed in unbelievable rags, and covered with every kind of running, infected sore. They were beaten, with or without reason, by all the more sturdy Germans (female guards in the SS or other prisoners—their impulses were the same); they would throw themselves flat in the mud to lick up the remains from an overturned soup bowl; without friends, hope, or dignity, and apparently without thoughts; transformed by fear and hunger, and finally destined to be gassed like rodents after one of those manhunts known as "selections." Each day of existence for these poor grubworms defied everything one might have believed about nature and hygiene. It was no surprise that they died; they were already removed from life.

> It seems to me today that they suffered a mental and moral decline before a physical one; I remember comrades who also died of hunger—no perceptible disease, but simply worn down—but who maintained complete self-control even during their last minutes of life.

The Frenchwomen followed after the Schmuckstück on the road to death, and I was determined to learn whether such an exceptionally high death rate among my compatriots was caused by living conditions harder than those of other nationalities, or simply by lower physical resistance. I discussed the problem quite often, especially with my Czech comrades in the Revier.[3]

There was an obvious answer for the Czechs: the intrinsic weakness of our people. They made this judgment with sadness, but without surprise, for, as in all of Central and Eastern Europe, they had been subjected for years to intense German propaganda on the alleged degeneracy of the French, without any contradiction or response from France. Since I had once taken the trouble to analyze the so-called facts behind such propaganda and had found most of them to be

[3] See p. 230 for a description of a similar situation at Buchenwald.

fundamentally false, I had the very strong desire to, first, compute the exact mortality rate for each nationality; then—and most importantly—to analyze the figures, taking living conditions into account. This became impossible for me, and, regrettably, I can only give approximations here.

Among political prisoners, the Russians, who, like the French, did not receive outside packages, suffered a higher mortality rate than the Polish or Czech women, but slightly lower than the French.

The Poles and Czechs, more senior in the camp than the French and mostly German-speaking, had all the "good spots," as kitchen workers, group supervisers, block chiefs, etc. Belonging to a "privileged class," they managed to have clean linens, a bed shared by only two persons (and sometimes even single beds), and ample opportunity for bathing, resting, and obtaining extra food. And they received packages from their families. On the other hand, the French—partly because of a peculiar border situation between France and Germany which did not exist between Germany and the other countries, partly because of deficiencies in the French Red Cross—did not, for all practical purposes, receive such outside aid; the rare few who did were usually the ones who survived. And one other factor: both out of patriotism and a sense of revulsion for German discipline, many French considered it a matter of honor to avoid working in the industrial units which were part of the war effort.

As I mentioned earlier, prisoners not enrolled in a work column were listed as Verfügbar (available). Remaining so for any length of time required all the wiliness and durability of a Sitting Bull, or, much to the contrary, one had to be a complete human waste, unusable and totally rejected—one of the Schmuckstück. I can say without much risk of contradiction that a wretched French Verfügbar was to our Blockovas and Polish prisoner-policewomen like the lowliest flophouse derelict would be to the Queen of England. A Blockova—fat, well-dressed, surrounded by her little "court"—enjoyed a rather tangible power over those who failed to submit: twenty-five blows of her club, or six months in the Strafblock (a hell within hell) for a prisoner who had done nothing more than displease her. And I can say flatly that many of my comrades were worse off than that tattered and starving flophouse derelict. Any compilation of "statistics" not taking into account these physical, moral, and social factors is little more than nonsense.

I have also already noted that the overcrowding precluded not only decent sleep, but even the barest minimum of hygiene—a deadly condition in itself. It killed quickly, more so than hunger. Lack of food, especially when combined with excessive work, is a sure killer, but still a slow one. The cold was fatal only by accident, and we were able to adapt to it.

The differences in living conditions explain, in large part, the variations in mortality rates among nationalities, but the reactions peculiar to each assuredly played a part.

Almost all the peoples of Europe were represented at Ravensbrück, and their characteristics were laid bare by the catalysis of the camp: English, Swiss, Spanish, Americans, and Italians[4]—in many cases arrested in France and French-speaking—were intermingled in the mass of Frenchwomen and seemed to have the same reactions. Nor were the Belgians perceptibly different.

The Dutch and Norwegians, generally German-speaking, were gathered in small, homogeneous groups, received many outside packages, and could be considered privileged compared to us. They were a dignified and admirable group, and we got along well whenever circumstances brought us together.

We had something very basic in common with the huge mass of Russians in the camp—horrible mistreatment—but we remained strangers; they were an almost incomprehensible jumble of humanity to us, if only because they were such a heterogeneous people. There was also an entire block of old peasants of uncertain nationality, touching in their gentleness and amiability, and continually at prayer, feeling obliged to

---

[4] Those whom I knew had been arrested in France, but after the change of power in Italy a convoy of Italians, arrested in their own country, arrived at Ravensbrück and was very quickly decimated.

thank God for every scrap of rutabaga they might find in their soup. And there was a great, unsorted hodgepodge (left-overs from the village raids, I suppose) who, as a group, amazed us with their adroitness at thievery, but who also un-fortunately exhibited an equally surprising savagery and fe-rocity.

The women of the Red Army were very impressive—highly organized and disciplined before their imprisonment, a defi-nite advantage—healthy, clean, honest. Somewhat rough and uncultured as a whole, but there were intellectual elements among them (doctors, professors), and they were almost all exceptionally likable and overflowing with kindness and good will. And we especially admired their spirit of resistance to the Germans.

Apparently, the camp administration didn't feel it neces-sary to distinguish the French from the Germans, at least as far as our "badges" were concerned. (We both wore red triangles with no other markings.)[5] But the Ukranians' tri-angles bore a "U," which kept us from blaming the Rus-sians for the Ukranians' indescribable savagery that easily made them the least desirable neighbors in the camp. It was impossible for me to conduct any kind of investigation among them, but I suppose they were mostly volunteer workers whose "contracts" had been broken, or streetwalkers who had fallen on hard times; there was a Ukranian state, theoretically allied with the Reich, and I think it likely that the true "politi-cals" among the Ukranians (those who didn't care for Ger-many) must have managed to take on the label of "Russian." In any case, the Ukranians' status as "ally" did them little good at Ravensbrück.

Therein lies an error: the Germans did not actually attempt to create a separate Ukranian state. On this point

---

[5] On arriving, each prisoner received a printed number, which was sewn on the left sleeve of a striped jacket and accompanied by a triangle.

A red triangle signified "political," the green was for the com-mon criminals, and black meant "social outcast"; this last bizarre category included gypsies and some Jews. All others wore a yel-low triangle.

the information available at Ravensbrück was indeed faulty.

The Polish women were, after the SS, the bosses of Ravensbrück. They held almost all the important and/or easy positions and guarded them jealously. In fact, they were at the same time the senior prisoners and the majority, and the camp had, in large part, been built by them. Our Stubovas (room chiefs), Blockovas (block chiefs), Lagerpolizei (policewomen), and *"bandes rouges"* (work bosses) included many from the Polish middle class, and the basic crudity of their country's proletariat (at least in the generation involved here) did the middle class the favor of preventing our confusing them with their compatriots who had been arrested for "common crimes." Unfortunately, there was always a mutual lack of understanding between the French and the Poles, while the French position of resistance was usually understood and appreciated by the other nationalities. Nonetheless, the attitude of my French compatriots had its own injustice, since these Polish women did possess some admirable qualities: courage, patriotism, and love of work and discipline—all unfortunately often marred by an exasperating snobbishness, infantile nationalism, and, above all, a shocking attitude of submission. One of them—well-educated, arrested for resistance activity—expressed it extraordinarily well: "Every master must be served, and all the work must be done"; no more need be said. This very restricted élite, which called itself "the Polish intelligentsia," administered Ravensbrück as it had its unfortunate homeland, with selfishness, futility, and a shameful absence of social awareness.

I hasten to say that today I am ashamed of this judgment, for I am convinced that in a similar situation, any other national group would have committed similar abuses. In fact, I have had occasion to watch my own countrymen utilize power (notably during the Algerian war), and that is why I can now admire, when the opportunity presents itself, those rare and scattered individuals of all nationalities who may be the strongest but do not abuse their power. One should not excuse the others, but I have since tried to avoid imputing to any one nationality what should be attributed to the evil instincts of humanity.

Two circumstances had placed the Polish women in a "position of strength" at Ravensbrück: their seniority in the camp and the fact that German was usually their second language, rather than English. (The opposite was more often the case among the French.) *Some* Poles abused this position of strength.

The Poles also knew how to organize an efficient system of mutual aid and, in some cases, true "resistance." One notable example: in the face of enormous risk they managed to get messages sent to the Allies telling of the medical experiments going on in the camp. There were also many admirable women among them who, in their direct relations with the French group, inspired unanimously favorable opinion: our dear Jadja, Stubova of the NN block—agreeable, quiet, efficient, and courageous—working constantly to maintain order, neatness, and as much justice as possible, continually putting herself between us and Knoll, the diabolical German Blockova, as when she would manage to get rid of the papers Knoll had made up to send one of us to the Strafblock (or worse). And I remember the courageous students from Lublin—some of them only children—and the dignity with which they collectively refused to allow any new martyrs to be taken from their ranks for the "scientific" experiments by SS Dr. Gebhardt. Then there was a very aristocratic old woman, certainly no "intellectual" by trade but the most contemplative spirit among them; she once said to me, with profound sadness: "We are now the last people of Europe, and by our own fault. When I was young, I lived on an estate we had in Russia. Today I met a woman who told me what's going on there now, the schools, the hospitals . . . Thirty years ago it was like that on both sides of the border." And I am not even counting the Polish friends who told me how much they preferred our attitude of systematic rebellion against the Germans to their own selfish complacency; I was very moved

when one of them told me: "All of the best people I hav
known in this camp have been French."[6]

On the whole, we got along best, by far, with the Yugo
slavs. Although we did not know their language, and few o
them knew ours, we felt a certain kinship whenever circum
stances brought us together, perhaps because of a simila
sense of national and personal honor, mutual civility, and
shared hatred of enduring the German yoke. What please
me most was that these qualities did not belong to one socia
class, but were, as with the French, a part of the people, a
all levels.

We found among the Czechs a much higher level of cultur
and political sophistication than in the other Central an
Eastern European peoples. And, the direct application of thei
talents to politics had developed a much more intense part
activity, especially among the Communists, whose party wa
exceptionally dynamic and disciplined.

Like the Poles, the Czechs were camp veterans and ha
certain "privileges": packages from outside and relativel
good jobs. But on top of that, they had an organizationa
and social genius which they used to make their life at Ra
vensbrück a clever mixture of sabotage (for the sake o
honor), work (to keep things peaceful), well-camouflage
"rest," and shrewdly arranged "recuperations." One of thei
finest successes was the conquest of the Revier: there, in on
of the most visible jobs in the camp (supervised by th
hateful and hypocritical Elisabeth Marschal), one Czec
woman always held her ground, never sacrificing her patrioti
dignity, always serving her comrades of every nationalit
(often with great daring), and, in place of the medicines sh
didn't have, giving everyone a maximum of personal atten
tion, a constant smile, skillful and gentle touches. All thi

[6] I hope I may be excused for this bit of naïve chauvinism
the words are not mine. I admit to having felt some satisfactio
on hearing them in 1944, but it is not without a degree of discom
fort that I reread them in 1972.

by someone named Zdenka, known by everyone at Ravens-brück only by her first name.[7]

Nevertheless, the Czechs had their own rather greedy and selfish petite bourgeoisie, completely Germanized and shame-lessly profiteering on the camp conditions. In Block 31 in particular, they applied (always methodically) the principle mentioned—but not recommended—in the Gospels: "To him who has will more be given, and from him who has not, even what he thinks that he has will be taken away." (St. Luke 8:18.)

The German "politicals" (with the exception of a very small number of Communists who had come from Austria and a few other isolated prisoners of international back-ground) were of a totally disheartening moral and intellectual level: vulgar, depraved, rapacious . . . and informers. But, to be just, one must note the point at which the "political" la-bel ceased to have real meaning: some women, for example, who had refused to work for Hitler's war (therefore quite "political") wore the same black triangle as the derelicts and prostitutes, while a prostitute who slept with a Polish man wore the red triangle of the "politicals." (All the French prisoners had red triangles, which made the situation I just described a considerable affront to the true "politicals.")

I felt the deepest compassion for the wretched gypsies in the camp. I often went into their block, and I had even begun a small vocabulary of their various dialects in order to engage them in conversation without seeming totally foreign. Thus I discovered two "families" of Belgian women and one old French gypsy, all bewildered and dazed by their incompre-hensible misfortune. They had a basic education and decent living habits, both of which made living with the German gypsies unbearable for them. The rest (except for a few Czechs) were astonishingly barbaric—less so than certain Ukranians, but noticeably more so than the African tribal

[7] I have since learned her full name: Zdenka Nedvedova, to whom unknown hundreds should be thankful.

women to whom my profession of ethnology had taken me. To be sure, I had never observed these latter in the atmosphere of a concentration camp.

The old Frenchwoman told me her story: they were itinerants, making the rounds of fairs and markets with some very good games and amusements, inherited from relatives. They were fourteen in all: She and her husband, their grown children, a son-in-law, and a married brother. But when the season was over they always returned to a nice little apartment in Paris, with radio and all the conveniences. One night the Germans arrested all the itinerants at a fair (in Lille, I think) and deported the dark-skinned ones. They were taken first to a prison in Belgium, where they learned they would be going to Auschwitz: *The others told me "Poor woman, that's hell where you're going," but what could I do about it? When we got to Auschwitz they put us in a big wooden hangar with black gravel for a floor, and nothing else—no straw, no blankets, and nothing to eat or drink for two days. . . . And we could see huge red flames through the cracks in the walls, but we didn't know what they were. After two days the order came that we would not be killed; then they gave us soup and tins of water and sent us somewhere else. . . .* Then came the real suffering, the beatings, the executions, and they died one by one, until none remained but her, and perhaps her youngest daughter in another camp; she didn't know. *But why? What did we do?* she asked over and over. *Why?*

Nothing else in the long catalogue of German crimes surpassed the slaughter of the gypsies (even the Jews often had the good fortune to die quickly). Every variety of murder was tried on them: more than any other group they were forced to serve as guinea pigs for "scientific" experiments, and at Ravensbrück, while some Germans might be sterilized as a form of individual punishment, only the gypsies were subjected to such treatment as a group, one after another—even the youngest girls.

Why? What were these poor people's crimes? If they were so culturally inferior, whose fault was it but the Germans', who had ruled most of them for centuries, doing nothing for them before they began the slaughter. The Germans—a shameful breed who knew only how to kill the defenseless.

The Frenchwomen, along with the Russians, were the favorite targets for SS hatred, and consistently produced the lowest profit for them. We were also systematically excluded from the easiest and most advantageous jobs, as well as from the most important ones; there were no French Blockovas, Stubovas, or Lagerpolizei; nor were there any among the cooks and gang bosses except for one or two Alsatians and one Frenchwoman married to a Pole, who used their positions to give all the help possible to their comrades. And they were not alone: Czechs, Poles, German "politicals," and Austrians, in numbers impossible to estimate, used their responsible positions in the same way, always at great risk.

The French were at cross-purposes with the camp authorities; the SS discipline, administered by the Poles, had the virtue of keeping all of us constantly enraged. Our shortcomings played as strong a role as our virtues in this obstinate stance; our worst elements (prostitutes and volunteer workers) were almost useless in the German scheme of industrial profit, partly because of their chronic lack of discipline, but also because of their unwillingness to act as informers. At the same time, one of our better elements (the Communist factory workers) applied all their courage and organizational talents to a cleverly methodical scheme of sabotage. The others (teachers, lawyers, professors, officers' wives) were "good-for-nothings" under any circumstances and could claim no great credit just for remaining themselves. . . .

One of the great misfortunes of the French political prisoners was our being thrown together with the ordinary lawbreakers or the miscellaneous foreigners. The NN section[8] and part of Block 15 were the only semiblocks where the French were a majority. The NN section was a "special" block for which the Germans had planned an initial period of harassment, to be followed by extermination; women from the Resistance reached a proportion of 80 per cent (never 100

[8] See p. 91 for details on the NN prisoners.

per cent, but no one knows why not). Our block was one of those which never saw the delivery of outside packages, thus one which experienced more hunger than most of the others. But it was the only block where a crust of bread could be left around without disappearing instantly; and it was relatively clean—and free of lice. Resistance to the Germans was always a common goal, and a woman trying to hide for one reason or another could always find accomplices. It was the only block where the *troc*—the camp's infamous black market—had been banished and replaced by a system of fraternal sharing; the only one with a regular system of helping the sick with small portions of extra food—hungry women would give up a potato or the spoon of ersatz jam they received once a week to help a tubercular live a little longer.

During the week following our liberation, I attempted to determine the number of Frenchwomen at Ravensbrück, having to use, obviously, very contrived methods.

The Swedish Red Cross, which delivered us on April 23, 1945, had grouped us in convalescent camps; we numbered 300. I was elected representative for my group and questioned each of my comrades on the date of her arrival at Ravensbrück and the number she had received, as well as the number of prisoners in their convoys (and names, if possible). From this I managed to arrive at an approximate total for the major movements of Frenchwomen, with no certainty of having identified all the transports involving relatively small numbers of deportees. My count of identifiable prisoners came to about 7,000, but the total number of Frenchwomen who passed through Ravensbrück was obviously greater: 8,000? 9,000? Perhaps 10,000.

The behavior of the various social classes would have been an interesting subject of investigation if it had been possible to conduct a really thorough study, since the entire social spectrum was represented. Of the 8,000–10,000 Frenchwomen recorded at Ravensbrück, no doubt almost a quarter were "common criminals": prostitutes who had infected German soldiers, housekeepers arrested for theft from their German masters, police informers who had become too deeply involved in the black market, workers who had gone voluntarily to the German factories and had been arrested for any number of offenses, etc. Although the prostitutes and the volunteer workers affected mutual contempt, there was usually very little difference between them. Except for the little scatterbrains who left for Germany on an impulse, or women who went to find their "man," the volunteer workers came from somewhere considerably lower than our society's élite; many had been in serious trouble at some time in their lives, and the rest were not much better. As for the prostitutes, they were all there for having contaminated the occupiers, which leads one to think that they "worked" for them with no particular sense of loathing; it would be difficult to think of their microbic accident as "sabotage."

The rest of the prisoners could all be considered political deportees, and they considered themselves as such. But not all of them had actually taken part in acts of resistance; they might have been sisters, mothers or wives of underground fighters, perhaps a concierge or servant in a "political" household—or even an innocent visitor; another might have been living in a nice apartment coveted by a Gestapo officer, or denounced by an impatient heir or jealous neighbor.

It was only natural that these women (who had become prisoners like one is struck down by a car—a stroke of fate in which their own will played no part) were not inclined to take risks and were, in many cases, dead weight to be borne by the others—the authentic resisters. Still, there were exceptions among them, but few to be sure. Some were moved to action by a love of adventure or to cover up shady dealings; there were others whose character and fortitude could not hold up under the violent strain of questioning, solitary confinement, and the temptations caused by hunger and fear, to which everyone was subjected.

It is all too common for the complexity and diversity of social groups to be oversimplified, or understated, for the convenience of political propaganda, perhaps, or out of simple mental laziness. This is a pity, as such an oversimplification makes a questionable point of departure for any soundly based inquiry. Better points would be the great number of studies that no one has ever taken the trouble to do: questions, for example, about how institutions form themselves and draw their "members"—a factory, government ministry, literary salon, brothel, political party, or newspaper readership. One might have been in a position to begin such an inquiry at Ravensbrück, but far too ill-equipped to carry it out coherently, which means that even concerning my own "institution"—the French Resistance—I have only approximate data.

It is possible, nonetheless, to make some rather simplistic observations: there were groups which, for the most part, performed their duty in this regard—the liberal and intellectual bourgeoisie (medical and teaching professions), the aged and impoverished military aristocracy (who had lived year-round in their magnificent but drafty chateaus), the Catholics from Brittany and Alsace, the practicing Protestants, the Communist organizations, in other words, the "socially adjusted" elements. They were all well-represented in our ranks, both in number and quality. On the other hand, the "misfits," obviously enough, were fewer and weaker. Thus we had with us a few very wealthy women from Paris "society," arrested because of bad luck rather than their own inclinations. They had a reputation of being dirtier than the others and harder to live with. Perhaps we just noticed them more.

There were various national groupings of Jews, but I was never able to discern any real bonds among them: Turkish Jews—educated, well-bred, pleasant to deal with, and very resourceful; Hungarian Jews—chronic complainers, totally at loose ends, and so abject that it is impossible to say what they might have been like under normal conditions; German Jews —impossible to distinguish from other Germans; a few Dutch and Danish Jews—impossible to distinguish from non-Jews; no Polish Jews. As for the French Jews, they had all been in the Resistance,[9] and none of us ever dreamed of considering them as a "special" category of patriot.

[9] In August 1944 there was one convoy of prisoners who had just been arrested in France on racial grounds; they did not remain long at Ravensbrück.

Compared with other nationalities, the French "society" at Ravensbrück particularly impressed me with its homogeneity. The difference between a Polish student and a Polish woman of the masses was so great that they seemed to be of different species, in their ways of eating, speaking, drinking, or blowing their noses. . . . But I would defy any foreigner to see—under those striped dresses—the difference between a Parisian student and a Parisian worker.

I have often noticed the point at which the intellectual classes transcend the borders of nationalism and come within a trifle of being a homogeneous class of their own. But the working class, so accurately called "the people," is always very much of its own country, providing a gauge of a nation's level of civilization—the heritage of carpenters and mechanics, not of professors. And the French working class I had contact with was, to my mind, intellectually, morally, and socially very superior to the others of Europe and, in an absolute sense, of a very high level.

In the women's camps, political and religious bonds played a less important role than the solidarity of nationalism, which, for every country, was quite strong. This does not mean, however, that Communists and Christians lacked conviction, or did not gather for discussion or prayer, or did not find great consolation in these embryonic communities which went beyond the borders of nationalism; in a sincere search for universality, many of the best prisoners found the most profound communion in ideology or religion. On top of this, the very nature of the camp created a remarkable situation: the mixture of cultures was so complete and the terrible living conditions were shared in such a way that ordinary conventions and hypocrisies were swept away and true natures revealed— the *"grande dame"* who turned out to be a thief, the Communist who showed herself as a cheat and hoarder, the Gaullist "patriot," zealously working for the German war effort in order to get her dish of soup. Negative reaction to these lapses was justifiably severe, especially since moral collapse was more of a threat to our collective dignity than simple physical decline. But these lapses had the beneficial result of spotlighting each person's intrinsic worth, and all of us were judged by the others according to this single criterion, quite apart from political or religious labels.

In the men's camps, where the physical situation was the same if not worse, reactions were different.[10] All of which leads to the possible conclusion that women are less sectarian than men, and traditionally accustomed to a more relaxed form of competition and less burdensome economic responsibilities, but at the same time perhaps more directly and deeply involved in the more human exigencies of life.

[10] See p. 223 for a commentary on Eugen Kogon's book on Buchenwald.

4

Extermination and Profitability

The mortality rate among men in the camps was higher than that of women, an inequality due at least in part to the different aptitudes of the sexes. Women have a greater ingenuity in many things touching directly on the simple preservation of life: nursing their sick, sewing and knitting clothing from scraps and discards, but less aptitude, I'm afraid, for things technical. I was often appalled at our incompetence in mechanical matters; of the 115,000 (or 123,000) who passed through Ravensbrück, I doubt that there was a single woman, say in 1943, with either the technical knowledge or enterprising spirit to put together a simple radio transmitter, or even to pick a lock.[1] In the women's camps, any enterprise involving wide-ranging collective skills was to be avoided.

Two other sets of circumstances, in my view, helped explain the difference in death rates: the first and most obvious was the greater proportion of extermination Kommandos in the men's camps; second was Ravensbrück's role as a center for the economic exploitation of female prisoners—it was a profit-making industrial enterprise which waited until the last minute to "settle" its labor costs and liquidate its "manpower."

This matter of the rate of consumption of human lives in the various camps is absolutely central; not only did it create a sort of staggering in the ineluctable march toward death by attrition, but, more importantly, it was the greatest difference and the only real form of gradation among the camps. There were camps where one might stay alive for two to five years

[1] Such is not so much the case today. (1972)

(Buchenwald and early Ravensbrück), others for a few months (late Ravensbrück, certain Kommandos at Auschwitz), others where one could expect to be dead within a few weeks (Bergen-Belsen, Jugendlager, Block 25 at Ravensbrück, etc.). I am speaking only of death by simple physiological afflictions; the camps where death came in a few days were those with organized extermination: gas, poisoning, mass murders, etc.

But of course it always came down to that anyway—that is, properly so-called "murder"—since in death by exhaustion and attrition, there is necessarily a more or less long period of "dying," during which some poor soul at the end of her strength no longer produces a profit; and during this period, which could last a few days or a few months, there is a cost, however small, to the "employer."

Given these conditions, one can very easily understand why, in order to keep the business of Ravensbrück prosperous, it was necessary to periodically destroy the human equipment that was no longer useful (at first, a quarter or one fifth of the population each year). But in order to maintain optimum efficiency, it was preferable to erect a façade of propriety, which meant that exterminations were not carried out on the spot. The transports noirs served precisely this purpose, removing the worn-out prisoners and disposing of them in some camp specializing in annihilation. So the work camps and death camps were "complementary."

Costs at Ravensbrück were negligible: since the camp was self-supporting, expenditures were kept to a minimum. Draining the marshes, preparing the land, raising the rutabagas, gardening, carpentry, plumbing, manufacture of uniforms and shoes, all were done by prisoners. Thanks to comrades who worked in the bookkeeping offices, I arrived at a figure of 35 pfennigs as the daily cost of individual upkeep, including bread, which came from the Oranienburg camp,[2] and margarine from the quartermaster. I have not been able to verify this figure since my return, so I give it without guarantee.

[2] The Sachsenhausen camp (near Oranienburg), which was the source of our bread until April 11, 1945.

Eugen Kogon, who was able to get access to the Buchenwald archives immediately after the liberation, has given us an accounting, drawn up by the SS, representing the average profit that could be produced by a deportee. I have summarized as follows:

Average daily revenue for a hired-out prisoner		6 marks
Deductions:		
Food	0.60	
Depreciation of clothing	0.10	
		0.70
		5.30 marks

which, for an average life span of nine months, comes to:

$$5.30 \times 270 = 1,431 \text{ marks}$$

This profit was increased between 200 and several thousand marks by the practical utilization of the dead (gold teeth, clothing, valuable articles). But these amounts had to be reduced by the costs of incineration, about two marks per body.

(E. Kogon, op. cit., p. 269)

In an undated document from Auschwitz cited by O. Wormser-Migot,[3] the cost of maintaining a prisoner was estimated at 1.22 marks for a woman and 1.34 marks for a man; this amount would include the initial cost and upkeep of the rags that passed for clothing, as well as general expenses (water, lights, building maintenance). Regarding Oranienburg, the same author wrote (p. 391): "Experts have calculated that food must not have cost more than 33 pfennigs per person per day, or about 15,000 marks. . . . The camp took in an average of three marks per prisoner-worker . . . or, with the food deduction, 120,000 marks per day. . . ."

[3] O. Wormser-Migot, op. cit., p. 282.

Of course a certain number of prisoners were always involved in the work of the camp, but the rest were hired out to various business enterprises nearby, or in the camp itself.

There was an economically independent manufacturing complex inside Ravensbrück, managed by a man named Opitz, who paid the camp administration 3.50–4 marks a day for each prisoner assigned to him. But I believe that he also paid a certain amount for the feeding of his prisoners—theoretically his responsibility, but carried out by the camp management as a matter of convenience. There were bitter disputes between Opitz and the quartermaster about this, of which the most obvious result was that the poor women of the *Betriebe* were more poorly fed than those of the camp as a whole, if such a thing can be imagined.

> Suhren (interrogatory, December 6, 1949) stated: ". . . the companies paid the camp the flat daily amount of 70 pfennigs per deportee for food, and, to my knowledge, the same amount still applies today in German prisons." Now it could very well be that he was telling the truth, and actually dunned them the 70 pfennigs on top of the work fee, to the likely indignation of businessmen who considered it theft when they received dying women in return.

Near the camp there was a Siemens factory which paid even more—4.50, 5, sometimes up to 7 marks for specialists or very productive workers. This resulted in a standing order at the Revier that the Siemens workers were to have top priority. For others, it was just as well not to ask for a consultation with a fever of less than 104°.

Ravensbrück not only furnished cheap labor for the nearby factories, but, on request, sent prisoner-workers throughout Germany. For a stipulated price the businessman or industrialist received the 500 or 1,000 women requested, along with Aufseherinnen who, equipped with trained dogs and clubs, could force twelve hours of work a day out of exhausted and starving women, right up to the point of death. They would be replaced with more of the same, without additional cost to the client. But thanks to the Aufseherinnen, the dogs, and the beatings, it was a perfect cycle, with no waste; the prisoners worked until they could work no more.

(Prisoners employed in the work assignment offices counted fifty-five factories and Kommandos using prisoners from Ravensbrück, but their lists were not necessarily complete.)

Most of these subcamps were under the administration of Ravensbrück, but some (Brunswick and Hanover, for example) were within Neuengamme's jurisdiction or attached to other major prison centers—Buchenwald, Dachau, Flossenburg, Mauthausen. In such cases the prisoners were considered as having left Ravensbrück, and, if they returned, were issued a new identification number. The number of these prisoners registered at least twice was estimated at 2,000 by our comrades in the labor registry and at 3,000 by comrades in the political office.

Following is a list of some of the outside Kommandos using prisoners from Ravensbrück:

Buchenwald exchange (some returns)

Altenburg (near Dresden)
Leipzig (AEG plant)
Leipzig (Hasag plant)
Meuselwitz (returns to Ravensbrück)
Neustadt (Cobourg) (returns to Ravensbrück)
Polte (Magdebourg) (returns to Ravensbrück after a bombing raid)
Schlieben
Taucha
Torgau

Dachau exchange (no returns to Ravensbrück)

Augsburg
Lebensbornheim (Munich)
Plausee

Flossenburg exchange (no returns to Ravensbrück)

Graslitz
Holleichen
Neurolau
Zwodau

Neuengamme exchange (very few returns)

> Bartensleben
> Braunschweig (one returning transport on April 14, 1945)
> Hamburg-Ost
> Hanover
> Helmstedt
> Salzgitter
> Salzwedel (returns)
> Wattenstedt (830 departures, 155 returns)
> Wittenberge

Sachsenhausen

> Belzig
> Berlin (AEG)
> Berlin (Pertrix)
> Berlin (Siemens)
> Genshagen
> Glöwen
> Königswusterhausen
> Oberschöneweide
> Oranienburg (Auer)
> Schönefeld (600 prisoners, 200 of them French)
> Velten
> About 100 women at Mülhausen and sixteen at Natzweiler.

Then there were the Sonderkommandos, the "special" Kommandos to which the SS chose to give no other name, but it was a terrifying name in itself. They included the prostitution squads, ten assigned permanently to six camps —Buchenwald, Dachau, Flossenburg, Mauthausen, Oranienburg, Sachsenhausen. Their number was replenished from time to time and must have totaled more than 100.

Some of the transports leaving Ravensbrück went to maintain the air bases at Königsberg and Rechlin, worked at the installations in Schönefeld, Neubrandenburg, Torgau, Barth, and at the Zwodau powder factory; more than 800 prisoners were used at Wattenstedt in the Hermann Goering factories. . . .

Here is something written by one of our comrades[4] during the month after her liberation. She was part of a transport sent to an underground factory (1,800 feet down) in an old salt mine at Beendorf.

I just learned about Miron's death two days ago. It was so sad. . . . We were miserable at Beendorf; every time the least little thing went wrong, I thought how lucky poor Miron was not to be there—she couldn't have put up with it. . . . We've lost so many good friends that way we wouldn't be able to count them all; we'll probably be surprised when we get back to France. In your next letter you must tell me about your own work, and the working conditions. As for myself, I left for my "job" on August 10 with some comrades from Auschwitz, except for Charlotte and Mado (there were thirty-five of us, and all good friends), not a bad convoy on the whole. From August to the end of April we had to work in a salt mine 1,800 feet underground, making airplane parts. There was plenty of rough treatment, but the beatings didn't keep us from doing our part in the way of sabotage—about 80 per cent of our "production" was sabotage. We drove our bosses out of their minds. They offered bonuses to encourage us to do better—rather tempting ones (food, etc.), which we would have loved to snap up. But we refused. I was among the first to refuse the Blockführer's offer; he looked amazed but didn't say too much. Still, he insisted that I take the stuff and tried to force it into my hands. I kept my arms at my sides; he finally gave up and let me leave. After the fifth refusal by my friends, he stopped trying to pass things out and went to look for the Scharführer. They talked things over and ended the matter by throwing everything out, and the Germans fell all over each other trying to grab it up. While all this was going on, the day shift had arrived; we told them we had refused the bonuses, and they all repeated the process. There were about thirty of them, and threats of twenty-five lashes with the rubber hose had no effect. Then the bosses

[4] Luce C., in a letter to her friend Maguy B., May 31, 1945.

*tried to change the method of distribution, but we all still re-
fused. . . . We saw the outside only during our night shift,
and that was terribly distressing. We continually wasted away,
every one of us, and looking at each other, with our sickly,
ghostly color, only frightened us. But now we're beginning
to recover, and it's such a relief seeing friends transformed
day by day, for the better. We're a long way from normal,
I'm afraid: we left quite a few comrades in the TB sanatorium
and hospital, and many of us are still sick—all because of the
mine. We all had swollen faces and legs from lack of air; a
few days in the infirmary was enough to reduce the swelling,
but we had to start all over again a couple of days later.*

*But the worst part of all for us was the transport from
Beendorf (near Magdeburg) to Hamburg. Still, we had some
unexpected good luck: they had intended to send us to the
gas chambers at the Neuengamme camp, but we got there
one day after it was evacuated; so many of our comrades had
already been gassed in that camp, men and women! The trip
had lasted twelve days and nights, and it was a nightmare,
believe me. They began the extermination along the way;
there were 5,000 of us at the start, and we lost more than
1,000. On the second day there were 380 bodies piled up waiting to be buried; of these, 120 had been shot, some others
died of hunger, but most of the Jews had died from beatings.
. . . It was terrible, terrible, even despite my constant opti-
mism, which somehow never failed me.*

One could, without too much trouble, make a rough calculation of the profits, based on what I have already shown, of
Ravensbrück as a working camp (before its main function
became extermination, in August 1944, for example):[5]

[5] The following passage is from a book (Guerber, *Himmler et
ses Crimes*, p. 63) which, unfortunately, is not precise enough in
citing its sources:

*Himmler had created certain camps, the revenues from which
were his personal property; the following seven concentration
camps, in effect, belonged to Himmler, not to the German state:*

1. Mauthausen: revenues of 67,000 marks per month
2. Dachau: 80,500

around this time, 58,000 women had been entered on the camp rolls; of these, perhaps 18,000 were already dead or dying. Some 8,000, in fact, had gone out of circulation by January 1943; eighteen months later one could estimate the additional "wastage" at 10,000. A calculation should be based on about 40,000 more or less able-bodied women, each producing 2.50 marks a day (allowing for certain deductions: camp services, which used some of the best-qualified workers, and the knitters and Verfügbaren, whose profit return was insignificant). Even so, this minimum estimate would be a daily gross of 100,000 marks, or an annual gross of 35 million marks.

Gossiping with an elderly prisoner employed in an administrative office in early 1944, I learned that Himmler was not only our administrative "superior" (as head of the police and SS), but at the same time either the owner of the land (which

3. Treblinka:	56,000
4. Ravensbrück:	59,000
5. Bergen-Belsen:	69,000
6. Sachsenhausen:	56,000
7. Auschwitz:	96,000

Other National-Socialist leaders had "shares" in other death camps. Goering, for example, received a quarter of the profits collected at Buchenwald. For a time before he fell at the hands of Czech patriots, Heydrich underwrote the "management" of the Siedle camp in Bohemia; SS General Sepp Dietrich was a "partner" in Treblinka, the worst of the prisons, where the Nazis exterminated up to 35,000 a day—men, women, children, the aged—mostly Polish and Hungarian Jews.

It would be interesting to find out exactly when the document citing these figures was put together. It would be equally interesting to know if the amounts were those actually received by Himmler, or were the total net profit for each camp.

The monthly gross profit at Ravensbrück in 1944 was at least thirty times that given here, but in 1941, for example, it was probably next to nothing. In the prison context, the difference between gross and net should not be too great. Would it really be necessary to deduct innumerable salaries, etc.? One could quite logically conclude that the profits shown in the Guerber book were only a small part of the total—perhaps the exact amount allocated to a private party or, conversely, the minor portion which reverted to the state.

he rented to the state), or the principal stockholder of a company exploiting the camp's prisoner labor. In any case, it is certain that, in a private capacity, he had a financial interest in Ravensbrück and took a share of the profits. At the time I was unable to determine either the exact form or amount.

I am unable to do much better even today, but I remain convinced:

1. that Himmler and his close collaborators shared *privately* in the profits produced by concentration camp labor;

2. of the sanctioned destruction of documents relating to these share accounts.

Indeed, at Auschwitz as at Ravensbrück, the prisoners whose job was to keep the books were quite emphatic on this point: they regularly recorded the profit shares going to these "stockholders" by name. It is a simple fact that these records were the subject of their daily work, and they were in these jobs for long periods.

When I discussed this information in the presence of a comrade who had returned from Auschwitz (Marie-Claude Vaillant-Couturier or Hélène Solomon, I do not remember which), she told me that at Auschwitz there were greenhouses belonging to a private individual and maintained by prisoners. The operation required special books, also kept by prisoners, of course. The private party was Heinrich Himmler.

I still recall the jolt I felt on first learning these things in early 1944. How clear everything became! Mr. Himmler, property owner, performed the service of relieving Mr. Himmler, police minister, of all his enemies. And in exchange, Mr. Himmler, chief of police, continuously furnished Mr. Himmler, landowner, with handsome dividends in the form of human livestock to replace what was being used up at an accelerating rate. A perfect utilization of uncultivated wasteland for an ingenious capitalist: where nothing grows, a concentration camp is built, and it becomes a veritable gold mine!

Equally remarkable, beginning in 1943 a concern over profits superseded the practical extermination of Germany's enemies. Properly so-called "executions" became fewer (what could they lose?); yet there were no more prisoner releases, even if one had been incarcerated by flagrant error. The result was that many violent terrorists, condemned to death under any number of laws, would be arrested, deported, and might still be alive, while thousands of totally innocent people (or some perhaps liable to a couple of weeks in jail) were also deported, beaten to death with clubs, gassed, or died of hunger. Until 1943, political executions (that is, of Germany's enemies) took precedence over economic executions (people used in the "service" of the country), but after that time they no longer executed someone for having a bomb in her handbag, but because she might show the white hair of age or look not quite fit. Mr. Himmler, policeman, was sensitive to the interests of his counterpart.

I was naturally very eager to pound my new-found conception of the system into whatever receptive heads I could find among my comrades. (Thank God there were some.) Mentally taking apart and understanding a system, even one that is crushing you, and stepping back and taking a clear view of a situation, even a desperate one, are powerful sources of consolation, composure, and spiritual strength. Nothing is more terrifying than a complete mystery. While tracking these mysteries, I was conscious of giving a degree of moral strength to my comrades, but I had another reason, which might be better understood when this account is complete. It seemed to me unhappily certain that few of us would survive, but I assumed that not everyone would vanish, and I wanted there to be every possible chance that the truth would emerge from this pit of desolation and crime.

After more than twenty-five years of searching, much of the mystery remains. Some documents refer to the enormous revenues at the disposal of the Wirtschafts und Verwaltungs-Hauptamt (WVHA), the organization responsible for the economic exploitation of deportees. These revenues were on the order of one million marks a day: 120,000 marks at Oranienburg (O. Wormser-Migot, op. cit., p. 391), 35,000–40,000 a day at Auschwitz (p. 381); these include only the amounts garnered from the victims' actual work, not the additional sum realized from their bodies and belongings.

But little is known about the use of these funds simply because of a lack of documentation.

5

The Exploiters

At the top of the hierarchy was the probable inventor of the system—or at least its principal administrator—Heinrich Himmler, simultaneously the main supplier, chief executive, and major stockholder.

Aside from the financial ties which bound us to him, we did not know a great deal about Himmler, except for two significant practices that began after one of his inspections at Ravensbrück: the authorization to receive outside packages (a great advantage for both the prisoners and the camp economy) and the use of corporal punishment and flogging. A reflective analyst will no doubt see in these apparent contradictions the same perverse puzzle as in another set of incoherencies I have already mentioned: the apparent leniency and forebearance which pardoned some terrorists (a direct turnabout from the death sentence handed down on deportation) and, on the other hand, the cruelty which filled the slave camps with innocent people. I have heard this called the "German incoherence," and "logic within inconsistency," but to me it is precisely this so-called contradiction which made up the "style" and peculiar genius of Heinrich Himmler, and it was along this borderline that the profits quietly flowed.

Here are some observations on Himmler by his boyhood friend Dr. Karl Gebhardt (part of Gebhardt's endless discourse in court—which filled 400 pages):[1] *He was neither an exceptional man nor a pathological case, and*

[1] Dr. François Bayle, *Croix gammée contre caducée*, pp. 218–20.

he wasn't two-faced either. He was never really interesting. On the other hand, if you will allow me to se aside for a moment all those unspeakable atrocities Himmler was a man with a very straightforward an full work plan. We came from the same city—Landshut— and our famous relationship of mutual confidence ha its origin in our fathers—mine, the Himmler family doc tor, and his, the principal of my school. We spent ou childhood, from the ages of twelve to sixteen, together . . . I lost contact . . . from 1919 to 1937. . . . H had no originality, but he was extraordinarily indus trious. . . .

It was during this trip [when they went to Austria to gether in 1938] *that Himmler spoke to me about the ver personal struggle in his life, which so many lies hav been written about; he asked for my help. He never reall got a university education; here was a well-balance man, but only half-educated; he couldn't have childre and simply never overcame these problems. . . .*

SS Colonel Wolfram Sievers, administrator of th Ahnenerbe[2] from 1935 to 1945, was in frequent contac with Himmler, and: *. . . We then decided to assassinat Himmler and Hitler, or if that was not possible, to ge at least Himmler, who was more powerful. Hitler ma have appeared to be the most important in the Reich but Himmler—because of the concentration of power i his hands—was actually the strongest. He was, in fac the principal figure in the entire Waffen SS, in most o the Allgemeine SS, and in all of the police bodies, in cluding the Gestapo Security Service. Even more, he con trolled the civilian internal organization of Germany, be ginning in 1943, as Interior Minister; and after Canari was disposed of in 1944, Himmler took over the militar counterespionage organization. . . .*

[2] The Ahnenerbe (Institute for Research into Heredity) was a organization created in 1933 with a goal of "examining the local ization, spirit, and deeds of the Nordic-Germanic race." It wa responsible for the cruelest and most lunatic human experiment in the concentration camps. F. Bayle, op. cit., p. 294.

Dr. Rudolf Brandt, Himmler's chief secretary and adjutant for more than ten years, with the title and salary of cabinet counselor (he handled some 3,500 letters a month and dealt mainly with personal matters), said of his employer:[3] *I disapprove of Himmler because of the crimes he committed and because he committed suicide. . . . He took me everywhere with him to finish whatever work he was doing; I was like his shadow. . . . It was a rare member of the party who did not play his role and augment his legal income with money from other sources. I could see how hard he worked. The performance of his duty and his work were his principal concerns. . . . I believed that a man who lived by these rules and had such goals could want only good and would take care not to commit crimes. . . .*

Dr. F. Bayle said of Brandt (p. 315): *Insignificant ideas . . . devoid of intuition or common sense. His judgment is childish, naïve and suggestible. . . .*

One can hardly doubt the above, but it is equally evident that Himmler was a maniacal double-dealer.

I often tried, from the depths of the unfathomable misery of the camp, to build a mental picture of those who had conceived and constructed that miserable world.

But I could not get past an image of a fat, manicured hand, pouring tea or coffee into a cup, taking a sugar cube from a dish—one of those small, daily gestures which are so human and so much a part of an atmosphere of civilization. Beyond immediate reality, the bounds of imagination are so confining and mental laziness so prevalent that it is difficult to react fully to an environment. You who read this should make the effort to imagine the scenes of terror, but those of us who lived in them had to think of the outside world of the living in order to maintain the burning indignation which was our only strength—an emotion in the exact middle between blind hatred and an equally blind self-surrender (the lassitude called resignation, which is all too often the result of extreme physical weakness).

[3] F. Bayle, op. cit., p. 310.

But I do have the book by Count Folke Bernadotte, i
which he relates conversations with Himmler in April 1945
to brutally revive this vanished hell for me.

After the Americans had liberated Buchenwald, Himmle
was indignant at their reactions: "It is outrageous," the Ges
tapo chief said, "that this camp, which in my view was i
model shape, should have become the subject of these shame
less accounts."[4] And this quiet, gentle man, the fancier c
runic inscriptions, might well have been thinking, "And if the
make such an issue of this, what are they going to say whe
they stick their noses into the extermination camps?"

He probably did not feel like laughing when he told Coun
Bernadotte that he was going to have an investigation mad
into the "totally ridiculous descriptions" of Buchenwald an
Bergen-Belsen by the Allies; these were, after all, extremel
detrimental to his interests. Rather grimly ironic to us nov
that these conversations took place in the clinic at Hohenly
chen administered by Dr. Gebhardt, Himmler's childhoo
friend, the very person to whom Himmler—always the goo
friend—had offered my little Polish comrades (a hundred o
so fourteen- to twenty-five-year-old students) for his vivisec
tion experiments.

Himmler's suicide fits well within the bounds of the pictur
I have tried to construct by using a tangible being—a ma
who actually lived and actually conceived and carried out s
many crimes. . . . It was not a suicide of temperament, o
a bizarre and "Niebelung" act of passion like that of his col
league Hitler, but the calculated and belated "resignation" o
a nefarious functionary who did not want to stand up fo
an accounting of his deeds. His death still remains a mystery
What was he up to when he was arrested by the Allied police
If he had intended to die all along, would he have waite
until his captors made him open his mouth for inspection t
bite the vial of poison he had kept hidden—actually the ver
last second he would have been able to take his own life?

One could also rightly ask what became of the enormou
personal profits the concentration camps produced for him

[4] Count Folke Bernadotte, *The Curtain Falls* (Knopf), p. 98.

d, besides these more or less straightforward "business"
ofits, there was the Ravensbrück "treasure": the treasures
the dead, the millions in gold which left the camp in trucks
few days before the debacle and of which nothing more
s ever heard. It has led to speculation that Himmler had
refuge all prepared in a neutral country, perhaps, or even
Germany, which was surely known to at least a few others,
rhaps only a few steps away. . . .

The other personnel employed in the operation of this sys-
n of exploitation are also worth examining.

Under Himmler's direct orders was SS Gruppenführer Os-
ld Pohl, an administrative official who also had a private
ancial interest.

He was the sole owner of a model farm on the very land
ich had been cleared and plowed by prisoners. The prop-
ty included a special Kommando of Dutch women and a
la which, from the outside, appeared extravagantly lux-
ious.

Pohl passed orders along to Lagerkommandant Koegel,
o was later transferred to Mauthausen. Koegel ordered tor-
res carried out and, during the winter of 1942, personally
rtured a large group of "religious" prisoners who had re-
sed to do any work or even answer roll calls on grounds
at such co-operation would be a form of participation in
e German war machine. A dozen or more of them had been
nt to Auschwitz in the autumn of 1942, only to come back
Ravensbrück shortly afterward to be executed. It was from
em that the other Ravensbrück prisoners received the first
tails about Auschwitz; at least they had time to tell us some-
ing before they were killed, particularly of the children who
d been burned alive there and of the smell of burning flesh
hich floated continuously over Auschwitz.

Those who had remained at Ravensbrück were locked up
a single block for two weeks without sleeping mats, blan-
ts, or coats. They got a bit of soup every four days. At
e end of the two weeks they received an admonitory lec-
re from Koegel and twenty-five cudgel blows. One of them—
ung, very pretty—only laughed under the beating; she died
om the twenty-five extra blows meted out for her laughter.

Then they were divided up, two or three to a block, and signed to Blockovas with orders to bring them into compl submission. In good time, most of them disappeared from camp; about sixty remained; there had been 500 of them 1941.

Koegel was replaced in late 1942 by Fritz Suhren. We s relatively little of him, but his actions as head of the ca were sufficient for judgment. He seems to have been an perienced and crafty official, avoiding compromising blund and always careful to keep his flanks guarded, even on most minor matters. His administration could take credit building the Uckermarck subcamp (Jugendlager) and the chamber. He was directly responsible for the murder of s eral thousand women who were guilty only of being old, worn out by the surfeit of work and lack of food, both which he so methodically organized.

It seemed unlikely to me that during the final phase of war, Suhren—for the first time, and without orders—wo have taken the responsibility of ordering the extermination prisoners on the spot.[5] His personal, and ingenious, role the camp's administration appeared as a sort of windo dressing propriety, which he tried to maintain as long as p sible with his clever machinations of faking the death t a form of "double accounting." He was always present at e cutions and floggings, but I don't know whether he consider them a diversion or just another drudgery of the job. C case: a group of German prisoners who for some infracti or another had been sentenced to a term in the bunker (hole). One day in December, Suhren came to inform th personally that, in observance of the holidays, they had be paroled from the bunker, and by the same token they wo

[5] I am not quite so convinced of this today.
I followed his two trials very closely and read all of the tr scripts. There was not a single point on which he volunteered truth spontaneously, but when it finally seemed impossible to de certain crimes committed at Ravensbrück, he tried to strength his defense by acknowledging that crimes existed—as in the nota instance when he admitted there was a gas chamber—while tryi to attribute responsibility to his collaborators. See p. 147. (1972)

receive for their little Christmas, three weeks in advance, the twenty-five lashes they were entitled to before returning to the merry camp of Ravensbrück. These fortunate ones, crying with pain, begged him to spare them his generosity, but, correct as always and apparently indifferent, he didn't deprive them of a single blow.

Fritz Suhren was born on June 10, 1908, in Vasel (Oldenburg). Questioned at Rastadt in December 1951 about his vital statistics, he answered that he was married, had four children, and earned his living as a businessman. His only conviction of any kind, he said, was a two-year term for currency smuggling, imposed in 1949 by an American military tribunal. He then acknowledged that he had taken command at Ravensbrück in October 1942 (which was correct) and said those duties ended in February 1945 (which was untrue and contradicted by his superior, Obergruppenführer Oswald Pohl, and two subordinates, Schwarzhuber and Binz). Suhren had good reason for lying on this detail of when he gave up command, since he could not deny the existence of a gas chamber at Ravensbrück beginning in February 1945. But he obviously decided to contend that at that date he no longer had the responsibility of command (his entire defense, detailed in careful steps, rested on this date) and that he was then replaced by Sturmbannführer Sauer.

An excerpt from the examination of Fritz Suhren at Rastadt, December 5, 1949:

Question: *Concerning the functions you performed at Ravensbrück between February and May 1945, I call attention to other testimony in these proceedings which contradicts your position; that is, several accounts whose importance you cannot deny. First, the testimony of your assistant Schwarzhuber, who, at the Hamburg trial (document no. 864, p. 3), said specifically that Sauer was not the commandant at Ravensbrück, but took orders from you.*

Answer: *I deny Schwarzhuber's statements on this point.*

Question: *And we have SS Obergruppenführer Pohl, currently in custody at the Landsberg prison, who testified (document no. 323): "Suhren was the chief of the Ravensbrück concentration camp. I don't remember the exact date when he took over these duties, but, to the best of my recollection, he remained in that position until the end."*

Answer: *I also deny SS Obergruppenführer Pohl's statements on this point.*

Question: *We have your codefendant Hans Pflaum, who testified on this issue twice during his first appearance before me. First, document no. 176, p. 1: "When I came to Ravensbrück in February 1945, around the fifth or tenth, Suhren was still Lagerführer, and he remained Lagerführer until the end." Then, document no. 176, p. 2: "Sauer and Suhren had the same rank—both had four stars; Sauer was older, but I maintain that Suhren was Lagerführer. . . . Furthermore, I always took orders from Suhren." But when you confronted Pflaum on this point on November 7 (document no. 201), Pflaum retreated from his earlier testimony and contended that he did not know who was actually the commandant of Ravensbrück between February 1945 and the German collapse, which seems totally unlikely, considering the level of Pflaum's duties there. Pflaum explained this change by claiming that the interpreter misunderstood him.*

Directly under the Lagerkommandant's orders was the Schutzhaftlagerführer, who was responsible for maintaining order in the camp. Of him we saw a great deal more.

When we arrived in November 1943, it was a huge and brutal man, named Edmund Bräuning,[6] who passed himself off as the lover of Oberaufseherin Dorothea Binz, a blond young flirt who would have been pretty if her face had not

[6] Before Bräuning, there were four Schutzhaftlagerführers at Ravensbrück.

always been literally contorted with hate. She always attended the floggings with her "lover"—without any official need, it seemed—and they were often seen in a passionate embrace during or after this type of "ceremony."

One Schutzhaftlagerführer, Schwarzhuber, inserted himself into the command hierarchy during the final winter. He came from Auschwitz, so he was naturally an expert at slaughtering prisoners. Elegant and relatively young, he had the manners of an officer from the Prussian aristocracy, seemed more intelligent and contemplative than the average German we had the misfortune to know, and was more temperamental than methodical. I personally watched him very closely during several "selections"—the arbitrary marking of women for death—and he displayed a hearty and brisk good nature, which contrasted sharply with his usual demeanor and belied his prematurely aging face. It is quite possible that, in addition to the material advantages of his position, he valued the "moral" advantages as well, if I may venture such an expression. And possible, too, that in this atmosphere of terror and despair he experienced a sort of expansion of personality.[7]

Johann Schwarzhuber, born August 29, 1904, in Tutzing, Bavaria, completed a secondary education and was a printer before enlisting in the SS on April 8, 1933. On May 5 the same year, he was assigned to Dachau, where he became Blockführer on March 1, 1935, and Unterscharführer in November 1938. As of September 9, 1941, he was inspector in the outside labor Kommando at Auschwitz, and from there he was promoted to Untersturmführer on November 9, 1941. In March 1942 he was named commandant of Auschwitz 2 (Birkenau) and attained the rank of Obersturmführer (April 20, 1944). He left Auschwitz at the end of October and in early November 1944 became a deputy commandant at Ravensbrück, where he remained until the dissolution of the camp on April 29, 1945, and where,

[7] This does not necessarily contradict two other brief references about him. (See pp. 60 and 185.)

despite the repugnance he was to express later,[8] he carried out all the extermination orders he received. He was arrested by the Allies on May 3, 1945.

Of all the Ravensbrück war criminals (some of whom went on trial at Hamburg under British supervision, while others were tried at Rastadt under the French), he seems to me to have been the most spontaneous in telling the truth. According to the British investigators, his was a lost cause from the very first, but he was very cool about the situation, and, either just to get things over with, or more likely out of weariness, fatalism, or the courage of a soldier, he decided to tell the truth and stick by it, regardless of the consequences to himself or his accomplices. He was not a beast (like Binder and Pflaum), and he displayed the articulateness, appearance, and conduct of a psychologically normal man. His biography shows, however, that from the ages of twenty-nine to forty-one (1933–45) he was an official in the extermination machine. He was, in short, a "specialist" in death and, by all appearances, came to the profession by choice.

Rudolf Franz Hoess, the commandant of Auschwitz, refers to Schwarzhuber fleetingly in his own confession,[9] in a passage concerning the gypsies: *About 4,000 gypsies were left by August 1944, and these had to go into the gas chambers. Up to that moment, they were unaware of what was in store for them. They first realized what was happening when they made their way, barrack hut by barrack hut toward Crematorium I* [on the night of July 31 or August 1]. *It was not easy to drive them into the gas chambers. I myself did not see it, but Schwarzhuber told me that it was more difficult than any previous mass destruction of Jews and it was particularly hard on him, because he knew almost every one of them individually and had been on good terms with them. They were by their nature as trusting as children.*

[8] See p. 149.
[9] Rudolf Franz Hoess, *Commandant of Auschwitz*, World, 1959, pp. 139–40.

Another, and equally formidable, camp personality was the chief of the work office (Arbeiteinsatz), who was, in a manner of speaking, the representative of Himmler the proprietor, while the commandants represented Himmler the policeman. I do not know the official relative positions of these men within the military hierarchy, but I do know that the commandants considered their principal role to be the execution of orders from the work office.

In 1943 the director of the Arbeiteinsatz was one Herr Dithmann, who was replaced in 1944 by the gross and bestial fiend mentioned above, Hans Pflaum, known as the "cow merchant"—the very model of a German brute who mercilessly abused every woman who came within reach and was almost always drunk. During the last three months, he made the "selections" himself: on the right those who would go dig the trenches, on the left those headed for the gas chamber. These were devastating scenes, for toward the end the women could no longer be ignorant of what awaited them. He would pounce upon a group of terrified wretches, his head thrust out like a rugby player's, throw them to the ground, trample on them, drag them around by the hair. It was an almost daily spectacle during those last months, one which I saw with my own eyes many times.

The other SS had a less significant administrative role, but that did not keep them from being savages. Quite bluntly, their ranks included a large number of physical misfits whose bodies seemed thrown together and who could have had personal grudges to take out against the female sex in general. But what was the exact role of these secret and individual impulses within the mass of cruelties they committed every day? I cannot say.

I remember a young SS known as "the Hungarian" who, while passing through a workyard unconnected with his official duties, slapped one of my friends[10] for no apparent reason. Quite calmly, and in an insolent voice, she asked in good German why he had struck her. I was standing only a few feet away, closely watching his facial expression, and ready

[10] Dr. Paulette von Zimmet, nicknamed Bérengère.

to try to intervene if necessary. He struck her a second time with a look of ferocity that I could liken only to that of an assassin at the instant of his crime. Physically, he reminded me of a dirty little urchin, thin and pale, but with murder very much on his mind. No doubt the only thing holding him back was the realization that he was outside his jurisdiction.

Of a totally different type was the big, bullnecked, alcoholic Bavarian whose workshop was the daily scene of brutalization of thirty or so of the women, over whom the reign of terror took every conceivable form. As soon as he arrived, for example, he leaped onto a table in the middle of the shop and, leaning forward, cast his malevolent look over the few hundred unfortunates who were completely at his mercy. Needless to say, all the machines kept working, and no one looked up. After a few minutes of this little comedy, he lashed out at someone totally at random and beat her black and blue; the ceremony was repeated several times a day. Whenever a victim was unconscious or half-dead, he became very pale and locked himself in his office for fifteen minutes or so. His name was Uscha Binder; he had a wife, children, an official mistress, plus a few unofficial ones. Several of the innumerable women from his workshop died under the blows. As far as I knew, this never caused him any great worry.

Sexual relations between the SS and prisoners were strictly forbidden, thank God. Probably for reasons of order and discipline. But it seemed that liaisons between SS of opposite sexes were encouraged, and they lived in a kind of promiscuity some might call "primitive," although their situation was anything but primitive. It appeared that all the Aufseherinnen, married or unmarried, had one or more constant SS lovers. And, so it seemed, they never overlooked an opportunity to talk comparisons with their colleagues. In addition to the lovers and the shop talk, their diversions (especially around solstices and equinoxes) were monstrous eating and drinking bouts, after which they were so far gone that men and women were unable to recall with whom they had spent the rest of the night.

One thing I found particularly striking: the close relationship between debauchery and cruelty among both male and female guards, but especially among the females. Those who, in front of the prisoners, had themselves fondled and pawed by a man (or men) or by other women displayed a very personal and bizarre cruelty, which was something quite different from ordinary physical brutality.

> I think now that the SS, both men and women, could not have shown such cruelty without feeling some degree of anguish, and that the debauchery was simply an expression of this anguish, or perhaps a palliative for it.

A brutal and selfish military feudalism had kept the German people in an exceptionally downtrodden and stupefied condition, in Prussia more than anywhere else. The overly rapid and formless industrialization of the late nineteenth century only worsened this condition in the apathetic atmosphere of the cities. Out of this, and the terrible crisis which followed the Great War, grew a proletariat which had all too recently been part of the middle class. Men of once great wealth, former intellectuals, officers, and businessmen, while retaining their contemptuous hatred of "the people," found themselves assimilated into the masses. No longer bound by the strictures of tradition, they relaxed all the old disciplines (military honor, bourgeois modesty, business honesty, and the catechisms of priest and pastor) without accepting the creeds of the masses (brotherhood, union discipline, solidarity, and social justice). But they kept their selfishness, narrowmindedness, idiotic prejudices, and intolerant patriotism, all magnified by the rancor of having lost their former status. All of this *possibly* helped prepare the marshy and poisonous ground from which the political monstrosity of Nazism would grow.

I have heard a great deal said about the cruelty and depravity of the "German race." How assuring it would be to simply think in these terms and thus limit the responsibility for all the calamities! The truth is, however, that racism and Nazism are phenomena whose causes can be neither "racial" nor "national." Hitler's personal and political adventures are only the occurrence and symptom of a cancer happening at the same time. It is sad to think that humanity, so competent and careful with its domestic animals, is so completely overwhelmed by the problems of its own species. Although the small and ostensibly stable societies of the good old days have crumbled to dust, the overgrown institutions of the present day build and destroy themselves on the same principles: "Take things as they come" and "It is God's will" . . . but with the monstrous catastrophes befitting the new gigantism.

Perhaps the Germans have some reason for disclaiming responsibility; they are the prey of the limping evolution of their civilization and, like many other criminals, the victim as well.

We knew very well the cool, detached harshness of some of our assassins and the alcoholic, loutish sadism of the lower animals, but we also encountered every other possible pattern of brutality: those who acted with all the conscientiousness and care of a loyal functionary; others acting on a whim, or through negligence; others who did so accidentally, out of fear.

Nonetheless, I did hear of one SS named Schmidt who beat no one and performed services for prisoners (while keeping such favors well hidden). He was aware of the atrocities, of course, and sincerely disapproved of them, but was most worried about their result: "What will they do with us when we've lost the war?" We were asked the same question in Paris in 1942[11] (in the Fresnes prison) by our German guards, when they dared. (We gave them little comfort, to be sure.) Schmidt had lived in Prague for many years before the war; enthusiasts of mass psychology might find some meaning in that. All the other SS abused us without pangs of conscience, or so it seemed.

Each work detail was supervised by both SS men and SS women (the Aufseherinnen). The latter were under the orders

[11] Strange as it may seem, almost all our German guards at Fresnes were convinced, in 1942, that Germany would lose the war and, accordingly, tended to go easy on us, while the Ravensbrück guards still believed firmly, even in 1945, in the imminent victory of the Reich.

of the men, who held them in total fear. (Even though they might be sleeping with them, sexual favors were no insurance against denunciation.)

Executions were carried out by SS squads, some members of which (a man named Pietsch, the tailor who supervised the fur workshop, for example) boasted of participating as volunteers. But I still hear echoes of some SS, dead drunk, beating their breasts and wailing, "I am no longer worthy of touching a woman. I am a murderer of women," etc. I should point out that the women executed were, in general, Resistance fighters, parachutists, and partisans, that is, usually healthy, courageous, and attractive young women around eighteen to twenty-five, and that the custom at Ravensbrück (as in the other camps) was to execute them nude, or clothed in a shirt at the most. Another point of interest: the execution squads received a special alcohol ration and certain food advantages; the SS canteen, like all other such services at Ravensbrück, was maintained by prisoners. The storekeepers were required to be German, but this was by no means a guarantee of discretion. (There were several Alsatians among them.) In short, the separate worlds of prisoners and their guards were not completely airtight.

6

The SS Women

My comrades who worked as administration secretaries found evidence in camp documents of about 3,000 Aufseherinnen (the uniformed female SS guards), including the following breakdown for some of the camps:[1]

Auschwitz	55–60
Gross-Rosen (including Kommandos)	about 490
Neuengamme (Hamburg)	150–60
Oranienburg	about 140
Ravensbrück (including Kommandos)	550–60
(excluding Kommandos)	300–50

Their pay was geared to age and seniority: a beginner, twenty-one or twenty-two and single, drew 125 marks a month, a married woman about 135 marks. If the husband did not receive a dependents' allowance, she would get another 10 marks per child.

Out of this, she had to pay taxes (7.50 marks a month for the single women, 6 marks for the married), dues for compulsory membership in the Nazi Labor Front (2.40), another deduction for the illness and disability fund (about 10 marks). She also paid 1.20 marks a day for food and drink in the canteen, and 5 marks a month for barracks lodging

[1] Since the Ravensbrück archives were almost totally destroyed, these data are practically all that remain. I personally believe them to be very accurate, as they were gathered by honest and intelligent women, and very well informed; their entire working day was spent typing administrative papers on SS personnel.

(or 15 for a private room). Uniforms, shoes, and stockings were furnished, but not laundry.

The chief Oberaufseherin, named Klein-Plaubel, was known for having her prisoners beaten or punished severely and ruthlessly. But whenever a punishment was considered unjust (according to her personal code of justice), there was always the hope that she would cancel it. By all appearances her conduct was guided by the idea that she was doing what she had to do.

Sometime after the evacuation of Auschwitz, she was replaced by Luise Brunner, an Oberaufseherin from that camp. This change passed almost unnoticed, but unless I am mistaken, Klein-Plaubel left Ravensbrück before the mass executions, or, at the latest, at the very beginning of them.

The personalities of these two chief Oberaufseherinnen were, however, completely eclipsed by that of their first assistant, Dorothea Binz, the camp's "star" character. Whenever she appeared somewhere, one literally felt touched by the breath of evil. She would walk slowly among the ranks, her crop behind her back, searching with menacing little eyes for the weakest or most frightened woman, simply to beat her black and blue. (She could not face up to courage, obviously.) I could not list all her exploits (and they occurred daily), but one particularly struck me because it was so unprovoked and psychologically symptomatic. It was witnessed personally by one of my good friends, a moderate woman of sound judgment, who had once received a long sentence to the bunker.

The classic punishment at Ravensbrück was twenty-five stick lashes, but there were sometimes fifty, sometimes seventy-five; in the two latter cases, they were generally meted out in two or three installments, but not always. Victims often died under fifty blows at one time; whenever there were seventy-five at once, death was almost certain.

After one of these sessions (I don't know how many blows), and when everything seemed finished, my friend hazarded a look out of her tiny window. The victim was half-naked, lying face down in the dirt, apparently unconscious and covered with blood. Binz looked at her a moment, then, without a word, stepped up on her victim's bloody legs, her two heels on one leg, toes of her boots on the other. Binz balanced herself there for a while, rocking her weight from heel to toe. The woman could have been dead by then—she showed no reaction. After a few minutes of this, Binz left, her boots smeared with blood.

Unlike the SS men, a sizable percentage of whom fell into that universal category of true physical misfits—bowlegged, slope-shouldered, etc.—the Aufseherinnen were, in general, stout, strong, and healthy women. They were not all volunteers; there were some labor conscripts, compelled by law to work, and who had not necessarily chosen the SS as their vocation. Many had never joined the Nazi party. I had reasonably complete personal data on about 200 of them, and a special interest in the social classes they had come from—and they came from all classes of German society. I encountered, among others, streetcar ticket takers, factory workers, opera singers, registered nurses, hairdressers, peasants, young middle-class women who had never worked before, retired teachers, circus riders, former prison guards, officers' widows, etc. The beginners usually appeared frightened upon first contact with the camp, and it took some time to attain the level of cruelty and debauchery of their seniors. Some of us made a rather grim little game of measuring the time it took for a new Aufseherin to win her stripes. One little Aufseherin, twenty years old, who was at first so ignorant of proper camp "manners" that she said "excuse me" when walking in front of a prisoner, needed exactly four days to adopt the requisite manner, although it was totally new for her. (This little one no doubt had some special gifts in the "arts" we are dealing with here.) As for the others, a week or two, a month at the most, was an average orientation period. But I did hear of a very young Aufseherin who was never able to adapt to either the debauchery or brutality of her colleagues. "She cried a lot," the inmates who knew her told me, "and we don't know how she ended up getting out." I never heard of another case like hers, and she had left the camp before I arrived. Then there were the rather frequent instances of Aufseherinnen who became prisoners themselves under various penalties, but these were usually for theft or for openly intimate relations with inmates—of either sex.

It would be a reasonable estimate that about half of the guards took visible pleasure in striking and terrorizing their prisoners, especially the weak, ill, and frightened. Others dealt their blows with the coarseness and simplicity of a peasant whipping her donkey, some simply acted for the sake of conformity, particularly in front of their colleagues or the SS men. In any case, even the best of them showed no adverse reaction when a prisoner was beaten in their presence.

It is quite difficult to report precisely on the ratio of guards to prisoners, since the proportions depended on several factors: a work Kommando (woodcutting) of ten prisoners might be guarded by one male SS and one Aufseherin, a ratio of 1:5, while a Betrieb (workshop) of 300 or 400 women could be guarded by three or four men and as many women (1:50). Movement of a transport noir (1,100 ill and aged inmates) required twenty SS men and twenty Aufseherinnen. As I have already noted, the camp as a whole had (under normal conditions) 300–50 Aufseherinnen, and there were most likely a slightly larger number of male SS, for an over-all ratio of one guard for twenty-five prisoners.

Whenever we lined up five-by-five for a roll call, I made mental calculations of the number of guards compared with our own numbers, and what our chances might be in an insurrection. It could have been possible, if absolutely necessary, to take control of the interior camp, but the walls were completely surrounded by fortified machine-gun emplacements aimed at the camp and blocking every possible exit. A few hundred men could thus easily wipe out several thousand women, either by a few days of enforced starvation, or by their guns within a few hours. Only if the authorities had begun a mass annihilation of prisoners would such a revolt have been worth while, loss for loss. The result would have been foreordained, but at least the Germans might have been inconvenienced.

And there was always a related and important factor: the administration at Ravensbrück, unlike those in the true extermination camps, was—even while carrying on a reign of terror and keeping prisoners in a constant state of extreme exhaustion—very careful to avoid the public atrocities that might cause a revolt or panic. They knew quite well that in such an event they would have to crush us, and thus shut down a major industrial enterprise.

7

"Medicine" by the SS

Even in a very brief examination of Ravensbrück, its medical personnel could not be passed over quietly. Medical attention was, to say the least, bizarre. There was no Revier until the summer of 1943—before that, only an infirmary for a few freakish operations. The sick were not even isolated from the rest of the inmates, and if children were born they were drowned immediately under the tender care of Gerta, a prisoner-"nurse" who also had the duty of administering fatal injections to the gravely ill—ministrations which seem to have been the only medications used in those days. Two doctors presided over these services, Dr. Schiedlausky and Dr. Rosenthal. Nurse Gerta was Rosenthal's mistress, and the strict prohibition against sexual relations between SS and prisoners once led the doctor to perform an abortion on his mistress. Someone informed on them, and both were still confined to the bunker when we arrived (October 1943). During this period, pregnant prisoners were required to undergo abortions, otherwise a child was killed at birth. So it must have been that Dr. Rosenthal was punished not for performing the abortion but for his liaison with a prisoner. Various rumors circulated about him: first that he was going to be shot, then that he had not been.[1]

Dr. Percy Treite[2] was named director of the Revier around

[1] He was condemned to death at Hamburg, but committed suicide before he could be executed. (1972)

[2] In retrospect I feel a certain pity for him; he had indeed committed crimes but did not enjoy doing it.

that time. He organized a system of medical service, insufficient to be sure, but more than one could hope for in a place like Ravensbrück. Beginning with his arrival, the seriously ill were hospitalized and received a degree of care, the contagious were isolated, and children gained the right to enter the world and stay there for a while.

The year 1943 saw the peak of the German war effort and, concurrently, the country's greatest need for productive labor. This fact most likely had a great deal to do with the creation of a medical service almost worthy of the name and the choice of Dr. Treite to organize it. He was forty-eight years old, but looked younger, blond, coolly detached, and properly mannered, a good doctor and a good organizer, very careful, and conscious of the "foreignness" of the SS atmosphere. (He once pointed out quite gladly that his mother was English.) This was obviously not the basically good, sensitive, courageous man one might find elsewhere, but at the same time he was not sadistic or brutal. Simply a proper doctor, a good technician, a believer in clean sheets and well-scrubbed hands, discipline and professional seriousness. For as long as he could, he carried on a personal struggle to maintain an outward propriety in his Revier, and he always effectively protected his staff. Working in the Revier was the prisoner's dream. Nonetheless, Dr. Treite himself performed, and had others perform, the systematic sterilization of gypsies (including girls as young as eight years old) and of certain groups of Germans. He presided over the organization and selection of several transports noirs (including one transport of 900 women in February 1944)[3] and of several transports of the insane and allegedly insane. He had sick prisoners poisoned in his own hospital and actively collaborated in the murderous hoax known as the Jugendlager. When extermination orders were issued he carried them out, all the while contriving to do as little as possible himself and leaving most of the responsibility to others. I would call him a coward—the

---

[3] We knew at the time that the SS were trying to round up 900 women; secretaries told me later, however, that 800 had actually been taken away.

kind of man, in my opinion, who was almost as dangerous as the real criminals.

Treite had two assistants: one, Bruno Orendi,[4] neither very intelligent nor capable, left for the Eastern front in February 1945. The second was Dr. Lukas, who merits special mention as the only one who openly refused to participate in the selections; for his trouble he was sent to the front. Even besides this act of courage, there were other factors to his credit: a genuine interest in the welfare of the sick, whom he examined himself (something his colleagues never lowered themselves to do), and even a degree of kindness.

I personally hope that if he is still alive, all this would be taken into account. But Dr. Lukas—the good doctor and honorable man—personally performed sterilization operations on the gypsies without discussion or protest, and apparently without remorse. But (and I say this in his defense) was there a single doctor in the entire Reich who would have refused?

The dentist, Dr. Hellinger, openly and publicly took part in the selections, although his duties did not require it. He was occasionally interested in real "dental cases," but more often in recovering gold teeth from the dead.

Selections were usually organized and supervised by, in addition to Pflaum and Schwarzhuber, two doctors who were seen only during these rounds of death—Dr. Trommer, short and thin, and Dr. Adolf Winkelmann, tall and heavy. Little Dr. Trommer had arrived in camp pedaling like a spider on his huge bicycle, while Winkelmann the giant moved around on a tiny motorbike. But none of this made anyone laugh; even those who placed no great value on human life detested the sight of them. I know nothing about their mental processes, and I would hesitate to speculate on the subject. What can one say on the thoughts of two medical corpsmen who murdered inmates in the so-called Revier in the Jugendlager and who had complete control over the gas chamber?

[4] He was not a doctor, having studied medicine for only two years, but he practiced on his surgical techniques at Ravensbrück. Young, elegant, healthy, and a very sheltered type, he spent almost all the war far from the front in his soft medical job.

In addition to these male personnel, there was a female group[5] known as "the sisters" (*Schwester*), who by no means belonged to religious orders but were simply the equivalent of nurses. Compared with the vulgarity of most of the Germans we had dealt with, the Schwester seemed to have had good bourgeois origins, or at least better backgrounds than many of our Aufseherinnen. They were quite strict about their appearance—no carelessness, no untidiness.

They took orders from Oberschwester Elisabeth Marschall, a square-faced, hard-eyed woman, strong and dignified, full of authority, respectability, and competence. Looking like the Mother Superior of a convent, she personally and actively participated in all the crimes of the camp. It was she who, the night before an execution, would go to the Revier's card file to choose the names of the condemned, she who kept the secret records of the murders, she who set up medical supervision of Dr. Gebhardt's "experiments."

Most of the Schwester were old and full of hatred—Sister Lisa, mean-tempered and cadaverous, soured by spinsterhood, looking like a scratchy, dried-up tree root; the diabolical Sister Erika; others who were quite passive and indifferent, such as Sister Martha, stolidly and impartially passing out pills of poison or aspirin—it made no difference to her. I knew two, however, who were pleasant, kind, and very sorrowful about their situation; one in particular, named Gerda, could only be blamed for having been a passive witness to so many crimes. . . .

A conscientious and cold chief surgeon who sacrificed his patients for his career; an incompetent and rather limited

---

[5] I did not know Hertha Oberhauser, a doctor and a "well-bred" young woman from a middle-class, Christian family in the Rhineland, who took part in the "rabbit" experiments and killed some ill prisoners with injections of oil and Evipan (according to testimony by her colleague Dr. Rudolf Rosenthal). On August 20, 1947, she was sentenced to twenty years in prison. She began practicing medicine again after her early release, as expected, but a resolution by the British Medical Association (July 12, 1958) attracted the attention of German authorities, and her license was revoked on November 22, 1960. (1972)

assistant; one honorable man; an old, rough, hypocritical, but dignified, head nurse; a majority of crafty and disagreeable old women, along with a few sleepyheads, and two decently human young nurses—not a very inspiring collection but, on the whole, not too different from what might be found in any hospital. These people were only the overly docile instruments of a larger machine, but, even so, this band of "average" citizens—traditional German middle class, educated, well-versed in proper hygiene and foreign languages—complacently directed the highly (and inventively) criminal enterprise of the Ravensbrück Revier.

In 1942, the medical services of the Revier were required to perform abortions on all pregnant women. If a child happened to be born alive, it would be smothered, or drowned in a bucket, in front of the mother. Given a newborn child's natural resistance to drowning, a baby's agony might last for twenty or thirty minutes. Beginning in February 1944, infants were no longer killed immediately, but simply allowed to die of the illnesses endemic to the camp. Then in October 1944 they were given a separate room, and Zdenka was even able to get powdered milk, which the nurses mixed with cereals donated by the prisoners who received outside packages. During this period some children might live as long as three months, but none survived beyond that.

During December 1944, a few mothers, along with their children, were sent out on a work detail, where French prisoners of war gave them extra food; two of the children survived—a French boy, Jean-Claude, and a Polish boy.

But in January 1945, the room reserved for infants was abolished; mothers and children were put in Block 32 with the gypsy women, who had children of all ages. The block was then encircled with barbed wire, and by the end of February it had been almost completely emptied. The most seriously ill remained, but the rest had been taken to Bergen-Belsen. During March the thirty-two surviving infants were gassed.

I have seen one estimate that from October 1944 to the end of March 1945, eight hundred fifty infants died or were killed under the circumstances I have just described.

8

The "Rabbits"

During the year August 1942 to August 1943, a number of young Polish women were forcibly taken to the Revier in groups of five to ten, anesthetized, and awakened with deep wounds on their legs. Some died shortly afterward; those who survived suffered serious aftereffects. It became known almost immediately that these "operations" had been performed by an internationally renowned surgeon, SS Professor Karl Gebhardt, director of the Hohenlychen clinic near the camp, which was reserved for the luminaries of the Reich.

This SS doctor's victims were very young, almost children, and chosen from groups of high school and university students. Some who had survived the operations were executed, but there were about sixty still alive when we arrived in October 1943.

They were all convinced that the Germans intended to kill them and burn the bodies before an Allied victory. And, indeed, the execution order did arrive[1] during the final winter, but right in the middle of the confusion surrounding the organization of a general annihilation, while every day hundreds, even thousands, of women were being brought in from the evacuated Eastern camps and while other hundreds, or thousands, were departing for unknown destinations. The order, which identified them by number, remained in effect, but the SS no longer knew how many detainees were in the

[1] Obviously, I never saw the order, but I knew through my Polish friends that a search would be made for them, and I saw the search going on.

camp, since women were dying anonymously every day. Now, with the help of bold sympathizers in the Revier, or of some spunky Blockova, one could change her number with one of these unknown dead and leave in a transport with a new identity (with the risk of becoming part of a transport noir and escaping from a "personalized execution" into a completely anonymous death. In all of the disorder, the "Rabbits," as they had named themselves, decided to "go underground" and take the false numbers. The most disabled ones were hidden in the contagious ward at the Revier, with the complicity of the prisoner-doctors, or in the rafters of the blocks. During roll calls, their young friends would occasionally let themselves be counted as "Rabbits" (especially Denise Vernay, who did it two or three times).

I am including here an account of this collective resistance, as written in 1972 by one of the "patients," Nina Iwanska, aided by notes taken by Wanda Kiedrzynska and published in Polish in April 1961. I had compiled an account of these same events, along with Nina, in 1948.[2]

In April 1942 the prisoners from the transport known as the "seven thousands" (which had arrived at Ravensbrück on September 23, 1941, from Lublin and War-

---

[2] A list of the "Rabbits" compiled by Nina Iwanska in 1948 included seventy-four Polish women, two Ukranians (both of whom died), one Russian (dead), one Belgian (who had been arrested in Germany; dead), and five German religion students (four died).

(The nine non-Polish women had been chosen from the so-called "insane" section.)

Sofia Magzka, a Polish deportee and a doctor, testified at the "Doctors' Trial" that there had been seventy-four young Polish women, one German (a Jehovah's Witness), and one Ukranian— seventy-six victims of the experiments. In a 400-page deposition, Dr. Gebhardt himself recounted having operations performed on sixty young women and fifteen men. (Bayle, *Croix Gammée contre Caducée*, p. 1031.)

According to Wanda Kiedrzynska, there were seventy-four victims of the medical experiments, of whom five died shortly after the operation, six were executed, and seven died after the liberation. (Kiedrzynska, *Ravensbrück*, Historical Institute of the Warsaw Academy, April 1961.)

saw) were gathered up and confined to the interior of the camp. And on April 18 the first executions took place: fourteen inmates from the "seven thousands." When six prisoners were "summoned" to the Revier (on August 1), we would rather have faced the executions than the medical experiments . . . which were taking place the same day. Although the first six "patients" were well guarded and separated from the others in the Revier, we learned the truth soon enough.

On August 14, nine more prisoners were called to the Revier, but this group decided to protest; I was among them, along with my sister Christine. We asked why we had been brought in for operations, since we were in good health. More strongly, we reminded Dr. Fritz Fischer that such repressive measures against political prisoners were totally illegal. Dr. Fischer sent us back to the Revier doctors for "clarifications," and, by way of explanation, they gave us injections which permitted them to operate on us once in the morning, then again in the afternoon. (We had been taken to the Revier after a morning roll call, which followed a full night's work!)

The experiments continued along the same lines until January 16, 1943; some victims were subjected to three, five, or six operations.

On February 11, 1943, the first two executions of "Rabbits" took place. (It was done in the Revier, since it would have been difficult to stand them up outside to be shot.) Four others soon followed. The last "patients" left the Revier on February 16, 1943, with official assurances that there would be no more vivisection experiments.

On March 6, 1943, five prisoners from the "seven thousands" were again summoned to the Revier; after an examination, they were sent back to the block. But the next day another summons came for the same five; this time, with the unanimous support of the other former "patients," they refused to go. We had decided to lodge a protest with Oberaufseherin Langefeld, and we approached her quarters in an impressive procession, on our crutches, with those who could not even walk that way carried on the interlocked arms of our comrades from Block 15. Langefeld did not come out to meet us immediately but called for Dr. Oberhauser. After a brief discussion, she decided to hear our representatives, Jadmiga Kaminska and Zofia Baj, who objected to the summons for new patients for the experiments despite official promises. They would not go, our representatives said, because they would rather die than remain invalids.

Taken aback, Langefeld claimed she didn't know that experiments were to have started again and that the summoning of our comrades to the Revier had nothing to to do with "operations."

That very afternoon, three others were ordered to go to the Revier—and refused.

The next day all the "Rabbits" signed a petition addressed to the camp commandant: "The political prisoners who have been victims of the Revier operations pose the following question to the commandant: did the commandant know that in the Revier of this camp, political prisoners were, without their consent, subjected to medical experiments which caused serious injuries? So far, seventy-one Polish political prisoners have had these operations; five have died" (names and numbers listed).

"Asked by the patients why such operations were being performed, Dr. Fischer replied only that all information would be provided by the Revier doctors. Up to now, we have received no answer, and we would like to know if these operations were a part of our sentences, provisions of which we do not know. We ask that you grant us an interview or give an immediate answer." There was no answer to our questions, and Commandant Suhren did not grant the interview . . . but he did order our "bed cards" taken away, which meant that all the "Rabbits" went back to work details.

So, after all that, there were no summons to the Revier from March until August 15, 1943. But on August 15, ten of our comrades received those same orders, five of

*them had been through the ordeal before, and all ten
refused to comply. Binz asked why they refused; all replied that they preferred death to the experiments. Their
protest was so effective that death sentences had to be
ordered. Binz and the camp police later tried in vain to
take the ten to the Revier, but they had been hidden
among their 500 comrades of Block 15. Seeing all the
uproar of resistance, Binz ordered all the Block 15 inmates confined to quarters. Half an hour later, she and
Hauptsturmführer Bräuning confronted us with the declaration that the entire block would be executed, and
that the machine guns were poised to put down any new
revolt. Binz demanded that the ten come foward; a few
of them did, trying to appeal their case to Binz and
Bräuning. They were dragged away to the bunker, where
five of them underwent operations. And Block 15, with
its 500 women, remained completely locked up—doors,
windows, shutters—and deprived of food, light, and fresh
air for three days and four nights. Despite all this, neither the inmates nor the trusty-supervisors (two Stubovas—one German, one Polish—and one Czech Blockova) gave up their resistance. But the camp authorities
finally yielded a bit, opened the block, and at the first roll
call offered to let outside anyone who had opposed the
revolt. Of the 500 women (not all of them political prisoners), not one stepped forward. They had decided of
their free will to stand by us, knowing in advance the
risks they were taking.*

So these five operations did take place, but in the bunker
(a dungeon), not in the Revier; they were the last. During
the following months, the "Rabbits" took bold and intelligent
advantage of the almost universal support of their fellow prisoners to get their stories passed out to the Allies. It was Nina
Iwanska who had the idea of undertaking this clandestine
correspondence by adding an illegal gimmick to legitimate
messages—invisible "ink," made of urine, used between the
lines of letters and on the inside of official envelopes. The
writing became visible when pressed with a hot iron.

Four of us assumed the task of getting news out of the camp to our families: Nina Iwanska, Krystyna Iwanska, Wanda Wojtasik (presently a psychiatrist in Cracow), and Krystyna Czyz (now a professor of geography at the University of Lublin). Our families took care of the rest, spreading the news to London (the BBC), the Vatican, Geneva (International Red Cross), Fribourg (Swiss Catholic Mission), and Lisbon (Piskovski).

So those were the targets of our messages—complete lists of the seventy-four "operations" victims, the 160 or more prisoners executed, the dates and number of deportees included in the transports arriving at Ravensbrück, as well as of the transports leaving the camp. We described the living conditions of the camp: work, food, hygiene, the gas chambers, crematorium, the "selections," etc.

Photocopies of these letters were among the documents collected by the Warsaw Commission on the History of Ravensbrück, and the letters were cited or reprinted by Wanda Kiedrzynska in her book Ravensbrück *and in* Beyond Human Endurance *(a compilation of personal accounts by the Rabbits), in which a twenty-page section contains complete letters.*

We could also send news out by way of the details working outside the camp (the Aussen Kolonne):

a) The detail responsible for taking care of the gardens at the Hohenlychen-Templin sanatorium: the trusty who led the work column (Teresa Taczukowa) managed to make contact with French prisoners who also worked there (including some whose job was to transmit news to the French Resistance). And, thanks to Polish agricultural workers, Taczukowa succeeded in sending and receiving letters to and from Poland, an operation that lasted for more than a year—until the farm workers were shipped elsewhere.

b) The Ladekommando (freight detail), supervised by Antonina Kotrowska, established contact with a group of Polish war prisoners (Stalag IIA at Neustrelitz); through

*them our news reached the outside and some Polish
books reached us.*

c) *A column working at Uppenthala (shoe factory)
even found a "legal" way to send letters. . . . There was
a mailbox near the factory entrance.*

d) *Contact with Polish officers (Oflag IID) was made
at Neubrandenburg (aircraft factory). When Oflag IID
was transferred to Gross-Born, the officers even set up a
"Committee to Aid the Prisoners of Ravensbrück" (letters, packages, family searches).*

*The "Rabbits" had friends in all of these work details
who took the responsibility of relaying their correspondence. Besides this, some of the "Rabbits" managed to get
into several of the columns (especially the Ladekommando, and the gardening detail at the Hohenlychen
sanatorium)[3] despite the official prohibition against their
working outside the camp.*

Nina Iwanska did not know about another exodus of information which was helped along, indirectly and by coincidence, by Grete Buber-Neumann (who was unaware of
the purpose of the "Rabbits'" ruses; thanks to this one success, the first list of "patients" got out of the camp, addressed
to the Vatican, the International Red Cross, and the British
Intelligence Service, and it reached them all.

It happened this way: sometime in 1942 or 1943 a very
small group of mostly Polish inmates went to a nearby forest
to cut wood, supervised by a nineteen-year-old Aufseherin
they had already won over. A forest ranger led them through
a potato field, which they picked clean and then had a family
picnic after roasting their booty over wood fires. Grete had
been a part of this work column for only a few days, but she
was there when a car pulled up and a Polish prisoner jumped
in. That night the poor Aufseherin was arrested and the work
column disbanded, but the correspondence reached its destinations.

---

[3] The clinic which, it should be remembered, belonged to Dr.
Gebhardt, and which was the site of Himmler's meetings with
Count Bernadotte. (See p. 54.)

As long-time prisoners, well-protected by their comrades, the "Rabbits" were able to get into the least-demanding work details. They received a few outside packages and had clean clothes, but they could never lose sight of the fact that the SS would never release them and that they had no chance of leaving the camp alive.

I remember my dismay when a special roll call was scheduled during working hours on January 18, 1945. During the call, the six or seven "Rabbits" unable to walk were hidden in the contagious-disease blocks with the help of prisoner-doctors; the others hid in the attics of their own quarters and in the block occupied by some Hungarian Jews who would never leave the camp—just arrived on foot from Auschwitz, they were all dying from dysentery.

Here is what Nina Iwanska learned about subsequent events: *On February 4, 1945, during the morning roll call, an order was read to the inmates of Block 24: the "Rabbits" were not to leave the block. Actually, the "Rabbits" had been warned of this move the night before by Grete Buber-Neumann.[4] There was no doubt that a massive execution lay ahead. Some Russian (Red Army) comrades, who lived in the same block and worked as electricians, decided to cut the camp's electricity in an attempt to delay the morning roll call. The Russians lived up to their promise, and the call could not go off on schedule because of the darkness. Block 24, meanwhile, was surrounded by Aufseherinnen and police. By daybreak the entire camp was aware of the danger to the "Rabbits." Then, one column of Verfügbar, along with the coffee detail (fifty Russians), "attacked" the Block 24 inmates to create enough of a diversion for the "Rabbits" to get away. With this, and the later collaboration of all the Blockovas, the "Rabbits" were very quickly hidden, except for*

---

[4] The source of the information was a Polish woman of German origin who had worked in the SS kitchen for several years; she had found out through Binz, with whom she had frequent conversations, and immediately told Grete Buber-Neumann.

That night, six women (one Belgian, two Norwegians, two French, and one Pole) proposed to the young "patients" that they exchange numbers and be executed in their place. (Nina Iwanska, 1948.)

Jadmiga Kaminska and Zofia Baj, who went to headquarters to negotiate with Binz and Schwarzhuber. These latter maintained that the special roll call was only a part of their effort to protect the "Rabbits" in case of "an evacuation of the camp."

As bad luck would have it, Schwarzhuber mentioned the Gross-Rosen camp (already occupied by the Red Army) in the course of negotiations. They tried several times to influence Kaminska and Baj to persuade us to go there, but, although we feared for our negotiators' lives, we decided not to yield, hoping that with the entire camp supporting us, Kaminska and Baj would return safely from each session with Binz, Suhren, and company.

Meanwhile, with the help of the Blockovas and workers in the political section (Politische Abteilung), we got rid of the old numbers assigned to us as part of the "seven thousands," taking those of our dead comrades (most of them from Auschwitz). But even with such "protection" the little game of hide-and-seek became increasingly dangerous for everyone. So we decided that eighteen of us would leave with some of the various transports going out of the camp in order to make it easier for our comrades to hide within the Ravensbrück blocks those of us who could no longer walk.

I went with a group of ten to the munitions factory at Neustadt-Glewe, where I finally escaped to the freedom which had been so long in coming to me.

The case of SS Professor Gebhardt, close friend and former classmate of Heinrich Himmler, tells the story of the medical "experiments." As one of the great doctors of the Reich he was the natural choice to be called to the victim's bedside when Heydrich, the Gauleiter of Czechoslovakia, was the target of a Resistance assassination in Prague in May 1942. Gebhardt's care did not prevent Heydrich from dying a week after the attack. Hitler's fury was unbounded: "With Heydrich I lose the equivalent of two divisions!"

"Hitler summoned me," Gebhardt said at his trial, "then refused to see me. . . ." Theodor Morelle, Hitler's personal physician, added to Gebhardt's problem: "If my modern sulfamides had been used, things would have been different. . . ." Consequently, Gebhardt's restoration of his own status depended on establishing clinical proof of the inefficiency of these sulfamides in the treatment of certain infections caused by war wounds. And thus, the artificial "war" wounds inflicted on our comrades' legs by this renowned surgeon, wounds which he then allowed to become infected naturally, or in which he ordered infections injected with, for example, the gangrene bacilli brought in from the Institute of Hygiene in Berlin. And, of course, the sulfamides used for "treatment" had to be ineffective. In May 1943, at the Congress of the Academy of Military Medicine (attended by 350–400 German doctors), Gebhardt detailed these "seventy-five experiments"—the "special experiments." Not one of the conventioneers questioned or protested the experiments, and, afterward, Gebhardt was named president of the German Red Cross.

Gebhardt's defense was based on the contention that these young women had already been condemned to death, but, in fact, they were sent to Ravensbrück precisely because they had *not* been sentenced to death. And Dr. Schiedlausky testified that six of the girls were executed only after a necessary delay for official correspondence: they had to obtain the consent of the governor general of Poland to proceed with the executions. It is almost certain that, in return, Gebhardt ordered the others rounded up for execution during the last days of the war.

We learned from one newspaper that got through to us (the Nazi propaganda sheet *Völkischer Beobachter*) that Hitler had personally decorated the illustrious Dr. Gebhardt for his worthy endeavors, without giving further detail. But on rediscovering in Count Bernadotte's narrative the same illustrious Dr. Gebhardt, peaceful and proper, inspecting his clinic and discoursing seriously and articulately on medicine and politics, I felt most strongly the reality of the man himself, as

well as another disturbing reality: an obviously aberrant and
monstrous "civilization" which had all the physical trappings
of the one I had always lived in: professors, automobiles,
newspapers, cinemas, conventions . . . and doctors. Doctors . . .

9

Night and Fog

Was it Himmler, one of Himmler's subordinates, or Hitler himself who invented the bizarre and forbidding terminology used by the Gestapo to classify their secret dossiers? One of the relatively well-known terms was "NN," of which we only knew that it stood for *Nacht und Nebel* (Night and Fog) and that it set us apart from other prisoners. We know now that it refers to an incantation in *Das Rheingold,* by which Alberich could make himself disappear. There was also a note in Hitler's own hand relating to treatment of the NN. According to a German military magistrate,[1] these notations only began to appear around the beginning of 1942, at least he could not find earlier evidence of them, and they were strictly secret, written in only by police authorities.

Ravensbrück's first NN arrived in July 1943 and for a time received the same treatment as other prisoners. It was not until February 1944 that special blocks—first Block 32, then Block 24—were set aside for them. On the other hand, all the prisoners in this perilous category had been arrested *before* July 1943. The exact dates of the orders concerning the use of the label remain unknown, but I do know that the Gestapo stopped using it around this same time, shortly before it began

---

[1] Military Judge Roskosten, who on February 17, 1942, pronounced death sentences on ten members of the "Musée de l'Homme" Resistance group arrested a year earlier. Seven were executed on February 23, 1942. This information comes from Roskosten's testimony in October–November 1949 at the Paris trial of Albert Gaveau, the traitor who betrayed them.

playing a major role in the camps. Should we infer that as of that time, since the final, complete annihilation of prisoners was already under consideration, it was no longer necessary, "in the night and fog," to sort them out? Then why keep up a system that was already outdated? Perhaps we will know some day.

And today very little more is known.

My present theory is that this category was invented as part of an effort to reconcile a set of interdependent circumstances: by the beginning of 1942, the German system of military justice, even with its summary proceedings, was no longer able to dispose of the many "Resistance affairs"; the backlog simply would not stop growing. At the same time, manpower needs were becoming a top priority. And finally, it was during this period that Himmler decided to assume direct management control of profit-making slave labor (or, more accurately, Himmler and his very small, totally dependent entourage). (See fn., pp. 46–47.)

The fact is, then, that all the important cases not amenable to an "immediate judicial solution" were classified NN, which permitted them to take quick advantage of the labor force made available.

Under this theory, Nacht und Nebel meant that concentration camp authorities had practical access to "human stock, to be utilized but closely watched in case of further investigation." This could account for the prohibition against the NNs working in any of the outside business installations or going outside the walls on work details for even half a day.

By the end of 1943, the police knew there would be no new investigations of prisoners, and they were so overwhelmed with work that it would have been impossible to resume retroactive actions on any cases. So at last the mysterious letters no longer appeared on new dossiers, while remaining as part of the "old" dossiers on file in offices in all the camps as an ominous and often fatal designation.

10

Extermination Within the Camp

A blunt memorandum, noting without further comment that the death rate was too low, appeared in the Ravensbrück offices *probably* around the last days of 1944. I cannot specify the exact date, as I made no note of it at the time, and in the gray sameness of a prisoner's daily life, I had no landmark of memory. The mortality rate was, however, considerably higher than in late 1943 because of the arrival of the Hungarian Jews and the evacuation of Eastern camps and prisons, which brought in women already near death. The secretary who first received the memorandum did not take it to mean a great deal, and I knew of no other, more detailed, instructions on the matter. Perhaps the commandant later received these instructions directly. The secretary added that it was the first time she had seen such a communication, and that her boss seemed annoyed she had seen it.

One night soon afterward, Sister Martha came to "attend" the sick in Block 10, offering sleeping medicine to any who were having trouble sleeping. Quite a few accepted the offer; most of them did not wake up the next morning. The rest became very ill but survived. (Needless to say, no one in the camp suffered from insomnia after that.) SS Dr. Treite contended that the problem was simply an "error in dosage."

This "white insomniac powder" was distributed shortly before Jugendlager was opened; that is, at a time when Suhren had obviously already decided that some form of extermination would be carried out but had probably not yet chosen the means of doing so. So it seems quite likely that the white powder was simply a "trial run." The Revier nurses said the poisoning incident took place on January 15, 1945.

During the same general period (November? December?), our captors requested that the ill, aged, and fatigued prisoners make themselves known so that they could be sent to a convalescence camp known as Jugendlager, a few hundred yards from the main camp. Many took the offer at face value despite the cruelties they had already suffered under the Germans.

> The decision to use the small Uckermarck camp as an extermination installation evidently predated its "opening," which took place in December 1944 with a convoy of prisoners from Poland. And in January 1945 (perhaps January 15), the ill and aged from Ravensbrück proper were transferred there. The little camp had been thrown together rather primitively to house German juvenile delinquents, who were evacuated during the autumn of 1944, thus the other name, "Jugendlager," by which it was more commonly known. The project to convert Uckermarck to its new identity—a death camp—was necessarily planned sometime before this evacuation, and it all more or less coincided with their preparations for the evacuation of Auschwitz. But there is no reason to believe that Jugendlager had been foreseen as a site for systematic extermination before 1944.[1]

Another contemporary event was the construction of a second cremation oven in December 1944, after which the two ovens blazed on without interruption, twenty-four hours a day. Even with that, they were unable to burn all the bodies, and the authorities ordered the oven temperatures raised to such a point that, finally, a couple of months later, one of the ovens exploded.[2]

[1] See p. 211 for Olga Wormser-Migot's views.
[2] As Suhren testified on December 8, 1949: *One crematorium existed before I took command in October 1942; a second was built under my command, but I cannot recall the exact date. Both*

When Ravensbrück was still a "labor camp" six months earlier (around the beginning of August 1944), the single crematorium burned twice a week, a few hours each time. Even considering the overpopulation and excessive incidence of illness during this period, the single crematorium, functioning only sporadically, must have maintained a sufficient death rate.

The gas chamber had been put into operation in December.

It had probably begun to operate only when the SS started rounding up prisoners in groups of 150, if one can believe testimony by Suhren and Schwarzhuber. Now, in January and February, prisoners were being removed to Jugendlager mostly in groups of fifty, sometimes groups of seventy or seventy-two.

To understand how we mere prisoners were so well-informed, and to gauge the reliability of our information, one should realize that Jugendlager was within short walking distance of the main camp, and that every day there were numerous movements between camps. Sometimes there were the nurses whom Suhren installed during the first days to build the impression of a convalescent camp; more often we had the Austrian Stubovas who took the roll calls for the political office.

The new procedures were totally different in principle from the transports noirs: exterminations were now "local." Some prisoners first assumed that a very small gas chamber was involved. (We even thought at the time of a railroad car hastily outfitted for that purpose.) If one can accept the very similar depositions on this point by

---

functioned simultaneously for a rather brief period, but one eventually exploded and was rendered unusable.
I learned that back in the main camp large graves had been dug for the "surplus" bodies during the last days of the war (but I have no landmark events to pinpoint the exact time). According to Erika Buchmann (*Die Frauen von Ravensbrück*, Kongress Verlag, Berlin, 1961, p. 106), a German political prisoner employed in Block 10 (insane and tubercular), some excess bodies were burned by flame-throwers in a forest near the camp; others were taken to the crematorium in Fürstenberg, a small town nearby. (1972)

deputy commandant Schwarzhuber and Dr. Treite, the disappearances of prisoners in groups of fifty was consistent with execution by firearms. According to Suhren and Schwarzhuber, the gas chamber had been intended for 150 persons and measured 29′ × 15′, but we are certain that sometimes as many as 170 or 180 prisoners were "transferred." It is impossible to know today exactly how they killed these twenty or thirty victims for whom, theoretically at least, there was no space in that room. Perhaps they were jammed in according to the whim of whichever SS was directing the operation, but perhaps the two methods of execution (gas and pistol) were used simultaneously.

The camouflage of these murders will be seen, in the overall perspective of the concentration-camp system, as Ravensbrück's only innovation: they could not risk provoking a panic which would paralyze a model industrial unit. Thus during the first days after Jugendlager's opening, every precaution was taken to inspire confidence in the ill and weakened women sent there. For example, the camp was endowed with a Revier administered at first by a French prisoner-doctor who was known to be completely honorable (December 5–10, 1944). To be sure, the charade was not effective for long, as it soon became known that this Revier had no medicines, no heat, not even any straw mattresses, and that sick prisoners entering Jugendlager were immediately stripped of all warm clothing and forced to remain standing in the snow for days at a time with almost no food. Similar practices were followed in some of the extermination camps, and for no apparent reason, since the most seriously ill prisoners were gassed every night in any case. This extra suffering was then completely gratuitous and did not even help them economize on gas usage.[3] I fervently hope that the judges who preside over the trials of Suhren and Schwarzhuber try to find out what principle or whose order these practices were based upon.

[3] There was, in fact, a reason for it: to step up the rate of extermination, which, even with the gas chamber, seemed too slow for Suhren. (See Schwarzhuber's deposition, p. 149.) (1972)

After only a few days, the doctors and nurses were recalled to the main camp, but, amazingly, the Revier was kept going under that name. Two military medics, Rapp and Köhler, served as medical personnel, along with a truly despicable prisoner named Vera Salveguart. Her responsibility was to dispense poison, and the two medics' only job was to beat the prisoners who refused to swallow. Whenever a contingent of women arrived at Jugendlager they were divided up among the various blocks and subjected to intense cold and hunger. But a small number of them, chosen strictly at random, were sent to the Revier and died there, either from illness, poison, or attendant afflictions. Such was the case of one of my friends —a scholar, a reserved and refined young woman, creative and meditative—who was clubbed to death for not swallowing her poison.

To me, the only plausible explanation for all these intricacies is that they were trying to maintain "separate accounts" of the death statistics, a sort of double-entry bookkeeping that was, I presume, an innovation by Commandant Suhren.[4]

Women sent to the gas chamber appeared on the camp rolls with notations of "sent to Mittwerda" or "sanatorium"; inmates who had been poisoned or beaten to death in the Revier were sometimes listed as having expired from natural causes —a few of these were needed, after all, for a degree of verisimilitude. But for whom? Who were they trying to deceive, the prisoners? Most of the inmates would rather have believed the Mittwerda story, did not concern themselves with statistics, and were much more likely to be appalled by the actual horrors of our sham of a hospital than by inconsistencies in the camp's figures, which they probably knew nothing about in any case. Was it some kind of administrative obsession? Perhaps. Our commandant no doubt dreamed of a complete extermination of witnesses—a cleansing by death— and of a totally empty camp, carefully swept clean by the last

---

[4] In light of depositions by the SS general staff at the Hamburg trials, it seems to me today that this "separate accounting" might have played a role, but only a secondary one, and that the goal of accelerating the exterminations by all possible means was the real reason for such cruelties. (1972)

prisoner. And good statistics proving there were fewer deaths here than in other camps, and that everything was perfectly proper.

But there were even women who came back from this waiting room for death, and there were even survivors of Jugendlager's Revier. One of these in particular—very handy with a needle—had begun some knitting job or another for the formidable Vera Salveguart. Every evening Vera insisted that the project be finished the next day, but every morning our resourceful friend invented some new ornament and, having gotten something to eat in the meantime, replenished her strength to keep going.

Not counting the women who were gassed or shot (included only on the Mittwerda lists), the official death count for 1945, as recorded at the Revier, was:

January	1,221
February	1,514
March	1,123

I do not know whether these totals include Jugendlager's "natural" deaths, but I believe—without being able to confirm—that Dr. Treite had ordered his functionaries not to count them. In any case, they definitely do not include those who died by gas or gunfire.

By the end of March 1945, there were no more than 11,000 at Ravensbrück, so the apparent death rate was about 10 per cent per month, but this was a complete fake, much lower than the actual rate.

As for that real total, we have never seen the exact figures.

11

The Final Days

During Ravensbrück's final weeks—a period of methodical extermination and horrors that defied imagination—I kept a daily account of the most important events, those for which I dared not rely only on memory. Much that I observed or heard about went unrecorded, but I made a special effort to set down those facts which affected me directly and those circumstances whose details I felt should survive. The following excerpts, for the most part, concern the camp as a whole. Even though they are only the barest of facts, one should be able to gauge the reliability of the information several of my comrades and I labored so hard to put together. While they may reflect only a minute part of the crimes actually committed, they have the virtue of having been recorded on the day of the event.

During December 1944 and January 1945, Dr. Treite's underlings in the main Revier very liberally distributed the pink cards signifying exemption from work. A few thousand women "enrolled" voluntarily.[1]

During the second half of January, the cardholders began moving up to Jugendlager, and deaths from cold and hunger began immediately. Every day during the second half of February, a group of fifty women (sometimes a few more) was selected at Jugendlager and taken to some unknown destina-

[1] The decisions involved in organizing the exterminations would necessarily have predated this new widespread distribution. I could venture a date of November 1944 at the very latest. The pink cards, in any case, had been around for several months.

tion. Notified immediately, my comrades in the Revier assumed this signified a small gas chamber somewhere. I would tend to believe now that this was the period when the prisoners were being shot, in pairs, by Sergeant Moll.[2]

Dr. Trommer and Dr. Winkelmann selected 2,300 Ravensbrück prisoners for Uckermarck. The women were already aware of the daily disappearances and the systematic starvation. A few tried to escape.

Friday, March 2—Selection in Block 28; immediately afterward those chosen, perhaps 1,000, began leaving, on foot, for Jugendlager.

The condemned are no longer leaving in groups of fifty, but in groups of at least 170, sometimes 180.[3]

Tuesday, March 6—A departure list for Mittwerda bearing today's date contains 700 names. My comrades help me check it immediately: the number is actually a cumulative total, a sum of the murders of the three or four previous days. This list has since disappeared, or so I believe.

Wednesday, March 7—Exactly 180 women are taken away this evening; the prisoner who counted them told me immediately. The same day another 1,200 inmates are said to have left Uckermarck for an uncertain destination, but the information is questionable (probably again a cumulative list of earlier deaths).

Friday, March 9—At yesterday's roll call there were still 870 women *actually* at Jugendlager; the *official* number was 2,895. I am sure of these figures.

Saturday, March 10—Discussion between the chief of the labor office and his staff. He then telephones in a rage; according to him, the 2,895 women are still up there.

Pflaum, the unspeakable beast who directed the Arbeiteinsatz, knew about the previous day's actual roll-call

[2] See Schwarzhuber's deposition, p. 149.
[3] These are accurate figures, given to me immediately afterward by the prisoners who, every evening, had to record the prisoner numbers of their condemned comrades. What agony!

figure, not directly but through a French secretary on his staff who lived in our block and who had also informed me. The tally, in fact, had been taken twice: once for the camp administration, a second time for Pflaum's "labor units," and the two figures were different. Now there were definitely 2,895 half rations of bread delivered to Jugendlager on March 10. (It was well known that the bread ration was a monetary unit in the concentration camps and the source of incredibly active black-market trading, in which the SS participated.) Pflaum was probably wondering what could have happened to those 2,895 half rations, and that would seem to be the reason for his anger.

If there were 870 women remaining there, what happened to the other 2,025 on the labor-office register who were supposedly not present at the roll call? I think they were actually there, according to information from the Austrian Stubova who took the roll call.

Sunday, March 11—During the morning roll call I found myself alongside an elderly Polish woman who had just come back down from Jugendlager. She said she was Mme. Ossendowski, the first wife of the author of *Beasts, Men and Gods.* She was not a "prisoner" but an "evacuee" belonging to the category the Germans had taken with them on leaving Warsaw, warning them to bring along all valuables and jewelry— "for protection from the Russians." They had been brought to Ravensbrück, stripped of everything (including the hair from their heads), and numbered; the younger, healthy ones were put in the trench-digging details, the others sent to Jugendlager, where they were murdered by the hundreds. Then came an order that those still alive were to be sent back down to the old camp, and thus Mme. Ossendowski was still with us.

She ventured to tell me a little of what she had experienced during those weeks in hell, and she literally fell into convulsions of terror while talking about it. I think her account is indisputably authentic and, if anything, understates the truth. Here is her brief story:

At one point during the winter (January or February

1945), the SS nailed shut all the windows of a block's wash-room, crammed in as many women as possible, then locked the doors and left them there. (Here there were a few items Mme. Ossendowski had recounted in considerable detail but which I dared not record for fear of compromising her position; consequently, I could not vouch for them today. These concerned the exact date of the incident, the number of days it lasted, and the food rations the women did, or did not, receive during the period.)

Be that as it may, when it came time to bring the "experiment" to a close the SS made all the other prisoners return to their quarters, with strict orders not to leave or look out the windows (all in vain, of course). Then they threw open the washroom door and set up a motion-picture camera to film the wretched survivors as they came out: these prisoners had torn away the chimney bricks to try to get air and had ripped off all their clothing; several had died or were unconscious, others had evidently gone mad. . . .

They filmed every detail of the scene at great length, then, their movie completed, the SS loaded all the women, dead and otherwise, onto a truck, which went directly to the crematorium.

Mme. Ossendowski was not absolutely sure of the victims' nationalities, but she thought some were French.

From all appearances, this movie set was so carefully prepared for only one reason, to enable them to shoot a few feet of film. But what was this film, an "entertainment" for someone, a propaganda tract? To determine this one would have to evaluate the complete cinema archives of the Third Reich (assuming they have not been destroyed).

This afternoon I saw the Stubova (Irma, as always), *who told me of a gas chamber "survivor." Tonight I vomited.*

This "survivor" was a strong, healthy young woman who had been placed with a group of ill and aged inmates, the kind of group taken to Jugendlager every night. Like the others, she was put into the gas chamber naked. Somehow, she found herself regaining consciousness later—on a pile of bodies near the crematorium oven. She still had the strength to get out through a few of the barriers, then managed to remain hidden for several hours under some dirty mattresses piled outdoors. She was recaptured and gassed again the same day, but not before telling her story to other prisoners. This happened at the beginning of the exterminations.

Monday, March 12—A list of 700 prisoners leaving Tuesday the sixth . . . but this figure is only a total and does not necessarily mean that they left on Tuesday. . . .

There are still 700 women up there, of whom fifty arrived yesterday. . . .

Several convoys entered Jugendlager during this period, and it is impossible to keep track of the number of prisoners involved; none went out, except for the regular groups taken out every night after the roll call.

Thursday, March 15—This afternoon I take my temperature with Rita's thermometer (stolen from the Bekleidung)— 104°; tonight I vomit, very painfully. . . . Next Saturday or Sunday they will be evacuating the able-bodied (on foot, of course, and those who cannot follow will be slaughtered on the spot).

Seeing my fever, my doctor-friends assumed it was blood poisoning and decided nothing more could be done; I thought it was typhus.

My legs would not support me, but at least I did not lose mental control. During those long hours of sleeplessness I made a rather thorough survey of my situation—not as disinterestedly as that phrase may sound—in that strange atmosphere where facts propelled themselves and intermingled with dreamlike ease. I felt immersed in death, like a diver. I cannot say precisely why, but this presence of death was a comfort to me, the first I had felt in many days. That night, after objective deliberation on my condition, I decided I had to live, while chiding myself for having the gall to think one could decree such a thing. At any rate, I decided simply to play it by ear and do what seemed most sensible as events progressed. This decision was all that sustained me until liberation more than a month later. For similar reasons, liberation was a frightening prospect for many of us, since the last remaining crutch of danger would be snatched away from those whose psychological strength had already been almost completely shattered.[4]

Friday, March 16—The hunt.

This "hunt," sometimes known as a "selection," was a veritable beating-the-bushes-for-game throughout the camp during working hours, when the SS gathered up for the gas chamber those women who, like me, were not in one of the workshops. With sufficient warning, one could hide.

Before and after the hunt I go to the Revier—rather difficult on these legs of mine (to try to get treatment from a nurse-friend).

Saturday, March 17—A hunt. In the morning, an alert in the block (that is, a general inspection in our own block; we had to hide our disabled inmates between the ceiling and the roof—which had been dubbed "the fifth floor"—or under the beds).

Monday, March 19—This morning, a truck across the way (Block 23). For several days the gas chamber victims had no longer been rounded up directly at the Revier. Drs. Trommer and Winkelmann made their ominous visits to the blocks housing the ill, and those thus designated, instead of being loaded up and taken directly to the complex surrounding the cremation ovens, were listed as "dismissed from the Revier" and confined to Block 23. And it was there that the truck came every day for its load of women. Many of them went screaming in terror; the ovens were located just behind the camp's main wall, and the truck's trips back and forth could

---

[4] Complete statistics are not available, but a male friend deported to Dora gave me an indicative figure: of thirty comrades from his camp he continued to keep track of, five committed suicide after the liberation. As for the Frenchwomen, I personally know of only one case of suicide after the liberation, and none before. While it is quite true that, at Ravensbrück, it was hardly necessary to commit suicide in order to die, this negligible figure is rather striking.

be heard clearly. By this time, everyone knew its destination.
A "selection" in Blocks 30 and 31 this afternoon.

Tuesday, March 20—Back to the "fifth floor" this morn-
ing. In the afternoon, the truck is back at Block 23.

*Wednesday, March 21—*About two o'clock in the afternoon
they emptied one of the Uckermarck blocks (Block 21?). The
police carried the sick inmates outside the building, then the
SS threw them onto the trucks like so many potato sacks.

Thursday, March 22—Visits to Blocks 23, 6, 7, and 9 by
"the big mustache." This was the dreaded Dr. Winkelmann,
who came to choose his victims from among the sick. Needless to say, the inmates he spoke to all said they felt very
good, needed no rest or medication and had only one wish:
to return to work. One of our comrades, a pretty, young blond
student, had a serious lung lesion, a collapsed lung and continuous fever, and was in particularly bad condition that day.
She told me later that Winkelmann had come up to her bed
—all smiles and very friendly: "You feel very good, don't
you?"—"Oh yes! Very good."—"You have recovered completely."—"Yes! Completely."—"Then you can go to Block
23," and he made the little mark in his notebook. (She managed to escape on the way to Block 23.)

Friday, March 23—The truck at 23.
And three trucks left Block 27 for Uckermarck.

Sunday, March 25—Moving day. We have a roll call in a
new block. A general roll call of the entire camp was expected
but has not happened yet.
Officially, all the NN prisoners had left March 2 for Mauthausen; at the same time a number of gypsy women and their
children (about 800 altogether, I cannot recall the exact number) were sent out, and this was a sure indication of the voy-
age's destination. Schwarzhuber, moreover, declared flatly that
they were sent to be gassed. They came within a few hours
of being saved by the Swiss Red Cross.[5]

[5] See Appendix II, p. 218, for an article by Serge Choumoff,
a prisoner at Mauthausen, on that camp's gas chamber. (1972)

About fifty of us remained in the former NN block (which had been officially assigned to the Warsaw evacuees), and we were far too vulnerable simply because of our large number. In addition to that, the atmosphere had become unbearable because of the innumerable alerts and the overriding feeling of being rats caught in a trap. A half-dozen comrades and I decided to hide ourselves in a woodcutting detail which left the camp every morning and did not return until nightfall. With the help of some Czech friends and one Frenchwoman, a secretary in the labor office, and partly because of the prevailing chaos, we succeeded, and this gave us the opportunity to get into a workers' block (quite peaceful by comparison) and get out of the camp.

Monday, March 26—First day of work.

Tuesday, March 27—A "selection" roll call in our absence. Returning in the evening, we find 2,000 women in front of Block 24, waiting to leave for Jugendlager. They were soon gone.

At the same time a convoy just in from Rechlin was on the Lagerstrasse.

We had passed near them as we returned from work. The women lay helpless in front of the shower building, and five or six had died during the few hours they had been left there. The others were appallingly emaciated, sun-blackened, cadaverous, with blank, defeated stares. . . .

Wednesday, March 28—Back from work at 2 P.M. (very unusual). "Go along quietly now. . . . Your heart's still beating, isn't it?"

There was a general roll call that day, and, one by one, all the blocks filed past Schwarzhuber. We had to walk barefooted so they could see if our ankles were swollen. Of course, no one had any illusions about the fate of those who would be chosen, and Schwarzhuber knew it. He was literally beaming, brimming over with gaiety and good feeling, and when my rank passed by he bowed sanctimoniously and said in German: "Go along quietly now" . . . then, with a depraved, conspiratorial look: "Your heart's still beating, isn't it?"

Thursday, March 29—Coming back from work at six we pass a truckload of elderly women on the way up to Jugendlager (one of three today from Block 27). One tiny woman waves quickly as they go by. She looks French and is obviously trying to appear brave—such tragic eyes, but she keeps them high, and looking straight ahead. . . . And so old!

*Good Friday, March 30—*A "gassing," the largest numerically (about 350 victims, fifty or so of them French), and the truck had to make seven trips between Jugendlager and the cremation ovens.[6] For the first time, the victims attempted to struggle; nine managed to get away and hide in various places but were recaptured after a dramatic search. The SS locked everyone in dungeonlike cells, where, as was customary, they had them stripped (not wanting to risk burning their filthy rags, which could be reused).

To get the victims onto the trucks, they had offered pieces of bread, which were taken back immediately; bread could also be reused. But for some, terror was still stronger than the inducement of a crust of bread; they fought and screamed. Only a few yards away their terrified comrades, locked in their blocks, followed everything through the windows. And at that very hour the white Ford of the International Red Cross was parked at the camp entrance. (The Swiss doctor leading the mission had taken the initial steps toward an exchange of 300 French prisoners, but had been unable to meet with Commandant Suhren, who was said to be "occupied.")

Saturday, March 31—Returning from work we pass behind Nicole's block (no. 6). . . . She tells us to get away quickly; the truck is in front. We see it as we get to the corner of the building, and we don't linger.

A half portion of margarine. A crust of bread. No soup.

At nightfall the ominous truck was waiting in front of Block 10 for its cargo of victims: the gas chamber is still working.

A few women at Uckermarck—some of whom had witnessed the previous night's events through their windows—

---

[6] See p. 156: testimony by Marie-Claude Vaillant-Couturier on the location of the gas chamber.

were chosen for a work detail: to take the clothing stripped from the execution victims to the storerooms. Of course they recognized the rags as coming from their closest comrades.[7]

Sunday, April 1. Easter—
Scrap of bread. Half portion of margarine. No soup.
No roll call. They say we will not be working tomorrow.
Tonight they announce that the French prisoners must gather on the Lagerstrasse at 9 A.M., including those from Siemens and the Industriehof.
We wonder why.

Had the 170 daily executions already taken place?

The French prisoners at Uckermarck were to be included in this special call; even so, the little camp was not empty: Poles, Russians, Czechs, Germans, and Dutch remained there, along with those from Belgium, Luxembourg, the Saar, Alsace, and Lorraine, whom the Germans refused to include in this first liberation. (Three weeks later, on April 23,[8] the surviving French inmates, including the NN, were rescued by the Swedish Red Cross.)

Monday, April 2—Everyone is there at nine o'clock. There is going to be an exchange.[9]

That day and the night before they executed 500 women. This figure of 500 deaths over two days must have been a maximum, but it is accurate nonetheless; the earlier total

[7] The Germans generally cremated the bodies of their soldiers, but only after removing their clothing. (There was a Kommando at Ravensbrück for the rejuvenation of these bloody, grimy uniforms.) In the concentration camps the SS always undressed the condemned before killing them, and the recycling operation furnished proof of their deaths, if none other was available. Thus everyone at Ravensbrück knew, for example, about the execution of the young English parachutists, and the subsequent confessions by the SS who had presided over their deaths only confirmed what had been ascertained almost immediately.

[8] See p. 110 for an account of the execution of eleven male prisoners whose labors had kept the crematorium, and thus the gas chamber, operating. The executions took place April 25, 1945, *after* the visit by the Swedish Red Cross.

[9] This was a repatriation of 300 Frenchwomen through the Swiss Red Cross; NN prisoners were excluded.

of 180 in one day is also accurate. These were the numbers recorded by prisoner-bookkeepers for the SS units which removed the victims. The numbers were given to me immediately, and I made note of them immediately.

All of the information I have outlined (except for that relating to the Struthof camp) had come into my possession at Ravensbrück, and I had already concluded that the difference between the labor camps (such as Ravensbrück before November 1944) and the death camps (Auschwitz) lay primarily in the variations in rates of extermination. I also came to the conclusion that many of the apparent contradictions in German police policies faded in light of the economic organization of the camps and the fact that the highest leaders of the Nazi regime profited from it. For example:

—the establishment of infirmaries in the labor camps (during the summer of 1943 at Ravensbrück;[10]

—appearance of the letters NN on some dossiers (1942) and creation of a special category of prisoners: Nacht und Nebel (at Ravensbrück in March 1944);

—cessation of most criminal trials and replacement by administrative decisions (1943); a reduction of death sentences and executions (replaced by the letters NN in prisoner dossiers);

—cessation of acquittals and light sentences—even in cases of obvious error—and the continued massive deportation of totally innocent people.

I also believed that a second guiding principle of the system, to sweat revenues out of us until our final breath, led the Germans to wait until the last moment of the war to liquidate us, since they would at the same time be closing down a profitable industry.

But I was wrong, to a degree. Although the Germans in the Western camps may have been surprised by the American advance, our captors at Ravensbrück, sheltered behind the lower Oder River, could have carried on their exterminations more or less at their leisure, and without such surprises. As

[10] See p. 225 in the summary of Eugen Kogon's treatise on the camps, his characterization of the peculiar nature of their development, and the relation with the value of human labor.

of April 2, 1945, the day on which the camp authorities apparently destroyed some of the gas-chamber machinery, they still needed forty-four days to completely exterminate the remaining 11,000 prisoners, assuming a normal extermination rate. This could have been accomplished by the Germans before the arrival of the Russians. Why did they not do it? Because, I think, of Himmler's notion, crazy or not, to take power from Hitler and make a separate peace with the Anglo-Saxons through Swedish intermediaries, using us as commodities of barter. This final exploitation of prisoners as fodder for the German machine failed completely.

Ravensbrück, 1944–45
Verbier, January 1946

A deposition concerning events of April 25, 1945, given at the Hamburg trials:

Mina L., a prisoner employed in the Bunker maintenance detail, testified concerning the execution of eleven male prisoners who worked in the crematorium. *During the final weeks, these men had been moved into the cell block, where they waited to be executed. . . . On April 25 the SS made some significant changes: the men's group was broken up into various cells, and at the same time their coffee jug disappeared. I looked for it but couldn't find it. But as I was going to the crematory workers' cells, Aufseherin Mowes saw me, put the missing jug in my hands, and told me to take them their coffee. At first I suspected nothing and began pouring the first few cups. Then suddenly I realized that the coffee could have been poisoned. The Aufseherin snatched the jug from me and poured the coffee herself.*

When they came to check for dead bodies at ten o'clock, we had to leave, and everything became strangely quiet. . . . Later, Trasser (an SS) came to help pass out the noon meal, dawdled a few minutes, then commandeered me to carry the mess tray for him. We went directly to one of the crematory workers' cells—no. 47—and he ordered me, "Serve them." I knew quite well that the prisoners had noticed something wrong with the coffee earlier and had refused to drink it; now the lunch was poisoned. So I refused to serve them. Trasser glared at me, astonished and furious, wondering what I knew. I turned and left. He followed but came back later to serve them himself.

Two of the prisoners must have found nothing unusual about the food and ate. They were dead by evening. That night I was again given the task of passing out the food. I looked into Cell 47 and asked if they wanted to eat. They all answered yes, "if you are serving us." They were very weak and said they would be executed in any case. . . . The next morning our fears were confirmed; the cell was empty. . . . There was a claw hammer on the table, and a bloodstain someone had tried to hide with dirt. And there were bloodstains on the walls. . . .

Part Two

ONE CONVOY
OF FRENCHWOMEN

12

A List of 959

For the most part, the Ravensbrück archives were not recovered after the liberation. I have attempted to reconstruct some of the various stages and landmark events of the camp, especially those relating to the final exterminations, by means of a German document, an SS "working paper" drawn up for their own use. This, I think, will help us follow the destiny of a convoy of Frenchwomen. The document came from the Ravensbrück Revier, saved from destruction by a Czech deportee who later transmitted it to me.

These twenty-nine typed pages had the mark of a careful hand—no erasures, no alterations—obviously not a rough draft but a final, definitive version, meticulously drawn up in several copies for the various, more or less autonomous, services of the camp. Our copy was a carbon, embellished with annotations added later by several different hands, but all in careful legible writing, as precise and cold as the facts laid out before us.

Much more than a bare description of a group of prisoners, the document gives the exact composition, with names, of a deportation convoy which left Compiègne on January 30, 1944. Since 1945 I have managed to pinpoint 245 separate convoy trains of deportees; I have been able to find such documentation for only two—the January 30 convoy dealt with here and another of June 15, 1944.

There are, of course, false documents, just as there are unreliable witnesses, but the authentic ones have the twin virtues of being, usually at least, contemporary with the events they relate to, and of not having been made up to fit some particular cause, such as buttressing someone's testimony. They are immovable and objective, like inanimate objects. As has often been said, their value is greatest in contemporary history, where the most intense feelings are involved.

Along with occasional falsifications, quite easily detected, these documents concerning the deportations (those that escaped destruction) are, unfortunately, extremely dry and impersonal accounts; they exist only in such forms as internal orders, administrative memoranda, prisoner lists drawn up for intercamp transfers, or, on the other hand, lists made up by prisoners for possible notification of families or the Red Cross, individual prisoner file cards, private and official correspondence, stock lists, diaries, and photographs.

Nonetheless, one should not proceed under the illusion that a history of the deportations could be written with these documents alone. They are, above all, very incomplete, since the Germans systematically destroyed potentially incriminating documents whenever possible. Those that escaped the Germans' hands did not always survive in the form of coherent collections: the United States and the Soviet Union kept most of what they retrieved in their own hands, and the remainder were scattered among other belligerent nations and among some non-belligerents. (I personally located some documents in Sweden and Switzerland.)

Even assuming we possessed the complete records of all the concentration camps, we would still have to rely upon eyewitness accounts, principally for the simple reason that bureaucratic paperwork, however precise and complete it might be, could not convey the human complexities of actual events. And in the situation we are dealing with here, these records were often juggled and camouflaged from the very beginning. For example, there was no specific notation differentiating an extermination list from a transport roll, and in official Nazi communications the most terrifying realities were hidden by bland and innocent terminology; one had to know the code to understand the meaning. Even when one had deciphered the codes, it was still necessary to investigate further to ensure that an interpretation was not erroneous. But none of these preparatory tasks was insurmountable.

Unintentional errors are more dangerous; thus in studying certain German administrative documents—supplemented by our oral inquiries—one can easily find indications that they are riddled with gaps and inaccuracies, although they might be unquestionably authentic, without deliberate falsifications, and conducive to almost complete verification. Many of these inaccuracies are important simply because of their number and nature, and all the more hazardous because a future historian might approach them with unjustified respect, which he would hardly have the means to overcome.

And I am dealing here with such a document. It includes twenty-nine pages and presents a list of 959 women, of whom 958 were deported from France on January 30, 1944. They arrived at Ravensbrück at dawn, February 3.

As I have already said, all of the ordinary services in the German camps, including secretarial, were performed by prisoners. I was thus able to analyze this list not only with the aid of a great number of the prisoners whose names were on it, but also with those who had been responsible for keeping it up to date; they knew the list and duly verified it. In addition to this over-all attestation, my inquiries established that there were no intentional falsifications when it was drawn up; nor were there such alterations afterward. The list was simply a result of the Germans' administrative needs, and I think it meets the demands of critical history.

The errors in the text are unintentional and, consequently, unsystematic, unbiased, and unpredictable—thus all the more difficult to discern. There are many, some serious, but one should not forget that such documents, whatever their deficiencies, can be of profound historical and social interest once they have undergone critical examination.

The title—A simple typed date (February 3, 1944) which corresponds with the date of the convoy's arrival, but not at all with the date the list was made up. (It should be dated around February 10.) At top right, in pencil, is the word "Revier"; the list was, in fact, retrieved at the Revier.

First registration: 27,030–27,988—We can consider it certain that 958 women were present on the Lagerstrasse at Ravensbrück on February 3, 1944, and that they were assigned numbers in the twenty-seven thousands. This is, in fact, the only sure thing in the entire document, but it is of considerable interest nonetheless. I have said 958, not 959, because opposite no. 27,260, after the prisoner's name, I found the notation *"ist nicht zur Einlieferung gelangt,"*[1] which meant a deduction of one for the total number arriving at their destination.

Second registration: 1–975—A second series of numbers, assigned beginning at "one" and continuing in numerical order, would seem at first glance to indicate a total of 975 rather than 958, a difference of seventeen.

Up to page 3 of the list the numbering systems match perfectly, but on that page—opposite no. 89—instead of a name corresponding with the twenty-seven thousands series, there is a line of periods and the word *"gestrichen"* ("stricken" or "deleted"). On page 4, opposite numbers 105 and 119, the dots and the mysterious word reappear. And so on—seventeen *"gestrichen"* in all.

It seems hardly likely that cancellation of seventeen deportation orders or seventeen deaths during the transfer process could have gone unnoticed by all the many survivors I questioned. On the other hand, several remembered answering a roll call by name shortly after arriving at Ravensbrück, indicating that the German guards were probably using a list made up before the convoy's departure from France. The discrepancies are further complicated by the method of name classification on the first list—five separate alphabetical groups —which certainly did not make my own research any easier. There is a series of 279 names[2] (27,030–27,309), followed by the other groups—(27,310–27,570: 261 names; 27,571–27,-

[1] "Did not arrive at transfer point." The prisoner in question was deported on a following train and died. I know no further details.

[2] Not including prisoner no. 27,260.

863: 293 names; 27,864–27,929: 66 names; 27,930–27,988: 59 names).

Questioning of the principals involved was obviously the only way of resolving these anomalies. Proceeding in that fashion, I learned that a few hundred of the prisoners deported on this train had been at Compiègne for about a month before their departure for Ravensbrück. As far as I was able to identify them by name and number, they appeared only in the first series.

I also learned that a large group had been transferred from Fresnes to Compiègne in three huge buses only a few days before the convoy departed. It seems that they were combined with another contingent arriving the same day from Romainville to make up the second series.

In the third alphabetical series I found others from Fresnes and Romainville who arrived at Compiègne forty-eight hours later, as well as those in a convoy from Clermont-Ferrand.

My investigation of the fourth series is not conclusive, but in the fifth and last were prisoners brought in from the provinces, particularly Poitiers and Toulouse.

Details provided by the subjects of my interviews gave indications of the answer: they recalled, for example, one old woman—Mme. Marie-Louise Monnet—whose name came up among the second series (transfers from Romainville to Compiègne). She had been put in the hospital at the last minute and removed from the departure list. In the alphabetical position which should have been occupied by Mme. Monnet, we find the line of dots, followed by "gestrichen."

We can conclude that this first set of numbers (the twenty-seven thousands) was assigned to the prisoners before the convoy left France. "Gestrichen" then corresponds to the names of those who, for one reason or another, managed at the last moment to avoid leaving.

Identification—These are as given by the prisoners themselves, first to the Gestapo, then to camp authorities. Some, arrested under false names (either because they had already known they were being sought under their real names, or because they were of Jewish origin), appear in this document

with these false identities; when they died, the identity went
with them. Tracking down and correcting these errors—which
obviously could not be blamed on German record-keeping—
demanded long and meticulous checking.

A thorough investigation I devoted to another convoy—the
fifty-seven thousands—uncovered eleven false, but seemingly official, identities[3] out of 593 deportees, but this does
not necessarily imply that proportions anywhere near the same
would apply in other cases, since the practice of altering official identities was almost unknown in the early days of the
Resistance (and it also raised serious difficulties for those who
had only private, limited resources—salary, commercial earn-
ings, miscellaneous income). But it became increasingly widespread, in proportion with the intensification of the "secret
war." The fifty-seven thousands convoy was made up of
those arrested during the last phase of the Resistance (1944),
while almost all of the twenty-seven thousands were arrested in 1943 (a few dated from 1942), a period when completely false identities were mostly used by those (not many)
who had already escaped one arrest, or by some who might
otherwise be identified as Jewish or of Jewish heritage. Even
so, the latter had not been confronted at the time with such
dangers that fears about their origins forced them to take
really efficient precautions: in 1943, a false identity did not
always prevent a police investigation.

Grounds for arrest—It was the same for the entire convoy:
"political," or "polit." as it appears on the document—a label
with no relation to reality. It was applied to women arrested
for Resistance activities, as hostages, or through pure error;
there were others seized for prostitution, vagrancy, or theft.
The word "political" seems to carry here simply a meaning
of "non-racial" and was no more than a general designation

---

[3] It should be understood that some simple pseudonyms actually
amounted to a new identity. But a "nom de guerre," used in sign-
ing a report or introducing a Resistance agent to his comrades,
did not at all prevent one who adopted such a name from walking
around with the original identification card in his pocket. How
could he do otherwise when he continued to live in his old home,
as was often the case until 1943?

for the convoy; there was no individual significance, as, for example, our Jewish comrades arrested for Resistance activities were fortunately not separated from the rest of the group. I shall try to follow the destinies of several of those in that convoy.

13

Handwritten Notes:
The Work Transports

This was all of the typed information, but it was accompanied by handwritten annotations which also furnished valuable data. Written opposite individual names were place names in 262 instances; the word *"entlassen"* (released) appeared by seventy-four names; a cross—eighty-eight cases; and finally, a single letter "U" appeared fifty-two times; in four cases the letter "U" was followed by a cross.

The place names indicated work Kommandos, including the following:

Bartensleben (6-23-44 and 8-7-44)

Leipzig (9-2-44)

Neubrandenburg (5-15-44 and 8-28-44)

Oranienburg (9-20-44)

Wattenstedt (8-28-44)

Zwodau (10-2-44)

Six Kommandos in all, eight transports, and 262 prisoners. (One will see later why I did not include the place designated by "U" among the Kommandos.)[1]

"Entlassen" alongside seventy-four of the names presumably meant that the prisoners in question had been released: six on isolated dates during 1944 (March 19 and 29, April 19, May 10 and 19, and August 3) and sixty-eight listed as released on April 2, 1945, which was, in fact, the date of an exchange involving 300 French prisoners, arranged by the International Red Cross. So, among the 300 there were sixty-eight of the twenty-seven thousands.

[1] See p. 141.

One would assume that the eighty-eight crosses meant that number of deaths. As for the fifty-two women whose names were accompanied by the letter "U"—four of them followed by a cross—the logical assumption would be that they were part of a "U" convoy and that only the indicated four did not return. According to these figures, then, we have accounted for 476 of the 958, of whom seventy-four were freed and only ninety-two died.

My questioning of the secretaries responsible for keeping this type of document up to date confirmed what had been immediately apparent: the prisoners marked "entlassen" had been released; names accompanied by crosses indeed meant death (and on approximately the date listed); the place names all corresponded with Kommandos. Accordingly, the other 482 women (more than half) must not have died. They must have been sent out in a Kommando or been liberated, and must not have been involved in that mysterious, horrifying adventure designated by the letter "U." What became of them?

Actually, all of these "official" figures are imprecise, and involuntarily so—which confuses the situation all the more.

Methodical questioning of the survivors among the twenty-seven thousands led to the quick conclusion that they went through other ordeals of which there is no record whatever in our document. For example, I am reasonably sure that 122 of them were sent to Holleichen on April 13 or 14, 1944. There is no plausible reason for this omission from the record: as a Kommando, Holleichen was no worse than Leipzig or Zwodau; the books were still being kept up to date when they were sent out, and I am sure that relevant information concerning this transport was included in other documents of the same type as we are dealing with, but these have disappeared. One might assume that the omissions were only a matter of oversight.

Nor are there references in the document regarding transports to:

Hanover-Limmer, June 22
Brunschweig, July 7

Schlieben, July 22
Neubrandenburg, August 9
Flossenburg, August 31
Graslitz, August 31
Genthin, October 15
Bergen-Belsen, February 3 and 28, 1945
Rechlin, February 14
Salzwedel, April 1 and 5

I know that some of the twenty-seven thousands were part of these convoys for the simple reason that I located and spoke to them. I was not able to question all the survivors or, of course, the dead, and consequently even my supplemented list of Kommandos cannot be considered complete. Finally, we should remember that personal names (sometimes fictitious) corresponding to these dates and Kommando names were not always those of the women who made up a given convoy. (All deportees knew of the last-minute substitutions which sent one prisoner on a transport in place of another.)

Releases—Whatever information we have is precise in itself, but incomplete. There were six prisoners among the twenty-seven thousands—and only six—who were released individually at various times during 1944 and duly noted on the list; there were the sixty-eight—and exactly sixty-eight—who in early April 1945 took their places on the Red Cross trucks.[2] But fortunately there were others—on different dates, in various places, and through devices not noted on our list—who also returned to the homeland; most of these were in the various outside work Kommandos.

The gaps in our information on the prisoner releases is less disturbing than the others concerning the makeup and departure of the convoys and mortality rates. The last meaningful date in our text is April 21, 1945;[3] it is no longer valuable for subsequent developments. (There is no reference to the

[2] An exchange involving 300 French prisoners, the first from Ravensbrück to see France again. Officially listed as "entlassen" on April 2, 1945, they actually departed on April 6 or 7.

[3] Mme. Jeanne Wagner's death.

April 23, 1945, liberation of the surviving French prisoners, negotiated by Count Bernadotte and Heinrich Himmler.)[4] And one could not reasonably expect documents maintained at the Ravensbrück Revier to keep track of events involving prisoners who had been sent out in Kommandos, often far from the main camp. Accordingly, we found ourselves faced with two sets of significant but understandable gaps: in time —after April 21, 1945, and in space—beyond the boundaries of the central camp.

It is not possible within the framework of this study to give a complete account of the many fates awaiting those prisoners whose dispersion throughout Germany I have mentioned in general terms. Nonetheless, a very brief sketch would aid in understanding the distribution-center role of Ravensbrück in the deportation and industrial exploitation of women from throughout Europe. Such a glimpse can be interesting from another point of view, in that it helps us envision the wide diversity of these destinies. To be sure, one can find certain fundamental facts repeated throughout the vast deportation experience: the moral ordeals of captivity, coercion, and criminal excesses; the extreme physical misery of constant hunger, excessive work, cold, and overcrowding. But these are the characteristics of all repressive systems. The unfortunate innovation of the German concentration camps came in their atrocities and in the unbelievable variety of them. Let there be no illusions: the system not only trampled the spirit, but it killed an incredibly large number of its captives—the majority of our dead succumbed during the last three months of the Hitlerian oppression, and the deaths were wholly intentional.

According to the best-informed, the scattering of prisoners among the work Kommandos must have lessened the risk of extermination, which, beginning in 1942, was a constant threat

---

[4] Beginning with three series of lists drawn up in Sweden through the good offices of the Red Cross (marked by unavoidable errors, unfortunately), I attempted to refashion an over-all list through which I was ultimately able to identify ninety-one from the convoy of the twenty-seven thousands.

in the form of the transports noirs. All who could possibly leave on a work detail (forbidden to the NN) tried to do so; statistically, they had good reason. Here is what happened to some of them.

When the final debacle came, some of the Frenchwomen who had been sent to Leipzig were simply let out on the surrounding roads, where they gathered in small groups and were taken in by the Allied armies. Those who stayed behind were there when the Russian troops arrived; they managed to explain their situation to one officer, who only pointed to the horizon and said in French, "Odessa is that way," and let them leave on their own. At the first crossroads, they turned west, hoping to find the shortest route to France; as luck would have it, they encountered American soldiers and were repatriated rather quickly.

At Schlieben, the factory manager took responsibility for the prisoners after the SS fled on April 15, offering to any takers the opportunity to leave on foot to join the Americans, along with two horse-drawn carts for baggage and a guard contingent of six easygoing soldiers. About thirty Frenchwomen and a few gypsies departed under those conditions. The others later had the pleasure of seeing a Russian tank smash the walls of the prisoner compound, then living "on the house" until their eventual repatriation by the Western Allies.

Three of the Holleichen prisoners—two French and a Polish woman—had been sent to Flossenburg and executed; one other (an informer) was also taken there, but at her own request. All the rest, whom the guards had locked up before fleeing, were freed by Polish resistance fighters and waited for the Americans under the protection of French war prisoners from neighboring villages.

At Zwodau the first evacuation took place sometime in April 1945—to Neurolau (see below), on foot, with the healthy women carrying the sick. There were about fifty Frenchwomen, 800 Hungarian Jews, and a few Czechs. On May 1, those who remained were marched off toward Dachau —1,000 women, in ranks of five. But the road had been cut by the Allied advance, and the Germans brought them back to Zwodau four days later. Liberation came on May 7, after an agreement between the Russian and American liberators, under which the Americans were responsible for prisoner repatriation and the Russians were allowed to occupy the camp.

The women at Wattenstedt likewise went through wildly diverse experiences. Some were sent to Hanover; others, after a six-day journey in cattle cars, found themselves back at Ravensbrück, having the good fortune to arrive between April 1 (when the gas chamber was deactivated) and the April 23 liberation by the Swedes. They were a part of that group.

Thus parts of these scattered groups escaped the more or less methodical executions of the last weeks of the Reich, and it was solely because of the peculiar circumstances of these work details that they showed a higher survival rate than the others, not because of any less difficult conditions of captivity.

On April 3, some 750–800 prisoners, who had been working in the gas-mask factory (Continental) at Hanover-Limmer (a Kommando attached to Neuengamme), were given a crust of bread and then endured a three-day march to Bergen-Belsen. Along the way their number was reduced by about eighty—some escaped; others died of exhaustion.

A large convoy of disabled prisoners was sent from Neubrandenburg to Ravensbrück near the end of March 1945. It is almost certain that they were marked for extermination, but the gas-chamber building could accommodate only 150. And for some administrative reason, it seemed that our captors could only rarely accomplish more than one set of executions a day. This bureaucratic problem was no doubt the reason these prisoners were temporarily confined to one of the blocks in the main camp. There a "selection" was carried out a few days later (March 25); some were sent in cattle cars to Neurolau, arriving April 1, fifteen days before their comrades from Zwodau. Neubrandenburg was evacuated on April 27, except for the ill remaining in the infirmary (who were simply abandoned) and the few who had managed to avoid the last German-led departure by hiding. (They finally ended up in Sweden.) The others, as in other camps, were put on the road for a last march; some escaped; many died.

At Neurolau (where, in a mass of grisly confusion, the dead and dying were thrown into immense pits, and where for several days one could hear scattered pistol shots at all hours, which meant that at least some of the victims would not be buried alive), the surviving women (about 1,600) and the men were marched out on the night of April 19. For almost three weeks this tragic procession roamed over mountain roads, leaving bodies along the entire route. On May 8, 1945, the survivors arrived near Prague, where they were rescued.

A train which left Ravensbrück for Mauthausen on March 2, 1945, ostensibly carried, along with some gypsy women and their children, the NN prisoners, most of them French. But in fact, a number of our compatriots from other blocks (including some of the twenty-seven thousands) had been added to the French NNs. On several occasions at Ravensbrück there were reports, seemingly coming from Deputy Commandant Schwarzhuber, of the extermination awaiting the convoy (rumors made all the more plausible by the presence of the gypsies). But when the International Red Cross entered Mauthausen, those who had survived the journey were in relatively good condition despite their trying ordeals. It should be noted, however, that the aged and ill prisoners had been kept at Ravensbrück. They were sent later to Bergen-Belsen, which had apparently become a major extermination center, in view of the fact that in numerous camps and Kommandos the aged, the ill, and those with "racial" labels were separated from their comrades and sent in that direction.

When the English forces finally entered Bergen-Belsen—several days after surrounding the camp—they found themselves in a gigantic charnel house where, amid 33,000 rotting, foul-smelling corpses, there were some 10,000 prisoners near death (mostly from typhoid), tortured by thirst. Even so, at Bergen-Belsen, as elsewhere, there were survivors.

The Beendorf salt mines, northeast of Helenstedt, appeared in the Ravensbrück records under the name of Bartensleben. The evacuation of these mines was a nightmarish journey lasting twelve days, in cattle cars, under such inhuman conditions that when the train arrived at Neuengamme (fortunately after the destruction of that camp's gas chamber), more than 1,000 dead had been left along the way.

Many of the prisoners in the Rechlin Kommando experienced some of the worst atrocities. At the evacuation, the most seriously ill were left behind and finally liberated by Russian advance units. But the rest were taken to Ravensbrück in trucks,[5] several of which went directly to the crematorium enclosure—without so much as a check by the camp authorities. Little is known about the final minutes of these victims' lives, but we do know that none escaped the massacre. Other trucks[6] dumped their cargoes of haggard women into an overcrowded camp whose population was steadily and methodically being reduced by "selections" for the gas chamber. I saw them: all with that same expression of dying animals, their bodies wracked with trembling. Five or six of them died between their arrival during the afternoon and the time when they were finally put in blocks. Some ended up at Uckermarck (the mysterious "U" of the document); others managed to survive until April 2, 1945, and I found them later among those rescued by the Swiss Red Cross.

After this brief and necessarily incomplete summary of the fates of those of the twenty-seven thousands who had left Ravensbrück in work Kommandos, we must return to the others who remained in the camp, and of whom our document says nothing.

[5] See p. 106.
[6] To understand these movements one should keep in mind that Ravensbrück was equipped to execute about 170 prisoners a day; 180 was the effective maximum. (To my knowledge, this figure was increased significantly on only one occasion.)

14

The "Transports Noirs"

As we have already seen, our list, kept up to date through April 21, 1945, included 262 prisoners who left in work Kommandos and fifty-two in the "U" Kommando (of whom only four died—officially), or a total of 314 inmates. One might then infer that the eighty-eight dead (not including those in the "U" group) whose names are given in the document represent the total death toll, in exactly fourteen months and three weeks, of the 644 Frenchwomen who remained at Ravensbrück.

One very basic error was uncovered in the course of my questioning: the number of prisoners among the twenty-seven thousands who never left Ravensbrück was definitely not 644. . . . But we should first examine another erroneous conclusion one might be tempted to make on the basis of the listed information: the figure of eighty-eight deaths.

First, to give proper credit to Revier bookkeeping, the women whose names were followed by a date and the symbol of a cross did indeed die, if not on the given date, at least within a week of it. But these names came nowhere near representing the complete death toll of the group they belonged to. The camp authorities, however, regarded the document as a valid record, and the Revier's SS doctor relied on it during his trial. (He used not only the document in question here but his recollection of comparable material maintained by his own staff for every convoy arriving in camp.)

The death statistics he has cited are no doubt something of an average compiled from these texts, which are no longer

available. Dr. Treite attempted to put a stamp of validity
on all these figures, as did Commandant Suhren. The latter
stated (p. 12, interrogatory dated 12/5/49): "During the year
after I took command, the death rate at Ravensbrück ranged
from 0.2 per cent and 0.23 per cent per month."

A simple reading of Dr. Treite's statements helps us locate, but not quantify, the causes of serious errors in the
figures given by him and Suhren: *The large number of deranged and mental incompetents was a burden on the camp
. . . Some fifty to eighty of these prisoners were selected by
a psychiatrist and sent to Linz, where they would almost have
had to be sent to the gas chamber.*

*At the beginning of 1945, the camp became tremendously
congested, and evacuation had to be considered; the prisoners
unable to work were to be held back. In my capacity as
camp doctor it was my duty to weed out these prisoners with
the least possible delay. Since the time allowed to do this was
not sufficient, I refused to make such choices—the meaning
of which was all too clear to me.*

Dr. Treite was hoping to justify himself during a trial on
accusations of war crimes; he consequently chose the course
of telling what he knew about areas involving the over-all
responsibilities of the camp command, and lying about only
those points where he thought he might be implicated personally. It is true, however, that Dr. Treite took no part in
the deadly "selections" for Uckermarck after the first one.
That being the case, why not concede that he refused to make
such choices because he foresaw the fate of those who would
be chosen? To accept such a position coming from him would
be naïve at best, since he had lied on other issues. (See below
on the transports to Linz.) Did this "weeding out" of prisoners
seem reprehensible to him only because it would be hasty
and unmethodical?

During the same trial I found a line of defense adopted by
one Aufseherin particularly striking in its similarity to Dr.

---

[1] I learned from the secretaries that, beginning around the end
of January, not even those in Uckermarck who died of hunger
or cold were officially counted, and these were the deaths that they
could, if necessary, attribute to "natural causes."

Treite's. It seemed to cause her no great difficulty to recount having chosen women for the gas chamber, emphasizing that all these prisoners were old or ill or incapable of working. This Aufseherin was ignorant and narrow-minded; Dr. Treite was a cultured and intelligent gentleman.

Then there was the transport to Linz, made up of mentally ill prisoners, according to Ravensbrück's chief doctor—his own "patients," in whom he had shown so little interest (in spite of the fate he saw in store for them) that he did not know whether there were fifty or eighty. There were actually one hundred twenty of them, and this figure is absolutely certain.

This procedure for disposing of undesirable prisoners was known in camp jargon as the transport noir, and it was the routine, essential regulatory element of the Nazi concentration-camp system used in the camps which were not organized for systematic, local exterminations.

In an industrial "enterprise" based on the heinous principle of a slave-labor force pushed by brutality and terror to maximum production (with a minimum of upkeep), it is obvious that human attrition would be appallingly high and would rather quickly reach a level where the brutality and terror ceased to be effective. At this point, the used-up slave would have to be disposed of, and these "disappearances" were the function of the transports noirs. Any assessment of mortality at Ravensbrück that disregards these periodic "purges" would be absurd. What value could there be in a concentration-camp death figure which failed to take into account those who died of "old age" (which at Ravensbrück began at fifty), of so-called "incurable illnesses," and of simple exhaustion? Not to mention those labeled insane only because fear or grief had put them in a state of confusion.

The task of choosing "fifty to eighty prisoners, probably sent to the gas chamber" at Linz, fell to Dr. Treite as a matter of course, which helps explain the diffident and reserved tone in which he recounted the incident. According to the Revier secretaries I questioned on the subject, there were approximately *sixty* separate transports to Linz during 1943 and 1944—more than two per month. The last and largest was in November 1944, and comprised exactly one hundred twenty prisoners.

> I also tried to learn how the transport-noir system functioned before my arrival at Ravensbrück: one veteran secretary told me that between February 3, 1942, and the end of March she had counted ten "small" transports to Buch and Bernburg. . . . Grete Buber-Neumann, who arrived August 2, 1942 (prisoner no. 4208) and later that year became Blockova of the "religious" prisoners, recalled being summoned along with the other block chiefs by the commandant, who instructed them to make up lists of the *biologischminderwertige*, a bizarre category which included amputees, bed-wetters, and those who had been declared deranged by some "authority" or another. The official explanation was that they would be sent to a "rest camp." Why, at that time, did some prisoners think that this "selection" was for execution? The fact is that there had already been discussion along these lines, but the majority still believed the "rest camp" story—one German woman in particular, a doctor who, being ill, was placed in the convoy. She promised to send back a message inside the lining of her clothing to reassure her friends. (The ritual return of clothing was perhaps already a common practice?) The clothing came back very quickly, and in the hem of the dress her comrades found the message: "They are making us undress. We are at Bernburg."

Among the victims thus "dealt with" were the women ostensibly deemed deranged, sometimes by Dr. Treite himself, sometimes by his subordinates (some of whom had no medical qualifications whatsoever). Other prisoners were placed in the camp's forbidding "asylum" simply because they were more or less disabled or fatigued or because they had refused to work or had displeased some camp official. Such was the case, for example, of a young Frenchwoman, the daughter of a Fontainebleau notary. She had a perfectly healthy mind but had been devastated by the death of her twin sister—and she happened to irritate one Carmen Mory.[2]

During 1943 and 1944 there were transports noirs other than those to Linz: a convoy of 800 women to Lublin in January 1944, the small, so-called "racial" convoy to Auschwitz (about which I know nothing except that it existed), those from Rechlin to Bergen-Belsen; and all had but one goal—to rid Ravensbrück of "surplus" humanity.

During the final stages of the concentration-camp evolution (December 1944–April 1945), the safety valve represented by the transports noirs no longer functioned (see p. 43); human attrition was increasing at an incredible rate, while at the same time the Russian advance in Poland was taking out of commission those camps best organized for systematic extermination. The ballet of "production-extermination," once so well choreographed by Ravensbrück, was simply falling apart; the workshops were using prisoners less efficiently, partly because many of the prisoners had actually become unusable, but no doubt also because new problems in the chain of production and delivery of raw materials precluded the total utilization of manpower which is the goal of all good "managers." Food and shelter for these unprofitable women did not present insoluble problems, but all events indicated that of all the possible solutions, the commandant was considering only one—"local" extermination. But a question remained: should they get rid of only the unusables whose mouths were eating into profits, or simply execute everyone? At the time (early December 1944), the gas chamber at Auschwitz had just been demolished, and the same would soon happen at Linz.

In a carefully documented study on the Mauthausen gas chamber,[3] Serge Choumoff, an engineer and former de-

---

[2] Carmen Mory, a professional spy, arrested in France in 1939 as a German agent; released by the Germans in 1940, then rearrested by the Germans after they had examined the French counterespionage archives; a Blockova at Ravensbrück, and sentenced to death for murder at the Hamburg trials.

[3] Serge Choumoff, op. cit.

portee, wrote concerning Linz: *The sinister role of the Hartheim castle at Alkoven (near Linz on the Passau highway) is well known: it has been cited numerous times as a home for the deranged, converted into a site for systematic extermination of the mentally ill in the name of "euthanasia." This was provided for in Hitler's personal order launching the operation as of October 1939 (backdated to September 1). This function was the responsibility of, among others, SS Reichsleiter P. Buhler, chief of the Führer's chancellery, assisted by K. Brandt, one of Hitler's personal physicians. The office created for implementation of the policy was headquartered at no. 4, Tiergartenstrasse in Berlin and designated by the code name "T-4." The director was SS Oberführer Viktor Brack, another of Buhler's assistants. . . . "During the summer of 1940, the efforts of a number of experts in such operations were spread among the concentration camps, which were visited by a medical commission after a preliminary selection by camp doctors."* (B-p. 726). On December 12, 1941, Himmler issued an order instituting euthanasia in the concentration camps, under the code designation "14 F 13" (B-p. 728). *This was in fact only a formalization of existing practices: since August 1941 some prisoners at Mauthausen and Gusen had been subjected to such a policy, as the transport lists will demonstrate.*

Meanwhile, some courageous protests were being raised in Germany: one was by Pastor Braune, a fundamentalist leader who wrote to the Reich Chancellery on July 9, 1940: ". . . As for the program of euthanasia, which is already being applied to prisoners . . . Exactly who is abnormal or asocial, and who are these hopeless cases? . . ." (X-1, p. 213). Pastor Braune was arrested by the Gestapo and imprisoned for three months.

The existence of a gas chamber at Hartheim was attested after the war in Austrian police documents and in French investigations, as Choumoff has noted. He also quotes Franz Ziereis, the commandant at Mauthausen, in this regard: *"SS Gruppenführer Glücks issued an order that physically weak prisoners were to be considered as mentally ill and gassed at an installation located in the Hartheim castle near Linz. . . ."* Choumoff continues that *much more recently, Dr. Renno, the chief doctor at Hartheim, had to admit at the beginning of his trial in Frankfurt, in February 1970, that the gassing operations at Hartheim included not only the feeble-minded but also some physical invalids sent from Mauthausen. (Cf. "Frankfurter Allgemeine," February 2, 1970, p. 25.)*

. . . Hartheim ceased operations as of December 12, 1944, following an order from the Chancellery, through Ziereis, stipulating that the castle was to be reconverted to a normal residential building. A document dated December 30, 1944, shows the demolition carried out by a work Kommando sent from Mauthausen specifically for that purpose. The Kommando consisted of twenty prisoners, a list of which has been available. We also have the testimony by Adam Golembski, no. 31,755 and a member of this detail, on what he saw of the Hartheim installations during their work. His account follows in full:

"On December 13, 1944, we went by truck to the Hartheim castle, 27 kilometers west of Linz. There we entered a hangarlike building made of wood and covered on the outside with tar paper. It could be sealed airtight, and there were no windows. From this building one could go directly into a passageway of the castle and into the courtyard. The first thing to catch my eye was a smokestack about 26 meters tall. The stack could not be seen from the outside, as it was hidden by the three-story walls of the castle. On the ground floor to the right were the kitchen and pantry. To the left were the central-heating furnaces, a carpentry shop, a liquor storehouse, a refrigerator room, and the room where we were housed. A door led from our room to the castle tower, where there was a photography shop, and from this small room another door led to what seemed to be

the baths. The entryway was very small, and the ste
door, with rubber molding, could be locked with hug
bolts. Also on the door was a small, round porthol
Tiles covered the walls halfway up, and there were s
showers. The next small room contained the gassin
equipment—gas bottles and various meters and gauge
Then there was a larger room, also with half-tile wall
there was a table, and we found documents outlinin
proper procedures for research on a cadaver. A door .
this room led to the crematorium, which had two oven
To the left of the door we found a pile of ashes an
human bones which would fill about sixty of our tras
barrels. We also found an electric mill which was used
grind the bones left after the cremation.[4] In the garag
of the castle there were about four carloads of clothing
men's, women's, and children's. In the yard was a tras
pit where we found a large number of identificatio
tags of Mauthausen prisoners, along with more huma
bones.

"The SS were lodged on the second floor. The con
mandant was an SS doctor with the rank of Obersturm
führer, and the crematorium chief was an SS Unte
scharführer—unfortunately, I do not know his nam
Everyone was in civilian clothes. Elsewhere, one ver
large room contained big reflector lamps and many bed
there were still bloodstains on some of them. This roo
was probably used for their secret medical experiment
One carrying case of surgical instruments had a tag wit
the name of Dr. Renno.

"We tore down the smokestack and took out some o
the ashes. In the 'showers' we removed the tiles from th
walls and dismantled the equipment used in their mu
ders. Our work lasted eight days. The masons restore
the rooms to their original layout and replastered th
walls. Some of the furnishings were sent to Mauthause
and some went to a hunting castle owned by Princ

[4] Use of this kind of equipment was also mentioned at Eic
mann's trial. (X-2, p. 221).

Starrenberg at Wiesenbach on Lake Ata, about 130 kilometers from Hartheim.

"We went back again on January 2, 1945, for ten days and continued the work of giving the castle its old look. We would brick in a door, make a new door, etc. The place was made into a children's home, with room for 400. Around the end of our stay they brought in thirty-five children, six nurses, and a teacher."

15

The Letter "U"

In November 1944 the gas chamber at Auschwitz was destroyed, and after December 13 Suhren could no longer use Linz for his killing. What was he to do?

Did Suhren himself, as early as November 1944, request the extermination orders which, according to his own testimony, did not reach him until the end of the following February? But while waiting for this clearance, and knowing he would receive it, he must have taken the precautions which, in his opinion, seemed necessary. Did he lie about the dates, and did he get Schwarzhuber to lie on the same point? It should be remembered that Suhren's defense centered on the contention that he was no longer commandant at the time of these executions. This assertion seems baseless in light of the testimony by his codefendants, especially Deputy Commandant Schwarzhuber, that he was still in command when the gas chamber was functioning. The only one to amend his testimony on this point was Pflaum, who made a short-lived escape the same time as Suhren, was detained before and after this escape in the same prisons as Suhren, and would have had ample opportunity to communicate with him.

In any case, it was only in January 1945 that the letter "U" began to appear on prison documents, signifying Uckermarck, better known as Jugendlager.

Some of the details about Uckermarck were given in Part One of this study (see p. 94); one will recall that in December 1944 the Ravensbrück authorities ordered an inventory of the aged and ill prisoners who were unable to work. Those so designated were issued the pink cards exempting them from work, then during January they were taken to Uckermarck. Immediately upon arriving, they were forced to give up all their underclothing and the few woolens they had managed to save, which were thrown in piles outside, where they could see them. Then, clothed only in thin cotton dresses, they had to stand in the swirling, icy snow of the Prussian winter for a "roll call" that lasted the entire day. They were not totally deprived of nourishment, theoretically being provided with half the normal Ravensbrück ration. This ration, such as it was, varied widely: in 1945 there was often one ladleful of thin rutabaga soup and "five's bread" (a single ration of bread for five persons), and sometimes "six's bread" or "seven's bread." During the final days the soup was replaced by a "demimargarine" (a piece of margarine the size of a large sugar cube); in the mornings the prisoners also received a ladle of a foul black liquid of no nutritional value, unsugared of course, but at least hot.

Here is what Dr. Treite had to say on the same subject (continuation of his testimony already cited): "The women who were still alive at Uckermarck were put on half rations and forced to stand outdoors five or six hours a day; the evidence would indicate that these practices had the goal of getting rid of as many prisoners as possible. About fifty died each day in these circumstances."

Until her death at Ravensbrück in late 1944, Milena Jesenska (a friend of Kafka) was required to go to the morgue every day to count the dead. In 1944 she counted about eighty new bodies per day, but this was almost certainly during the months of October, November, and December. At the time Jugendlager was probably still occupied by the evacuees from Auschwitz, and it is also likely that the Jugendlager mortality statistics were never counted at the Ravensbrück Revier, except for a few from the Jugendlager Revier during the brief period when that inaptly named institution had real nurses and a legitimate doctor, Dora Rivière. (See p. 96.) But were the total Jugendlager rolls counted among those for Ravensbrück? I do not know, but one can presume that the dead were stored in the same morgue.

Whatever the death rate, Suhren evidently did not consider
it sufficient. The number of those wiped out by cold and starvation was, according to Treite, fifty per day, or, in five
months, about 7,500. But Treite's information dealt with the
early days of the subcamp, a period which does not cover
the time of greatest population density or the days when the
cold and hunger were most deadly. Nonetheless, we can accept his figure as an average, since it seems that on various
occasions Uckermarck was almost empty. The rate of deaths
attributable to simple exhaustion could not have been steady,
as it depended on both the severity of the exhaustion itself,
which was constantly increasing, and on the number of victims suffering from it. Thus the exhaustion, and the numbers
associated with it, diminished when there were no new victims.

It is even more difficult to estimate the total number of
women passing through Uckermarck than the number who
died, principally because of the numerous transports that entered and left there without being accounted for in the main
camp records. It would not be productive to even hazard a
numerical estimate as to the importance of these movements;
we know only that they existed, that they were large, that
they were followed by on-the-spot exterminations, and that
some of the convoys were reshipped elsewhere, perhaps to
Bergen-Belsen.

This "master plan" for death—that is, the measures taken
to record an almost equal number of dead bodies for each
day—could possibly explain the movements in and around
Jugendlager, which (to venture a guess despite reservations)
could have involved 5,000 prisoners. Counting poisonings, the
"roll calls" in the snow, the gas chamber, and "natural"
deaths, our camp authorities managed to achieve a daily total
of 280–300 bodies to be disposed of.

I attempted to learn what became of the fifty-two women
(forty-eight French, two English, one Belgian, and one Pole,
all arrested in France) on the twenty-seven thousands list
whose names were followed by the "U." Theoretically at least,
their stories could have had any of four possible endings: liberation by the Swiss Red Cross on April 5, 1945, by the

Swedes on April 23, or by the Russian Army when they occupied Ravensbrück, or they might well have died. There is no difficulty in checking the first liberation: we have a list of the 300 prisoners included therein, correctly spelled and accompanied by dates of birth, a list which is probably a copy of the one prepared in the Ravensbrück offices, in that it uses the same means of identification used in the original. Many of the women on that release roll were well-acquainted with the horrors of Uckermarck, but not one of them was among those marked with the "U" on the list of the twenty-seven thousands we have been examining.

There are no such absolutely verifiable lists for the subsequent Swedish and Russian liberations; one problem lay in the fact that these releases included some prisoners who died within a few days or a few hours, often without having given their names, and the Swedish Red Cross and the Russian medical units had no resources whatever for checking their identities. Even so, the very small number of French prisoners who would have been required, as a rule, to remain in the Ravensbrück Revier after the Swedish liberation were secretly double-counted by our comrades among the nurses when the rescue was being prepared. Using this clandestine list I was able to locate several prisoners who actually arrived in Sweden (where a few of them died), and thus I was able to place a date on the list: it was put together contemporaneously with formation of the liberation convoy, and after construction of an official list from which the most seriously ill were excluded. Some of these latter, with assistance from the nurses, escaped and took refuge in the white trucks of the liberators. This kind of accounting "error" could have been corrected easily enough through comparison with the Swedish lists and, above all, through supplemental questioning.

I was indeed able to consult the lists put together by the Swedish Red Cross concerning the liberated prisoners who owed their lives to the intervention by Count Bernadotte. To one who was well-acquainted with his efficiency and conscientiousness, the trying conditions under which these three groups were formed became immediately obvious. Incorrect spellings were everywhere, and the reliability of personal information was irregular at best. On the other hand, the three sets cross-checked among themselves, but not completely, which would indicate that they related to different dates and different places. An over-all list was attainable by way of a comparison of the three; it is not totally accurate, and probably not complete, but at least I succeeded in making a positive and complete identification of one of the fifty-two victims I was searching for—and only one. This was Mme. Louet, born Marie Chassot on August 15, 1879. She died, but she was still alive as of the end of April 1945, even though she was the senior member of the group marked by the "U."

(The age breakdown of the other fifty-one prisoners was, as of December 1944, one aged twenty-seven; two at thirty-one; one each at thirty-three, thirty-six, and thirty-seven; fifteen between forty and fifty; twenty-three between fifty and sixty; and seven older than sixty.)

The fact that I could find only one soon-deceased prisoner of the fifty-two on the three liberation lists did not establish conclusively that the remainder died unnatural deaths. (One must allow for errors in the Swedish documents.) But the documentation service of the French Veterans Ministry, at my request, kindly agreed to conduct an inquiry into the fate of the fifty-two women, using the identification material I was able to provide. The ministry had access to voluminous information, gathered from many sources (arrest records from the various provinces, prisoner registers from Compiègne, lists provided by the French repatriation mission in Poland, etc.), and the final, undeniable result sifted from all these resources was that all of the women in question died as prisoners. The ministry's records contained twenty-five official death certificates, eight certificates of disappearance, and documents declaring fourteen legally dead. The remaining five are also listed as deceased, but it seems that surviving families, if there were any, had not requested official documentation.

In addition, I was able to establish through my own oral investigation that some women from the twenty-seven thousands who were not marked with the "U" were actually sent to Uckermarck; some of them died there, although their names were not followed by the symbol of a cross, and I know of others who returned and are still alive.

The information in our list is often incomplete, sometimes imprecise, but the errors are never simply erratic or whimsical. Our data are based on very tangible reality, and the errors themselves help us grasp that reality. In these circumstances, what could be the meaning of the four women whose names were accompanied by a cross as well as the "U"? Why the cross? And why only four? These four crosses were listed with four dates in the last half of February 1945—2/18, 2/23, 2/25, and 2/26.

This is the last of the information I could extract from the twenty-nine typed pages of the list from the Ravensbrück Revier, but I did attempt to measure its reliability against some of the other (all too few) documents which escaped destruction.

16

Mittwerda and the Gas Chamber

There is an original document, dated April 6, 1945, which is one of the departure lists for the mythical camp called Mittwerda[1]—perhaps the last such list, but in any case the only one which, to my knowledge, remains intact. It includes 480 names.

On the last page, the date, "Ravensbrück, IV-6-45," is followed by the notation "Nachstehende Häftlinge wurden nach dem Schnonungslager Mittwerda i. Schled. überstllt." (The listed prisoners have been transferred to the Mittwerda transit camp.) The same page bears the original signature of the Ravensbrück commandant: "Suhren SS Sturmbannführer u. Lagerkommandant."

Having learned that such a document existed, I requested and obtained three copies from Mme. Helena Dziedzicka and Countess Plater, two of which I transmitted to the French judicial authorities during Commandant Suhren's trial. Suhren had adopted a line of defense which contended, in paraphrase, that there was a gas chamber at Ravensbrück, but he knew about it only by hearsay since it had not even existed until March, at which time he was no longer the Ravensbrück commandant. It was then that he was confronted with the Mittwerda list, dated April 6 and carrying his title and signature.

The identical meaning of "Mittwerda" and "gas chamber" had been obvious from the first to the prisoners who had the responsibility of maintaining the Mittwerda lists, since they

[1] The "camp" was spelled Mittweida on other lists which have since disappeared.

recorded the names and numbers of the victims as they were taken away.

I searched the ominous document titled "Sent to Mittwerda" for some of those that had also been recorded on the register of the twenty-seven thousands, a task eased by the fact that on both lists the names were accompanied by registration numbers and were classified in numerical groupings. I managed to find nine, and all nine names on the Mittwerda list were followed on the Revier document by the handwritten notation "U. 4-4-45." The difference between the two dates: only two days.

Other differences led to the conclusions that these two texts came from two camp services that were complete strangers to each other, that there had been no trading or copying, and that they were based on distinctly different sources of information. Among the nine names common to both lists, there is one shown as Berthe Boucher on the twenty-seven thousands register and Bertha Beudet on the other; of the nine prisoner numbers, one is incorrect on the Mittwerda list (27,806 rather than 27,993). In both cases the twenty-seven thousands list is more reliable.

The nine Frenchwomen could not actually have been sent to Uckermarck on April 4, 1945 (as shown in the Revier document), in view of the near certainty that all the French prisoners still there as of April 1 came back down to the main camp the next day, and none returned to Uckermarck. Nor were they gassed on April 6 (as might be inferred from the Mittwerda list), since all of our information is in agreement on setting the date of the destruction of the gas chamber as April 2. But we do know through countless oral accounts that these nine women were murdered, by gas or gunshot, on March 30, 1945–Good Friday.[2]

There was another list of ninety-six names, copied secretly in the main camp at the time of a "selection" of sick prisoners to be sent from Block 10 (tuberculars) directly to the gas chamber, without passing through Uckermarck. Two of the ninety-six belonged to the twenty-seven thousands. And on

[2] See p. 107.

the twenty-seven thousands document these two names have no supplementary notations—no letter, no cross, no date.

Questioning of my comrades confirmed, however, that these two women did indeed die, and at the very time the secret list was made up; they were taken directly from the Revier to the cremation ovens, and everyone knew it. (One should remember that this same Revier was the source of our principal document.)

The few cross-checks of the twenty-seven thousands document I have just mentioned demonstrate amply that, in spite of its unquestionable authenticity and richness of information, it demands strict verification. But neither the other documents that escaped destruction nor the personal accounts of the surviving prisoners would have sufficed alone. We needed the testimony of the executioners.

On August 15, 1946, at the Hamburg trial, Deputy Commandant Schwarzhuber testified as follows: *In late February Dr. Trommer and I were summoned by camp commandant Suhren. He told us he had received an order from Reichsführer Himmler under which all women who were ill or unable to walk were to be killed. Before telling us this he asked how many ill there were in the camp.*

I told the commandant that I was happy to have left Auschwitz and that I did not want to start the same thing all over again. To that, he replied that Sturmbannführer Sauer had been assigned the task of carrying out the order. Sauer was another deputy commandant of the camp. During the following days Dr. Trommer selected 2,300 women from various blocks. At the beginning, these women were shot. The executions were carried out by Hauptscharführer Moll. Eight internees helped him. But this method did not seem to do the job quickly enough for the commandant. He once said in my presence, "This is not going fast enough; you will have to use other methods." Sauer then gave the order to build a gas chamber.

I was present at one "gassing." A hundred fifty women were put forcibly into the chamber together. First Moll told them to undress for a delousing, then they were herded into the gas chamber, and the door was bolted. An internee wear-

ing a gas mask climbed onto the roof and threw a capsule through an opening, which he very quickly resealed. I heard sounds from the inside, mostly grunts and moans, but after a while everything was quiet. I do not know whether the women were dead then or had just passed out. I was not there when the room was emptied, and Moll only told me that the bodies had been taken directly to the cremation ovens.

All of this was done under the direction of Sturmbannführer Sauer, Dr. Trommer, and Hauptscharführer Moll—all of whom always attended the "gassings." All of the actual "work" was done by internees from the men's camps.

Hauptscharführer Moll came to Ravensbrück from Auschwitz, and we encounter him in the horrifying account by Dr. Miklos Nyiszli (*Auschwitz, A Doctor's Eyewitness Account*, Frederick Fell, 1960, pp. 86–88):

In the courtyard a terrified crowd of about 5,000 souls; on all sides thick cordons of SS, holding leashed police dogs. The prisoners were led, three or four hundred at a time, into the undressing room. There, hustled by a rain of truncheon blows, they spread out their clothes and left by the door at the opposite side of the house, yielding their places to those who were to follow. Once out the door, they had no time even to glance around them or to realize the horror of their situation. A Sonderkommando immediately seized their arms and steered them between the double row of SS who lined the twisting path, which, flanked on either side by woods, ran for fifty yards to the pyre, which till now had been hidden by the trees.

The pyre was a ditch fifty yards long, six yards wide and three yards deep, a welter of burning bodies. SS soldiers, stationed at five-yard intervals along the pathway side of the ditch, awaited their victims. They were holding small caliber arms, six millimeters, used in the KZ for administering a bullet in the back of the neck. At the end of the pathway two Sonderkommando men seized the victims by the arms and dragged them for fifteen or twenty yards into position before the SS. Their cries of terror covered the sound of the shots. A shot, then, immediately afterward, even before he was dead, the victim was hurled into the flames. Fifty yards farther on a scene similar in all respects was being enacted. Oberscharführer Moll was in charge of these butchers. As a doctor, and as an eyewitness, I swear that he was the Third Reich's most abject, diabolic, and hardened assassin. Even Dr. Mengele showed from time to time that he was human. During the selections at the unloading ramp, when he noticed a healthy young woman who above all wanted to join her mother in the left-hand column, he snarled at her coarsely, but ordered her to regain the right-hand group. Even the ace shot of the number one crematorium, Oberscharführer Mussfeld, fired a second shot into anyone whom the first shot had not killed outright. Oberscharführer Moll wasted no time over such trifles. Here the majority of the men were thrown alive into the flames. Woe to any Sonderkommando by whose action the living chain, which extended from cloakroom to pyre, was broken, with the result that one of the members of the firing squad was forced to wait for a few minutes before receiving his new victim.

Moll was everywhere at once. He made his way tirelessly from one pyre to the next, to the cloakroom and back again. Most of the time the deportees allowed themselves to be led without resistance. So paralyzed were they with fright and terror that they no longer realized what was about to happen to them. The majority of the elderly and the children reacted in this way. There were, however, a goodly number of adolescents among those brought here, who instinctively tried to resist, with a strength born of despair. If Moll happened to witness such a scene, he took his gun from his holster. A shot, a bullet often fired from a distance of forty or fifty yards, and the struggling person fell dead in the arms of the Sonderkommando who was dragging him toward the pyre. Moll was an ace shot. His bullets often pierced the arms of the Sonderkommando men from one side to the other when he was dissatisfied with their work. In such cases he inevitably aimed for the arms, without otherwise manifesting his dissatisfaction, but also without giving any previous warning.

Logically enough, Ravensbrück commandant Suhren was questioned several times on the subject of the gas chamber. He would begin by denying that it existed, then admit that it did, but not while he was in command. And he stuck by this position despite all the evidence to the contrary. Interrogated on December 8, 1949, he said: "I would estimate the number of women who died by gas at Ravensbrück at about 1,500. This is the number I have already mentioned in the account of my conversation with Dr. Trommer. In fact, this figure of 1,500 I have given as the death total for Jugendschutzlager is the actual total for the gas chamber."

And then we can juxtapose these statements with an account by a Red Cross representative[3] who was invited by Suhren himself to visit Ravensbrück:

After dismissing his orderly, Suhren began giving me a detailed defense of the concentration-camp system, telling me about the remarkable results they had achieved—all attributable to work, "enlightenment," and "education."

. . . Suhren said that to demonstrate the injustice of the unfavorable reports circulating in the outside world, he was prepared to give me a tour of the camp. . . .

Suhren would summon a prisoner and ask if she had been mistreated, how many times a day she had been beaten, and if she had any complaints to make. No one complained, of course; they had only praise for the camp commandant. After each response, Suhren turned to me and said with a serious expression: "Bitte." The SS women were also questioned. Suhren asked if they mistreated the prisoners, and they all answered as if offended by the question: "Aber das ist uns doch verboten" (But that is forbidden)—And if they ever beat the prisoners?—"But then we would be punished."

[3] Activities of the International Red Cross Committee on behalf of civilian prisoners in German concentration camps (1939–45), Geneva, 3rd edition, 1947, pp. 114–16.

17

Four U's with the Cross of Death

As Dr. Treite said in his deposition (p. 142), Uckermarck was at first a camp where extermination was accomplished by cold and starvation. When it was decided that these methods did not kill quickly enough, a team of nine men (see Schwarzhuber's statement, p. 149) assumed the task of shooting a certain number of prisoners each day. But then even this method did not seem sufficiently expeditious, and a gas chamber was constructed and outfitted about five yards from the two cremation ovens; it began functioning on March 1 or March 2. So the little camp presented us with three types of murder: by cold and hunger (often indistinguishable from natural deaths), by gunshot, and by gas.

These last two—carried out behind walls, beyond the view of most of the other prisoners, and officially passed off as transfers to the Mittwerda "rest camp"—obviously could not be recorded on the same public lists as the more or less natural deaths, for which the bodies (and the lists) were openly displayed. There was a fourth method (of which I have already spoken, p. 93) which was equally secret—execution by poisoning. The poison technique had one point in common with the "natural" deaths: the bodies were not concealed and, because of this, such deaths could have been "officialized." For some reason I have never learned, this was not done.

Whenever it became necessary to remove old and sick women from the camp, certain reassuring arrangements were made in such a way that prisoners "volunteered" to be "selected," as we have already seen (p. 96). It is in this context that we find one French prisoner—a doctor and completely honorable person (Dora Rivière)—and several prisoner-nurses, well-regarded by their comrades, who were given the responsibility of organizing a hospital operation at Jugendlager. Toward the end of January they took over a building for that purpose, and it duly became known as the "Revier," but there were no medicines, no blankets, not even any straw mattresses. Even so, they had charge of sick and dead prisoners—listed nominally on the rolls of the main Revier—for at least two weeks.

At the end of this period they were recalled to the main camp and replaced by a woman named Vera Salveguart and two SS "medics," who immediately began distributing a certain number of poison dosages each day. The poisons they were using were not instantaneously effective, and the sick soon realized what the results would be of the "medicine" they were being given. Some refused to take it; Salveguart and her assistants simply forced them to swallow.

According to Suhren and Schwarzhuber, Uckermarck held 5,000 prisoners as of March; at the same time, secretaries (I knew several who made the daily shuttle between the administrative offices of both camps) counted 6,000. These secretaries maintained for only a few days an account of the dead in the bizarre hospital at Uckermarck (for the main Revier records), and they were understandably horrified by the seemingly routine task; they recounted these experiences to their comrades in the main camp when they returned from work at night. They were even more astonished that the other "official" dead at Uckermarck (from cold and starvation)—who were openly carted away each morning—were not supposed to be included in these figures.

The last cross is dated February 26, which confirms what the secretaries had told me: the books of the dead ceased being kept up to date at the Ravensbrück Revier before March 1; those for Uckermarck had never been kept accurately.

A comparative evaluation of Suhren's various statements demonstrates plainly that, to be doubly sure, he lied at every opportunity, and that the truth finally crept into his testimony only after months of argument and, above all, after confrontation with evidence he could not deny; thus I mention his figure (1,500 killed by gas) only as a reminder. Schwarzhuber estimated the number of prisoners who were shot at 150–200 and the gas chamber victims at 2,300 or 2,400 (but he said he was directly involved in this process only on one occasion).

There were two prisoners—both completely trustworthy and in excellent positions to know the truth—who placed the number of gas chamber victims considerably higher; one has said 3,600, the other, 3,660. These two women were acquainted and almost certainly discussed these estimates together; the first, a secretary in the labor office, was normally a part of the typing pool that made up the Mittwerda lists; the second, a Blockova at Uckermarck, actually saw women taken to the gas chamber, and no doubt helped compile the figures recorded by the first.

> Wanda Kiedrzynska, a senior Polish prisoner and very well informed, says[1] that before 1945 prisoners were gassed at Ravensbrück in small groups, using at first a *Grüne Gina* (a prisoner van) and later an old Dutch military transport car; both had been set up in the forest. She also cites an invoice dating from 1943 and showing that the firm Tesch und Stabenov had provided the camp with 351.5 kg of Zyklon B (hydrogen cyanide). Kiedrzynska has also estimated that between January 22 and April 14, 1945, about 5,500 women were gassed (under the supervision of Unterscharführer Schäfer), and she cites February 9, 1945, as the date when a group of seventy-two prisoners of all nationalities *except German* were executed by gas. The number of women taken away and the orders received by those who selected the victims are firsthand information, since Wanda was in a good position to gather it, and she performed her task carefully. It is possible, however, that the prisoners executed on February 9 were not gassed but were part of the groups dispatched by Moll and his eight male prisoner-assistants (most likely common Ger-

[1] Wanda Kiedrzynska, *Ravensbrück Kobiecy Oboz Koncentracyjny* (Warsaw, 1961), pp. 106, 125, 127, 247.

man criminals) with their pistols. (This was before the gas chamber was put into service.) All this has to be viewed in light of the fact that Germans were excluded from this selection, an altogether unusual "privilege" which shocked all who knew about it. In any case, a non-gas theory for this particular set of executions would correspond with the dates given, however vaguely, by Schwarzhuber.

It is still possible, however, that neither Schwarzhuber nor the prisoners providing our information knew the actual number of deaths—Schwarzhuber because this was not a direct part of his duties (this was the domain of Sauer and Moll), the prisoner-secretaries because they did not necessarily check all of the gas-chamber convoys. (Not all of the women sent to Uckermarck were gassed, and not all of the women who were gassed passed through Uckermarck. The little camp was a way station for extermination, but not an extermination camp itself.)

My comrades who worked in the main Revier saw their patients taken away for execution, selected by the two sinister doctors, Trommer and Winkelmann. These prisoners went directly to the assigned place, which was located, along with the cremation ovens, just outside the wall encircling the camp. It was not difficult to hear the trucks going back and forth, and everyone listened. Uckermarck was situated in the opposite direction and much farther away; thus it is certain that these victims did not pass through Uckermarck.

Marie-Claude Vaillant-Couturier gave the following testimony at the Nuremberg trials (session of Monday, January 28, 1946):

. . . *Marie Rubiano did not seem to be dying quickly enough in the opinion of the SS, so one day Dr. Winkelmann, the selection specialist, entered her name on the black list, and on February 9, 1945, along with seventy-two other tuberculars (including six Frenchwomen), she was loaded onto the truck for the gas chamber.*

During this period they carried on such selections throughout the entire Revier, and all of the sick who were thought

*to be unusable for work were sent to be gassed. The Ravens-
brück gas chamber was just behind the camp wall, alongside
the cremation oven. The whole camp could hear the noise
of the truck when it came to pick up the sick.*

*When we were liberated I made my own way to these places
and saw the gas chamber itself—a sealed wooden hut, with
the odor of gas still present. I know that the gas pellets they
used at Auschwitz were the same as were used to disinfect
for lice, and that it left traces of evidence behind—little pale
green crystals which were swept up after they opened the windows. I am sure of these details because the men who disinfected the blocks for lice were in contact with those who administered the gas to human beings, and they said the two
materials were the same.*

(In fact, Zyklon B was originally manufactured commer-
cially as a strong disinfectant, but the Germans found a fiend-
ish new use for it.)

Other sick prisoners were taken directly to the tubercular
block, during the day, in much the same manner. This fact
was well established at the Hamburg and Rastadt trials by
numerous witnesses who actually saw these movements.
Shortly afterward, they also began taking sick prisoners to
Block 23, but at night, and I witnessed this myself, since the
NN prisoners were confined to Block 24 at the time. Through
the darkened windows of the block one could observe under
the SS floodlights the scenes of despair caused by these selections and removals.

Personally, I am convinced that some convoys were not
processed through Uckermarck or Ravensbrück but proceeded directly to the gas chamber. It is certain, for example,
that several trucks carrying French prisoners among their
cargo (including Dr. Peretti della Rocca) had left Rechlin
for Ravensbrück but never entered the latter camp. The
trucks were parked for several hours along the roadside in
front of the enclosure where executions were carried out, and
Dr. Peretti exchanged a few words with prisoners who walked
past, and they relayed the message. The only other indisputa-
ble fact about this incident is that the women on the trucks
were killed that same day. Were they included on the Mitt-

werda lists and, if so, when and how were their names and numbers gathered and recorded? Was there another "Mittwerda" list made up at Rechlin? Or was there no list at all?

According to Deputy Commandant Schwarzhuber, the gas chamber measured $29' \times 15'$ and could hold 150 persons, while on every occasion that the Austrian "bandes rouges" (who kept the "accounts") were able to arrive at an absolutely certain execution total, it was higher: 170 or 180. Could it have been that some overzealous subordinates (Hauptscharführer Moll, for example) figured that, given a place with an official capacity of 150, one could, with a bit of effort, make room for 170 or 180? Or perhaps Moll's pistol team carried on its work even while the gas chamber was functioning? There will always be doubt on these questions. But we do know that there are incontrovertible figures, verified by knowledgeable prisoners, which contradict those given by Schwarzhuber. This does not necessarily mean that he deliberately gave false testimony; since such executions were not directly under his jurisdiction, I believe that his statements were more on the order of "general impressions." But on the other hand, the recording of the victims' prisoner numbers was the direct responsibility of our Austrian comrades, a task they performed with loathing and fear, but with intense care.

If we make the simplest estimate of the total number of gas-chamber victims—based on the duration of its operation (March 2–April 2, 1945 for the official gas chamber alone) and the daily totals of 150 or 170—we arrive at a minimum of 4,500 and a maximum of 5,270. But was there a "gassing" every day? And were there not a few occasions when the gas chamber functioned at capacity twice in one day? We are sure of one such instance—Good Friday—but it might not have been the only one.

In brief, it is impossible at present to choose among the various figures we are confronted with: Suhren's estimate (1,500) can be dismissed, but what about 2,300 or 3,600 or 5,200? In any case, they took measures for wholesale extermination, but only those compatible with such practical considerations as burning or burying all the bodies, and perhaps with a view toward possible reactivation of the camp's industrial production. Had it not been for the German military collapse, the extermination machine would have continued to function like a gigantic two-speed motor, accelerating when industrial orders fell and raw materials were lacking, slowing down a bit whenever orders and supplies were plentiful.

Part Three

SOME REMAINING QUESTIONS

18

A "Routine" of Extermination

While at Ravensbrück I had attempted to look beyond the obvious atrocities to isolate and explain certain inconsistencies in the system, and I managed to form a hypothesis which would have helped clarify some of the principal contradictions. I presented it one day in 1944 during a conference with a group of my comrades—a meeting whose circumstances and environment I should describe a bit in order to prevent misimpressions.

We were a group of French NN who had since our arrival at Ravensbrück clung doggedly to the particularly difficult and dangerous designation called Verfügbar,[1] principally because in that category we would produce almost nothing for the German war effort; our work entailed, for example, maintaining the streets of the camp by pulling a heavy iron roller about for twelve hours a day. Our Auhseherin did not seem to find great enjoyment in supervising these labors, and she seemed constantly on the lookout for the opportunity to disappear, that is, when the SS were not patrolling the immediate vicinity.

We took advantage of such a situation that day to talk through the windows with another group of Frenchwomen who had been quarantined in Block 15 (which would place the date of our "meeting" sometime in March 1944). At the time, I was unaware of certain details of the system—the program and organization chart of the WVHA (Wirtschafts und Verwaltungs-Hauptamt) dated March 1942, and the secret

[1] See pp. 14, 25.

memorandum dated April 30, 1942, in which Pohl explained the principle of "extermination through labor."[2] But I had been reasonably successful in deducing the general outlines of the system from the beginning—and not from simple observation of the insane world we had been thrown into, but with a systematic juxtaposition of my own observations with the scraps of information I received from courageous and reliable comrades who were also senior inmates of the camp—those who typed the correspondence, kept the books, and counted the inhabitants of each block twice a day.

I shall never forget the open and enthusiastic response of my comrades when I offered my theories and observations that day,[3] and many have since spoken to me about it. My conclusions were a reasonably logical explanation of the absurdities and contradictions of at least part of the concentration-camp hell, and, very importantly, they took into account our meager chances of survival. Understanding one's situation is exhilarating in itself, perhaps because awareness of a burden is one way of overcoming it, perhaps also because awareness and comprehension are the more profound vocations of the human species, and one of the goals of humanity's place on the evolutionary scale.

Knowing today about the two texts relating to "extermination through labor" and the manner in which they were applied, I feel justified in asserting that the same events could have occurred at the same time in all sectors of this fundamentally absurd and incoherent system: that is, the statutory official establishment of an unchecked conspiracy among a very small number of people, including first and above all the thirteen commandants of the major concentration-camp centers. Each of these, a Führer within his domain, was accountable to only three persons: Heinrich Himmler, the great master of the police and the concentration camps, and two missi dominici, Oswald Pohl and Richard Glücks.

This intimate conspiracy among such a small number of

[2] Secured by prosecutor Dodd for the indictment of Pohl at the Nuremberg trials (vol. III, p. 470).

[3] One will find these explanations in similar terms on pp. 48–49

accomplices could have helped them adjust to the problems of those years when their ideas were inconsistent. It might also explain (if one recalls the personal participation of this group in the profits of the system) why related documents were selectively destroyed.

On the other hand, the conspiracy is not a sufficient explanation of the synchronism in the extermination measures taken late in the war in the Western camps, where extermination was not openly practiced before. It is even less of an explanation for the absence of simultaneity between these measures and the orders that supposedly set them in motion.

It is not my intention here to attempt an explanation of these contradictions but simply to underscore them, because on these two important points—as important today as they were twenty-five years ago—I believe that one should go no further than saying: "Everything was happening as if . . ."

Judging from surviving fragments of orders issued at the level of power—Himmler and his closest associates—the system was administered "as if" several differing points of view were in operation.

One indication of future events appeared in November 1944, when Himmler ordered that the gas chamber at Auschwitz be destroyed and that no more Jews were to be killed; instead, they were to hold hostages for possible negotiations, and camouflage the crimes already committed. . . . We can label this move "politics," I think, and note that after the order went out the exterminations at Auschwitz continued.

A second tendency could be summarized as follows: *We are not yet sure that the war is lost, so we must keep up production: evacuate the healthy prisoners and liquidate the useless.* This is a fair interpretation of the ideas of the apostles of "extermination through labor" and remains, for the most part, within the definitions of the system.

A third indication, if one wishes to cite one, might be found in Dr. Gebhardt's own words: *Toward the end we received Himmler's order to prevent any concentration camp detainees from falling into enemy hands; Kaltenbrunner was the one who circulated the order. I personally overheard heated tele-*

phone discussions on this subject between Himmler and Kaltenbrunner. As far as I know, this order was not carried out at Ravensbrück.[4]

It seems very likely that these orders came from the same group of men and that they were signed and issued after discussion of various "ideas" among the same functionaries. And one should not dismiss the possibility that all three tendencies coexisted in one brain—Himmler's.

As far as Ravensbrück is concerned, the order issued by Kaltenbrunner corresponds as to date and content with the policies cited by Schwarzhuber (see p. 149), but this similarity does not clear up all of the questions raised by events of those final three months. It does not explain, for example, why the Ravensbrück commandant, beginning in December 1944 if not earlier, took preparatory measures for executing an order which was not received until the end of February 1945.

Notwithstanding the authenticity of all these contradictory orders, one might easily believe that Himmler's entourage, burdened by other worries, largely left the major camp commandants to themselves, and events at that level indicated that the possibility of allowing the "unusable" prisoners to survive was not even considered.

We can now examine in more detail some of the contradictions in the operation of the system.

When the Allied advances forced the SS to evacuate certain camps, thus overcrowding others, the latter camps were faced with the very real problems of housing and feeding the new arrivals. Even in view of these problems, the mass murder of prisoners was a monstrously criminal solution, unimaginable in a civilized society. But in Hitler's Germany, the policy was consciously planned and executed.

This was not the only alternative; there was no lack of space around the camps, or of free labor, for the construction of additional barracks, and the raw materials were there. At Ravensbrück, there were nine well-built blocks which, as far

---

[4] Dr. F. Bayle, *Croix Gammée contre Caducée*, p. 232.

as I know, were used until the end as warehouses for blankets and old clothing. And it took them only a few days to erect a large army tent on the site of Block 25 as large numbers of new inmates began to arrive. Food stocks were still ample; some comrades liberated later by the Russian Army told me of having seen immense bins of foods and grain and many undistributed packages from outside. Even during the last months of the war, Germany's over-all resources remained infinitely more plentiful than those of many other countries which, faced with analogous problems, never contemplated such heinously criminal solutions.

The operation of the extermination machinery at Ravensbrück began in full force in January 1945; it follows, then, that certain preparatory measures had to be undertaken in December 1945, at the latest.

As for Commandant Suhren, who set the machine in motion, had he, or had he not, received the extermination orders by that date?

Schutzhaftlagerführer Johann Schwarzhuber, his immediate subordinate, has been very precise on this point: *In late February . . . Suhren told us he had received an order from Reichsführer Himmler under which all women who were ill or unable to walk were to be killed* (Hamburg trial, August 1946).

We also find this order mentioned in the long depositions by Himmler's intimate friend Dr. Gebhardt, who noted that it had been circulated by Kaltenbrunner—"at the end . . ."— which in fact means the end of February. Suhren himself has confirmed the terms and date of the order (particularly in his statement at Rastadt on December 8, 1949)—a note of harmony which merits attention in itself, since on most other points Suhren and Schwarzhuber gave contradictory testimony.

The very nature of the order left considerable maneuvering room for whoever was responsible for executing it, since it seems he was to be the final arbiter in defining who should be killed and in choosing a suitable date for the operation to begin.

Now, even if this order supposedly dates from the end of February, its execution at Ravensbrück began on January 15. It was January 15, in fact, which was marked by the transfer to Jugendlager of the aged and sick prisoners, of whom a census had already been under way for several weeks. And at Jugendlager their food rations were cut to half of what they had received at the main camp, which was little better than a starvation ration in any case. As has already been described, they were also deprived of most of their clothing and were forced to stand for hours in raging snowstorms. Each evening during this period, fifty to seventy of these women were "selected" and carried away, half-nude, to some unknown destination (according to Schwarzhuber, they were then shot by Moll and his pistol squad). It was also on January 15 that the first doses of poison were administered at the Ravensbrück Revier. In all cases, the dates of the new extermination measures coincide, but they do not correspond with the date of the official orders—preceding these orders by at least a month and a half. Now, the execution of hundreds of prisoners at a time, disposing of increasing numbers of bodies, and preventing panic among the other thousands who could not be killed on a given day—these were tasks requiring complicated and numerous arrangements that could not have been improvised overnight. How much time was necessary? In 1972, I'm afraid, one can no longer consult those who were responsible.

We should also examine what transpired in other camps, and the dates of orders relating to survival or extermination of the prisoners.

Auschwitz was evacuated on January 18, 1945, a normal course of action under the circumstances—the Russian Army occupied the camp six days later. . . . But why were exterminations suspended at Auschwitz two months earlier, beginning November 17, 1944, and on Himmler's personal orders?

Here is how Dr. M. Nyiszli[5] recalls the event (Dr. Nyiszli, deported as a Jew, was a specialist in forensic medicine and pathological anatomy, and in those capacities he was used by

[5] Dr. Miklos Nyiszli, op. cit., pp. 190–92.

SS Dr. Mengele to perform dissections and autopsies, which permitted him to see things few other men have seen): *Early in the morning of November 17, 1944, an SS non-commissioned officer came into my room and informed me confidentially that, upon order of higher authority, it was henceforth forbidden to kill any more prisoners, by any means whatsoever, in the KZ. . . . A new life began in the KZ. There were no more violent deaths, but the bloody past had to be hidden. The crematoriums had to be demolished, the pyre ditches filled in, and any witness to, or participant in, the horrors perpetrated here had to disappear.*

Many miles away, on December 13, 1944, following an order from "the Führer's Chancellery" relayed by Mauthausen Commandant Franz Ziereis, the extermination facilities were demolished at Hartheim castle, near Linz. Linz, in Upper Austria, was just as likely to be liberated by the Western Allies as by the Russian Army. Can we infer from these orders that the leaders of the Reich were envisioning defeat? This would seem to be a reasonable assumption.

These facts should be compared with Himmler's order[6]— issued by telephone on April 2 to SS Captain Olderburhuis, Commandant of the Ohrdruf camp—to liquidate "the criminal convicts and especially dangerous political prisoners," but with a strict command that the Jews were not to be touched. These Jews had to be evacuated along with other camp survivors, about 12,000 prisoners, to Buchenwald. What can be said about Himmler's sudden concern for the Jews (for whom he felt an insane hatred), except perhaps that he was beginning to worry about showing that some Jews were still alive; perhaps also he was beginning to distrust, rightly, the bureaucratic zeal of some of his subordinates. It would also seem that he did not foresee killing all of the "non-racial" prisoners, only the "few" individuals deemed dangerous, who were to be chosen by the commandant at his own pleasure. It should

[6] Cited by Eugen Kogon, who attributes the information to SS Dr. Ding-Schuler, op. cit., p. 250.

be recalled that April 2, the date of Himmler's order, was also the date of the International Red Cross' first entry into Ravensbrück. . . . These facts are consistent.

We should also try to understand why some "responsible authority" (Himmler, or some other level of command?), after giving the order to halt the exterminations at Auschwitz and doing away with the gas chambers there two months before actually compelled to do so, and after ordering destruction of a gas chamber at Linz which was not threatened by the enemy, then outfitted gas chambers at Ravensbrück and Dachau and attempted to do so at Buchenwald—that is, in three camps where they had not existed previously, and where they might have tried to attribute the thousands of deaths from hunger and sickness to simple mischance.

To comprehend what happened in these circumstances during the first three months of 1945, one should probably first consider the special nature and "careers" of the personnel who were responsible for running the concentration camps, keeping in mind the fact that the personnel in the Western camps (the so-called work camps) were never really different from those in the death factories such as Auschwitz; Schwarzhuber and Moll, for example, learned the basic "skills" at Auschwitz before serving at Ravensbrück. They had become killers by profession.

Even so, these very specialized functionaries moved in two apparently different worlds: the so-called "racial" camps in the East (such as Auschwitz) and the "work" camps of the West. In the first, a deportee was supposed to die quickly or even (theoretically) immediately; in the second, a prisoner was also supposed to die, but (theoretically) more slowly. In actual fact, there were many who died slowly in the first and very quickly in the second.

And why did the theories of the system have it that captives would have a short life in one sector and the privilege of living longer in the other? Because the two systems were governed by two different "ideas" and, probably, two different idea-makers. Under one guiding principle, known as the "final solution,"[7] the mass murder of entire populations, mainly Jews—men, women, and children. This principle had been directly inspired by the mythology propagated by Hitler himself, and the implementation was well under way by 1941. The other, conceived as "extermination through labor," became a working idea in March 1942 and definitely originated from Himmler or his closest collaborators.

The camps established by Hitler's Germany in Poland had one unequivocal goal from the beginning: to kill, to become death factories. Considering their original conception and the actual mechanism of carrying it out, it is amazing that we saw survivors returning. But in the Western camps, typified by Buchenwald and Ravensbrück, what was to be the final solution for most of the prisoners?

In all their monstrous absurdity, these two "grand ideas" of the Third Reich were completely contradictory: If it was so profitable to force a prisoner to work until his death intervened, why was this element missing from the "final solution" pursued in the Eastern camps? And in the Western camps, the opposite problem: When the "human stock" was exhausted, but not quite dead, how could they dispose of it?

The formulas of the system did not provide specific answers to these questions, but more important than the arid formulas, to me at least, was the fact that the entire framework of the concentration camp system—the "final solution" and "extermination through labor"—was legally and practically managed, directed, and controlled by the same people. A very few people.

[7] The expression *"die Endlösung der Juden Frage"* was used by Heydrich in a secret memorandum dated September 21, 1939, and the first signs that Jews were being executed by gas appeared in August 1941; these were from the Netherlands, and they were murdered at Hartheim (according to a document preserved at Arolsen). The first large-scale gas chambers began operating at the end of 1941. At any rate, the commandant of Auschwitz has written: *I am unable to state the precise date on which the extermination of the Jews began. But this probably would be in December 1941, perhaps in January 1942.*
The "final solution" for the Jews *who were unable to work* was entrusted to Karl Adolf Eichmann on January 20, 1942.

At the most powerful decision-making level was one man: Himmler; at the next level, where orders were received directly by those who would execute them, we find the commandants of the thirteen major concentration-camp centers.

For the latter, the insoluble conflicts between the final solution and extermination through labor were considerably more noticeable than for the other levels of the hierarchy: those above had no real conception of the practical problems imposed by economic production, and to them the practical advantages of the exploitation of slave labor existed mostly in the abstract; those below the commandants were only expected to obey orders.

At the power center, Himmler and his deputy Pohl could not have been completely unaware of the nonsense inherent in the dual system, and it is possible, if not probable, that the extraordinary powers delegated to the camp commandants under the "extermination through labor" structural plan of March 1942 was an attempt to reconcile the two principles. Beginning in 1942, in fact, the commandants were endowed with extremely broad responsibilities within their own domains, the types of powers that, in saner circumstances, would not have overlapped. They were at the same time "chain-gang guards" (who had life-and-death power over their convicts) and "captains of industry" (who organized the work, arranged utilization of the labor force and supervised finances and profits). Who controlled them and called them to account for the exercise of their powers? Only Himmler, or sometimes his closest associates.

Despite this monolithic leadership and the "purity" of the orders which filtered downward, the camp commandants were torn between two basic conceptions—one represented by Pohl, Sommer, Eicke, and Glücks (maximum production), the other by Eichmann, Günther, and Müller (extermination of the Jews as the primary goal). The two principles could not operate in the same place at the same time; the commandant of Auschwitz explained the situation in his memoirs (Hoess, op. cit., pp. 178–79):

The subsection concerned with the Jews, controlled by Eichmann and Günther, had no doubts about its objective.

In accordance with the orders given by the Reichsführer SS in the summer of 1941, all Jews were to be exterminated. The Reich Security Head Office raised the strongest objections when the Reichsführer SS, on Pohl's suggestion, directed that able-bodied Jews were to be sorted out from the rest.

The Reich Security Head Office was always in favor of the complete extermination of all Jews and saw in the creation of each new work camp and in every additional thousand Jews selected for work the danger that circumstances might arise that would set them free and keep them alive.

No department had a greater interest in raising the Jewish death rate than the Jewish subsection of the Reich Security Head Office.

As against that, Pohl had been authorized by the Reichsführer SS to provide as many prisoners as possible for the armaments industry. Accordingly he laid the greatest emphasis on the delivery of the maximum number of prisoners, and this also meant that as many Jews capable of work as possible were to be removed from the transports earmarked for extermination.

He also attached the greatest importance to the preservation of this labor force alive, although without much success.

The Reich Security Head Office and the Economic Administration Head Office were thus at loggerheads.

Nevertheless, Pohl appeared to be the stronger, for he was backed by the Reichsführer SS who, bound in his turn by his promises to the Führer, was constantly and ever more urgently demanding prisoners to work in the armaments factories.

On the other hand the Reichsführer SS also wished to see as many Jews as possible destroyed.

The commandant of Auschwitz had his problems, since he could not put to work the same people he was supposed to be killing at that very time; yet, as of 1942, he knew that he was not expected to execute everyone.

But also as of 1942, the commandants at Ravensbrück, Dachau, Mauthausen, and Buchenwald knew they could kill as they pleased, with no problems.

Finishing off the sick, eliminating the "biologically inferior," executing the prisoners who would not, or could not, work, getting rid of the troublemakers—all became part of the ordained program in the "ordinary" camps; that is, those which were not officially death camps. And beginning in January 1942, a small convoy left Ravensbrück for the Linz gas chamber roughly every two weeks. (See pp. 40 and 131ff.) Then in January 1944, when it became necessary to make room for new arrivals, Suhren used the gas chambers at Lublin and Auschwitz as the dropping point for 800 or 900 prisoners who were hampering his operations. (See p. 18.)

It was also in 1942 that they began administering fatal injections of oil and Evipan to "patients" in the Ravensbrück Revier. Zdenka Nedvedova-Nedjedla, a doctor and Czech Resistance prisoner, has recounted the story of the Evipan injections, and SS Dr. Rosenthal has spoken of the use of oil.[8]

Again at the Ravensbrück Revier and, again in 1942, there occurred a notable incident related by Grete Buber-Neumann, of whom I have spoken earlier. It was standard procedure at the time that upon the death of a German prisoner, a proper death notice was sent to the family. As it happened, two German prisoners with identical names and of approximately the same age were being treated in the Revier, one for a simple abscess, the other for typhus. The latter died, and a Revier secretary sent SS Dr. Rosenthal the patient card so that he could sign the death notice for the Politische Abteilung (the political office), which kept the rolls up to date and notified surviving families. The secretaries noticed shortly afterward that the wrong card had been sent, and they understandably trembled at the thought of confessing an error to Dr. Rosenthal. But, thinking of the anguish of the improperly notified family, they decided to tell the doctor. To their amazement, Rosenthal heard their confession without showing particular concern. He simply gave an order to Gerda Kuernheim, who left immediately to give an injection to the patient suffering from the abscess. "The error is taken care of,"

8 Cited by François Bayle, op. cit., p. 1,037.

Gerda Kuernheim said when she returned. "That one is also dead."[9]

When the transports departed for Linz, officially designated as having left for "a rest camp," the applicable lists which had been drawn up at the Revier were transmitted to the Politische Abteilung, and we should make special note of the fact that this office immediately sent death certificates[10] to the families of those on the lists, dated and captioned as having come from Ravensbrück.

It goes without saying that the secretaries from the Revier and the Politische Abteilung, quartered in the same blocks and speaking the same language, were acquainted with one another and also knew the sick prisoners sent out for "convalescence." As a result, these secretaries had no illusions about the "rest homes" of the Third Reich, nor about the constant danger of murder which threatened every prisoner in the camp. . . . These facts are fundamental to an understanding of how the prisoners received their information.

Whether one was part of the 10 per cent condemned to death in the labor camps or the 80 per cent in the extermination camps made little difference to the person involved; what mattered were the brutalities and terrorism which preceded death. For the others, the difference between the operative death percentages in the two types of camps existed all too strongly, and it determined the proportions of agony for the prisoners: whenever an extermination was to take place outside one's own camp and would involve a small, more or less well-defined number of inmates—and when one wanted to remain uninformed—a prisoner could hold to this small straw

[9] Margarete Buber-Neumann, *Als Gefangene bei Stalin und Hitler* (Stuttgart, 1958), p. 284.

[10] Serge Choumoff has noted that death certificates for prisoners sent to "a rest camp" were found at Mauthausen, and the documents were captioned as having originated at Mauthausen. The dates of death given to surviving families were the same as the dates of departure for "convalescence" listed at the camp. (Choumoff, op. cit.)

of hope. But it was impossible to be unaware of the horrors in the death camps; it was there for everyone to see and threatened them all.

The killers themselves must also have been fully aware of this difference: whenever inmates were to be exterminated locally, it was these men who selected the victims, led them to the slaughterhouse and executed them, and it would have been equally impossible for them to harbor illusions. When the murders were to be carried out elsewhere, and the same men had to force their victims onto the railroad cars with blows of their heavy boots and truncheons, they were not departing from their usual routine, and the destination of the trains meant little to them. The variety created by the difference in assigned death percentages might have been apparent to the eyes of some important members of the Hitlerian hierarchy (high-ranking officers who thought they knew everything but were aware of only the "facts" recorded in the files). But the difference did not exist for Suhren or for Himmler and his entourage: they knew what would happen to the "exhausted" prisoners. . . .

With the evacuation of the Eastern camps beginning in December 1944, Ravensbrück became vastly overloaded with these "exhausted" prisoners, and the new arrivals were no longer counted by tens, but by hundreds. And Suhren could no longer lighten his load by way of Auschwitz or Linz: the Auschwitz gas chamber had been out of commission for two months, and the facility at Linz was no longer available.

It is not necessary to attempt an explanation of why the orders from the centers of power concerning extermination or non-extermination of prisoners were delayed, and contradictory when they did arrive; the chaotic situation in the Germany of 1945 is sufficient explanation in itself.

But there is another matter which merits reflective consideration: the conduct of the SS responsible for running the camp during the final three months of the war.

Is it possible that Suhren, the commandant of Ravensbrück, did not envision Germany's defeat a mere month before it happened; that is, at the time in early March when e first utilized the gas chamber which, according to him, killed a total of 1,500 women? (The lowest estimate, of course, among those made by officers and prisoners in positions to know.)

At the time, the German defeat was rapidly approaching and easily foreseeable—at least for someone with that intangible facility for "common sense"—and in such a perspective the wholesale slaughter of prisoners must have seemed to some who organized it both a criminal act and an exercise in dangerous stupidity, since they, individually, and their fatherland would be called to account. How did it happen, then, that this crime of folly was perpetrated with such accord among the actors?

Commandant Suhren was by no means a fool, nor was he a fatalist, and while he did not place great value on the lives of others, he was extremely conscious of his own, which he defended during two long trials with a relentless mendacity that his codefendants could never hope to emulate. And none of them were as responsible or guilty as he. But except for his gas chamber—which he ordered built some two months before the debacle, possibly on his own initiative—he might have saved that life he defended so blatantly.

Suhren was otherwise quite capable of taking initiatives contrary to orders if his personal interests were at stake. A prime example occurred on April 23, 1945, the date the last surviving Frenchwomen were liberated by the Swedish Red Cross. Himmler's explicit orders notwithstanding, Suhren attempted to hold back a group of Frenchwomen whom he considered valuable hostages for his own possible negotiations. He finally gave in only because Swedish Colonel Ankarkrona —who had been warned by our comrade Danielle (Anise Postel-Vinay)—demanded that the women be turned over.

One will find in three brief appendices that the conduct of the commandants of three other camps belonging to the same "category" as Ravensbrück was almost the parallel of Suhren's.[11]

---

[11] Regarding Mauthausen, see p. 218; Dachau, p. 221; Buchenwald, p. 223.

These disturbing similarities of conduct might be explained some day by a definitive document or someone's incontrovertible testimony, but for the present I think we can comprehend them only in the context of the prior habits, the careers, and the "styles" of the men who commanded the major concentration camps.

One of those who observed Himmler's men with the most penetrating insight was Eugen Kogon, whose origin (German-Austrian), learning, and seniority as a Buchenwald prisoner placed him in an advantageous position within the camp hierarchy. As Kogon wrote in 1945: *Branching on down below like a nerve system was the chain of command in curious fashion allowing scope for individual judgment and thus for responsibility. The SS leadership expected obedience of its subordinates, but it also expected independence. Later on, when too many had learned that they were not backed up when the inevitable difficulties arose, SS men became reluctant to assume responsibility and failed to take any action without written authority. But . . . a curious mixture developed, compounded of a cult of obedience and complete lack of control. In a sense the subordinate had to feel his way between these two attitudes. As a result he was reckoned the best SS member who "knew what had to be done," who did not wait for long-winded orders but acted "in the spirit of the Reich Leader SS."*[12]

Thus "everything was happening as if" SS Reichsführer Himmler—better informed than his subordinates concerning the actual progress of the war and the rapidly shrinking chance that the Third Reich might win—had an advance inkling that live deportees might be needed for negotiations, all of which resulted in the orders he issued (or had issued) on various occasions that the principal gas-chamber installations be destroyed and that a few Jews be allowed to survive. . . . But his vast "death machine" had been thoroughly programmed, and it continued to grind onward under essentially the same program.

[12] Eugen Kogon, op. cit., p. 270.

19

"Ordinary" People

Between 1945, when I wrote my first account, and 1953, when I completed the study entitled "One Convoy of French-women," the occupation authorities in Germany conducted the major war crimes trials under a system of divided responsibility. The first Ravensbrück trial had been allotted to the British and took place in Hamburg in December 1946 and January 1947; the subsequent trials, assigned to France, were conducted at Rastadt.

The British had refused our prisoners' associations the right to send observers, but they did accept a permanent representative—one only—and the two French organizations involved (Association of Deported and Interned Resistance and the Ravensbrück Amicale) chose me to represent them officially. Because of my status, I did not testify, but of all those who were thoroughly aware of the issues involved, I was alone in following the trial from beginning to end. Alone with the accused, of course.

During the recesses, with the courtroom almost empty, I remained there facing them, looking at them silently, over-whelmed with pain and sorrow before these creatures who had committed so much evil and who now, aligned only a few yards from me, were having to answer for the thousands of cold, deliberate murders of defenseless women. There were fifteen of them, and I was very aware that what I knew personally barely scratched the surface of their crimes, and that no man, no legal proceeding, nor any historical study could ever give the complete account. And they, the best-informed, the only ones who had known the entire story, had already forgotten part of it. . . .

Should I say that I was horrified at the sight of people fighting for their lives against the constantly frightening, clockworklike process of the judicial machinery? But at the same time I knew each one of them, and I thought of how a single gesture from any one of them could have saved people quite dear to me. But they had not made these gestures; they had hurried about in zealous pursuit of one overriding goal—eventual death for their captives. And now, there they were, and I was watching their own agony.

This dismal sorrow I felt, could it be called "hate" because it was so discerning, so rooted in fact, that it allowed no deep compassion? Day after day, I saw them weaving the same obscure conspiracies that had been so familiar to the camp inmates, and I watched, not without pity, as they communicated with looks and gestures over the heads of their British guards with their own loved ones in the courtroom. . . .

All the while, the representation—re-presentation—of their crimes unfolded, and I became all too aware of the widening gap between what really happened and that imprecise representation known as "history."

And there they were—well-dressed, well-groomed, well-scrubbed, proper. A dentist, doctors, a former printer, nurses, middle-level workers. No criminal records, normal educations, normal childhoods.

Ordinary people.

At Santé Prison, then at Fresnes, we had been supervised by male and female German guards. Some of them had been on prison staffs before the war (FHA, Führungshauptamt) but most had been mobilized from the general population. The experts who conduct opinion polls would have considered them, I suppose, "sociologically" analogous to the guards at Ravensbrück: same nationality, same general levels of education, similar religions, comparable standards of living and social class. . . .

I neither asked nor expected anything of the guards at Fresnes, but I watched them, having nothing else to do. I remember that while I was in solitary confinement (and denied walks, outside packages, books, and letters), a guard of whom I knew nothing except that she had red hair, did not understand French, and was leaving that same day on furlough, suddenly opened the peephole of my cell door and thrust in a book only a few minutes before she was to leave; this was October 20, 1942. And there was one Sunday when our ration inexplicably included a small slice of meat—the only time in three years. I also noted the rarity of thefts from our packages, despite the abundance of them and the general poverty of the staff. Above all I remember the commandant's look of consternation as he counted and lined us up the day of our departure for Ravensbrück.

To be sure, many of the guards would watch their prisoners for hours, waiting to catch them at any small infraction—talking through the windows or the heating pipes—and have them condemned to a dark cell or deprived of their soup; these guards were even in the majority. Even so, I recall one German overseer who came to tell me of the landings in North Africa; I called her (to myself) "the good woman of Cologne"; she was tall, dark, and spoke French quite pleasantly.[1]

Neither of these types, the "good" and the "tough," could be considered as outside civilized norms but represented, together, the two boundaries of behavior one could expect to find in a prison, or probably even in any group.

But those at Ravensbrück—who drowned infants in pails, poisoned the soup fed to the sick, planted gangrene in the wounds they had opened in the legs of schoolchildren—did they fall within these norms?

Although the French people neither followed very closely nor fully understood the major international trials at Nuremberg, the French study by Dr. François Bayle on the Nuremberg "Doctors' Trial" is the best demonstration of the extraordinary interest of all the proceedings, including the "Doctors' Trial." Historical interest because of the enormous amount

---

[1] No doubt she knew the names of some of my comrades who knew mine, for in 1945 I was informed that she had requested a passport for South America; I took steps to help her get it.

of material;[2] and human interest because they dealt with an area in which humanity is in danger: everything our generation has seen in the past thirty years adequately demonstrates that man's moral frailty is constant and widespread—and increasingly out of balance with his material power.

In his book, Dr. Bayle added to an objective account of the trial an exceptionally thorough documentation of the histories and personalities of the twenty-three defendants.

They were all doctors, and all bore part of the responsibility for unusual and heinous—but specifically medical[3]— crimes: the program of extermination by gas, and the bizarre and cruel experiments, many of them fatal, on human subjects. Other doctors, who themselves played roles in the crimes in question, testified as eyewitnesses. One of the latter, Dr. Mennecke, former director of the Eichberg asylum, said in part: . . . *I was summoned to Berlin, where I participated in a meeting with about ten other doctors. There, Dr. Hefelmann, Dr. Bohne, and Mr. Brack told us that the leadership of the National Socialist State had promulgated laws and decrees designed for the extermination of those unfit to live. It was made very clear . . . that doctors participating in the program would not be committing any kind of crime.*

Among the characters described by Dr. Bayle, we find one who had a "completely vindictive nature and a constantly venomous state of mind," another who exhibited "moral licentiousness and basic faults of character," still another who was "mediocre, disorganized, and violent," and an "aggressive, treacherous liar, a manipulator of human feelings, vain and bursting with self-importance, with excessive and irrational ambitions hiding behind a guileless exterior. . . ."

[2] Thirty-two testified at the "Doctors' Trial" for the prosecution and fifty-three for the defense, including the twenty-three defendants. The prosecution used 570 documents (copies of which comprised nineteen volumes of several hundred pages). The proceedings were filmed, and the complete English transcript totaled 11,538 pages. Dr. Bayle devoted almost four years, full time, to the subject of the trial, from November 1946 to June 1950.

[3] The doctor-criminals, who made the "selections" for the Ravensbrück gas chamber, were tried at Hamburg (Dr. Winkelmann), or were never found.

But these men, whose individual and basic characters lay behind the acts they committed, by no means represented the majority. Quite the contrary, the majority showed no long-standing characteristics that might logically explain their actions. For example, Dr. Karl Brandt, Reich health commissioner and a close associate of Hitler, ordered "euthanasia" for 200,000 to 300,000 people; we learn that he was "intelligent," "sensitive," "energetic," "intuitive," and "sincere."

Dr. Conti, president of the Nazi party's medical organization and a principal figure behind the vivisection experiments in the camps (and, according to his close collaborator Dr. Blome, he also had a scheme in 1941 to sterilize the Polish élite), committed suicide in prison, but not before recording his thoughts about justifying his actions: *I am killing myself because I gave false testimony. . . . I had no good reason whatsoever for giving such testimony. I am not a criminal. I cannot believe that concealing the fact that Blome had often talked to me about his intentions to conduct experiments on humans constituted a serious omission. . . . It is very sad to put this kind of end to a life of good intentions and devotion to duty. . . .*

Such admirable characteristics—"good intentions"—which seem in this context to be only laughable affectations of style or the musings of unrealistic self-evaluation, might be somewhat more justified for some of the other defendants: for example, the general practitioner who directed the Wehrmacht health services is described as "intelligent, alert, and orderly, basically a courageous and judicious man, compassionate." Dr. Bayle pictured him as one who did not make "heroic" gestures in denouncing practices which might be reprehensible but were "potentially useful for a nation at war, and effectively concealed by the omnipotent Reichsführer."

There were many of these professionals who secretly disapproved of "certain practices" but, out of patriotism, refused to create "scandals." Behind them operated another level with fewer compunctions, including, for example, Dr. Gebhardt, very well-known at Ravensbrück for his role in the "experiments," and Professor August Hirt, who requested that eighty Russian war prisoners of Jewish origin (about thirty women and fifty men) be transferred for execution; he preserved the cadavers in alcohol as his personal "research collection."

At the next level down, behind the professors and renowned practitioners, were the bloody-handed executioners. Here is one of them as he described himself:[4] *My name is Joseph Kramer, SS Hauptsturmführer, thirty-nine years old. Until 1932 I was a bookseller in Augsburg, then I became an SS volunteer with the responsibility of guarding concentration-camp prisoners. Before the war broke out, I was a lieutenant at Esterwegen, Sachsenhausen, Dachau, Mauthausen, and Auschwitz. In April 1941 I was assigned to the Natzweiler-Struthof camp as a deputy to Commandant Hüttig. I became commandant in October 1942 and remained in that position until April 1944, when I was sent to Auschwitz. In December 1944 I commanded Bergen-Belsen. . . . I went to the Strasbourg Anatomical Institute, where Professor Hirt was based. He told me that a group of prisoners were to be executed in the gas chamber at Struthof, and the bodies were to be taken to the Anatomical Institute for his use. He gave me a bottle containing about a quarter liter of salts—I think they were cyanide salts. . . .*

Early in August 1943 I received eighty inmates, and one night, around nine o'clock, I made a first trip to the gas chamber with fifteen women in a small truck. I told them they had to go into the chamber to be disinfected. With the help of a few SS I stripped them and pushed them into the gas chamber completely naked.

When I closed the door they began to scream. I placed a certain amount of the salts in a tube under the peephole and then watched what happened inside. The women breathed for about thirty seconds before falling to the floor. After turning on the ventilation I opened the door. I found the women lying dead on the floor, covered with excrement. . . .

I had no particular feelings in carrying out these operations because I had received an order to execute the eighty prisoners in the manner I have described. In any case, that was the way I was trained.

[4] F. Bayle, op. cit., pp. 866–68.

Some of the men who tried to explain their actions before an official tribunal did not always fit their own descriptions of themselves. But even when they had plainly abandoned their attempts to argue with the facts, and even when they expressed themselves in posthumous letters, we saw only the façade.

What road had the former printer Schwarzhuber traveled before he came to Ravensbrück to watch his prisoners die? And what of Joseph Kramer, between his bookstore in Augsburg and the peephole of the Struthof gas chamber? We can only speculate about a complete account of their behavior.

The only one to give a lengthy confession about his own life was Rudolf Franz Ferdinand Hoess, the commandant of Auschwitz from May 1940 to October 1943. His testament is extraordinary. Hoess tells us that he was a believing and practicing Catholic, scrupulous, serious-minded, married to a young woman who shared his goals; that they had five children whom they brought up lovingly and according to "proper" rules of conduct. . . . We also learn that at Auschwitz he presided over the deaths of three million civilians who had been innocent of any crime.

Like Joseph Kramer, he had undergone an "education," first at Dachau (1934–38), then at Sachsenhausen, moving finally to Auschwitz.

Regarding the beating of prisoners at Dachau, he wrote (pp. 71–72): . . . *I avoided them as best I could or at least always left the parade before the actual whipping began. I found it easy to do this, for some of the block leaders were only too eager to attend. . . . Why did I have such an aversion to this form of punishment? With the best will in the world I am unable to answer this question.*

There was another block leader at this time who was affected in the same way and who always tried to avoid attending these affairs. This was Schwarzhuber. . . . The block leaders who hastened to these whippings . . . were almost without exception sly, rough, violent, and often common creatures, whose behavior toward their comrades and their families was in character with their natures. . . . (p. 88) *Al-*

*though I became accustomed to all that was unalterable in
the camps, I never grew indifferent to human suffering. I have
always seen it and felt for it. Yet because I might not show
weakness, I wished to appear hard, lest I be regarded as weak,
and had to disregard such feelings.*

At Sachsenhausen, Hoess organized the executions of men
from the army (and not without feeling, since some of them
had been his comrades), and of Jehovah's Witnesses. Some
Witnesses were forced to watch the execution of their comrades, and Hoess noted that *these Jehovah's Witnesses became
even more fanatical in their faith as a result of the martyr-
dom of their comrades. Several of them who had already
signed a declaration that they would cease to proselytize, a
declaration which helped them to obtain their freedom, now
withdrew it, since they were anxious to suffer even more for
Jehovah.*

When Loritz became commandant of Sachsenhausen, he decided that he preferred to have a subordinate more capable
of taking "drastic measures"—this was Fritz Suhren, the future
commandant of Ravensbrück. Hoess was then named commandant (on May 4, 1940) of a small quarantine camp sixty
kilometers from Cracow—Auschwitz.

During the summer of 1941 he met with Himmler, who
explained what was expected of him—mass extermination. *It
was certainly an extraordinary and monstrous order. Nevertheless the reasons behind the extermination program seemed
to me right.*

Acting on the suggestion of one of his collaborators
(Fritsch), Hoess utilized the cyanide-based Zyklon B gas, very
rapidly effective. His first victims were Russian prisoners of
war, then, in enormous groups, the Jewish civilians. He accompanied them personally to the door of the gas chamber,
and, as this gentle father figure has noted: *The smaller children usually cried because of the strangeness of being undressed in this fashion, but when their mothers or members
of the Special Detachment comforted them, they became calm
and entered the gas chambers, playing or joking with one another and carrying their toys. I noticed that women who either*

guessed or knew what awaited them nevertheless found the courage to joke with the children to encourage them, despite the mortal terror visible in their own eyes. (p. 165)

Hoess writes further on (p. 197) that *in Himmler's view, Germany was the one state in Europe that had the right to exercise supremacy. All the other countries were second-rate. The predominantly Nordic races were to be favorably treated, with the aim of incorporating them into Germany. The Eastern races were to be split up, to be made insignificant, and to become slaves.*

He concludes by saying: *I have had two lights to guide me: my fatherland and, later, my family. . . .*

Let the public continue to regard me as the bloodthirsty beast, the cruel sadist, and the mass murderer; for the masses could never imagine the commandant of Auschwitz in any other light.

They could never understand that he, too, had a heart and that he was not evil.

How could this man and hundreds of others, who by origin and upbringing belonged to the "average" levels of German society and were apparently sheltered by its protective elements (family, religion, patriotism), have tortured and coldly slaughtered defenseless humans by the thousands? That, indeed, is one of the primary questions posed by what we have learned, either firsthand or by hearsay, about the unique world of the concentration camps. Experience and custom would dictate that one delve into German history or the psychological characteristics normally attributed to the German people—even into Tacitus' *Germania*—for something which, while distinguishing the contaminated segment of humanity from everything else, explains the contamination itself; or something in the sociological design, perhaps like the famous excess gene which, according to some psychiatrists, indicates certain types of aberrant behavior.

It has always seemed preposterous to say that there have been savage or depraved "races," even in 1945 (and when I say "race" I mean "peoples of comparable lineage"). But it is true that certain societies have allowed certain savageries, and between 1939 and 1945, I, like many others, yielded to the temptation to put these phenomena into words: "they" did such-and-such; "we" would not do such a thing. . . .

I no longer think in these terms and, quite to the contrary, I am convinced that no "people" is immune to the kind of collective moral disaster[5] of which this study describes only a part.

Even so, I could never go so far as to say that other contemporary moral collapses were like what happened in Hitler's Germany; nothing else could be the same. But it is no less true that the difference between the Germany of Hitler and some major democracies which adopted his methods (more or less temporarily) was primarily statistical. But these other nations were, at least, not completely contaminated by the criminal elements they had fostered and patronized.

In this regard there are some who, enthusiastically and exclusively, point to the atrocities of the Stalinist era; others seem unaware of this but dwell upon the wars in Algeria and Vietnam. For my own part, my knowledge of atrocities in Vietnam is limited to what I have read in the press, but in 1951 I was part of a jury which conducted a public inquiry in Brussels into Stalin's crimes; concerning the war crimes in Algeria between 1954 and 1962, my information was detailed and direct.

No one would dare deny that in both the U.S.S.R. and France the state encouraged and concealed certain crimes, but in both countries a tenuous fiction has managed to endure: that they did not torture or slaughter the innocent, but only those who constituted a threat.

The cover-up was hardly effective, and the innocent were still tortured and murdered, but there was always the prospect of effective condemnation or refusal to accept the fiction, and such a public reproach allowed some form of recourse. The possibility did not exist in Germany. There, because of the myths of racism, institutionalized criminality permeated every

[5] It is because of this conviction that I decided to include as an appendix (p. 233) an account of certain aspects of the Algerian war, in which some of the principal characters were formerly in the SS.

aspect of society. Without the crushing military defeat, Germany would have had almost no chance for its own liberation.

There is an inescapable conclusion: whenever men, for reasons of "patriotism," create, encourage and conceal the activities of a criminal element, they are fostering and concealing atrocities against humanity, and any democratic country that has consented to this process has also taken the risk that the resulting damage cannot be neatly compartmentalized. It is well known that in both France and the U.S.S.R. the walls broke down and a fatal infection very nearly set in.

It is not my intention here to philosophize on contemporary history, but to contribute in any way possible in seeing that the same history is not falsified. But I also wish most fervently to call attention to the tragic easiness with which "decent people" could become the most callous executioners without seeming to notice what was happening to them, and to the dangers inherent in such actions, especially to those who might think they could profit from them. And, finally, everything points to the necessity of establishing broad definitions and sanctions, internationally accepted, for such crimes against humanity.

Part Four

METHODS
OF INVESTIGATION

20

Reliability of Testimony

Over the past sixty years or so there have been many studies analyzing how personal accounts and testimony stand up as forms of history, and, for the most part, these studies are broadly disparaging in nature. In my view, however, their negative conclusions have been vastly overstated.[1]

These conclusions are, basically, that an entirely accurate account is an exception, that errors, when made sincerely, can be asserted with as much confidence as accurate facts, and that "mental habits" of a witness can easily override what he has actually perceived, without his being the least bit aware of what has happened. Agreement among several narratives would not necessarily be a criterion for veracity, since it is normal for identical mental images to occur in the minds of individuals belonging to the same social group. This contamination of the "real" by the "probable" would grow in direct proportion with the amount of time between the event and the testimony—time during which the witnesses would have opportunities to reflect and discuss the event among themselves.

[1] This campaign began to spread during a time when the means of measuring and recording by machine were beginning their own period of spectacular growth: the phonograph and tape recorder for the voice, the camera and cinema for the image—all the mechanical (and today electronic) methods of scrutiny, which have led to the inevitable comparisons with our imperfect cerebral mechanism. The result has been that we have finally attained such an enormous hodgepodge of paperwork and red tape that a return to human proportions is almost impossible.

But in a very different situation—the exploration of a relatively distant past rather than recent history, utilizing accounts written by persons to whom the investigator has no direct access (and such is the normal situation among historians)—one might readily think that the likelihood of inaccuracy was even more disturbing.

In the situation we are concerned with in this study, the comparison of analogous testimonies would be of limited usefulness, since, during the same period and in the same place, atrocious living conditions coexisted with conditions which under the circumstances could be termed almost normal. On any given day one might see a relatively sound human being, who would probably survive, alongside another undergoing the most extreme suffering, which would soon end in death. In any case, an account by one can neither confirm nor weaken related testimony by the other, except in relation to certain details which many eyewitnesses all too rarely thought to give.

During the eight years following the war I attempted a systematic search for these details, questioning numerous qualified informants, directly and at length, on many precise points. I was thus trying to recreate, bit by bit, a vast body of fact, and the nature of my operation was often unknown even to those who were aiding the process. One can see that this allowed a degree of "regulation" over the amount of imprecision in each account, and at the same time demonstrated that some were extraordinarily accurate and pinpointed most of the incorrectness in the others.

The *authentic* documents examined in Part Two of this study could be wrung dry of every drop of information, to the point where even the errors provided precious material; in much the same manner a witness can be valuable both for what he knows and for what he does not know, so long as the questioning is adapted to his peculiar characteristics. One thus obtains from him a body of information more complete, more human, and often more exact than provided by certain documents, the fallibility of which has already been amply demonstrated.

The tests which pinpointed the inaccuracies were devised for precisely that purpose, and in doing so they served the cause of truth and inspired an observer's necessary caution. With that accomplished, it would be easy to devise "counter-tests" to demonstrate a different, but complementary, result—that one can arrive at the truth by using certain selected testimony.

For someone seeking specifically to document past events which have since ceased to exist except in memory, simple statistics of erroneous answers are valuable only to the extent that they form a basis for defining his areas of research; his goal is not just to gather testimony but to comprehend the past. With that purpose in mind, one would have to devise hierarchies of probability for each account, according to the subject of the account and the witness who gave it, but above all according to the relationships between these two (professional, emotional, or purely accidental relationships). It would then be necessary to classify the information in line with the demands of previously revealed history. With these constraints and classifications, plus the customary simple cross-checking, one has means of control almost as reliable as "machines," and much less likely to break down. There are no real problems if the subject of a body of testimony is an established, institutionalized entity; in those circumstances even the most elementary methods of investigation can quickly discern basic facts. Such a base of information is the foundation of the science of ethnology, and those who have tested its methods know that they are sufficiently reliable.

When an element of investigation is related to conditions which were temporary but lived in by a given group for a certain period of time (for example, day-to-day living conditions in a concentration camp, the organizational structure and certain other details of such a camp, or the approximate composition of a prisoner transport), valid reconstructions of fact are possible through a simple examination of the numerous accounts gathered by the Subcommittee on the Deportation of the World War II Historical Commission.

We begin to feel uneasy, however, when we encounter the most hazardous aspect of personal testimony, telling of a specific "event," but even on this uncertain terrain we have means of recourse.

The type of "event" I am speaking of is by nature brief and random and, consequently, must be recalled by the non-intellectual, non-abstract portion of memory; that is, by concrete recollection, the reliability of which varies all too widely from person to person. One questions disjointed and sometimes seemingly dishonest observations, but it is normal in these circumstances that the errors outnumber everything else, thus confirming one of the basic criticisms I have been reluctant to accept. Errors might abound, but they are not universal.

Especially inexact are the observations dealing with minute details, many purely physical: movements, shapes, colors, numbers, estimations of time. But even here there are degrees of imprecision: information about the forms and colors of prisoners' clothing would probably be more accurate if it were told by a dressmaker rather than an accounting clerk. If, for example, we might question the seamstress who made or repaired a garment, or perhaps the laundrywoman who cleaned and ironed it, we have correspondingly decreased the margin of error, and the police were well aware of this. In short, neither the possibility of error nor, conversely, the reliability of a witness' testimony was a matter of chance.

The basic veracity of witnesses was always questionable and, to some extent, distinct from their sincerity. Whatever the case, this is one of the primary areas to be examined, and it goes without saying that the liars had to be identified from the first.

There are two types, one of them difficult to discern, the other relatively easy. Contrary to popular opinion, the purposeful and self-serving falsehood can create the greatest difficulties, despite the often obvious self-interest which should alert us immediately, since it is generally a considered effort, thus well-constructed and plausible. It can also call upon the most trivial details, better known to the liar than to his audience, and as a result is difficult to verify. And of course its author is only an "ad hoc" liar, which makes him all the more formidable.

The accidental or gratuitous falsehood presents fewer problems, primarily because of certain indicative characteristics I have encountered on many occasions: it usually relates to comparatively well-known events, about which other information is readily available; it is rarely an isolated occurrence but part of some long narrative in which the perpetrator trips over his own contradictions; and, similarly, it is an effort by that special type of person who, I have found, is rarely successful in sustaining a lie.

To be sure, such persons are more numerous than might generally be supposed, and a world such as that of the concentration camps (the perfect stimulus, unfortunately, for sado-masochistic imaginations) provided them an extraordinary field of action. I have known of some unstable types, half-swindler, half-lunatic, who exploited a tale of an imaginary deportation; there have been others (authentic deportees) whose unsound minds worked overtime to embellish the monstrosities they had seen or heard about. And, inevitably, there have been publishers willing to dignify these meanderings and fabrications, and more or less official researchers willing to use them. For these there are no excuses, since the most elementary investigation should have been sufficient to uncover the deception.

Before explaining my efforts to alleviate the effects of both types of testimonial error, I should insert some observations on "bias," a debilitating element in contemporary history.

21

Commitment and Impartiality

Personal testimony on the deportation must be totally incompatible with "neutrality"; one of the basic characteristics of the world of the concentration camps was that no one viewed events as an indifferent "spectator."

The British soldiers who liberated Bergen-Belsen, the Russians and Americans who entered Auschwitz, the neutral Swiss and Swedes of the International Red Cross—none of these "lived" in this world. They saw what remained of a camp, but they could hardly be considered "unbiased"; quite to the contrary, they often felt immediate identification with the feelings of the victims, and perhaps even felt them more strongly simply because they had more strength.

The German guards witnessed things known only to themselves and to the dead. As yet, no pious autobiographical apologias for their conduct have been published, and we know their feelings and opinions mostly through the testimony they gave before the tribunals which tried them as war criminals. This form of testimony is doubly suspect; not only did they enter these proceedings with an inherent "bias," but the obvious and immediate demands of self-preservation impelled them to be less than truthful. This was true for the most part, but not always and not on all points, as I have tried to show in Part Two of this study. And the solution of some problems might not have been possible without this source of information. The criterion of individual morality (which plays such an important role in the a priori judgments one forms about a body of testimony) has not been included among my reasons for taking a wary approach to this category of testimony precisely because I believe that no testimony should be judged a priori.

The factor of time, while it might have softened one's inquisitiveness, has too often hardened chosen positions. The elements of society most directly affected by the camps have been especially susceptible in this regard: anything that might help blacken the reputations of participants in the criminal system has often been accepted without question, and the slightest expression of reservation has provoked indignation. On the other hand, those elements which reached an "accommodation," even a remote one, with Hitler's Germany have exhibited the opposite reaction, trying to cast doubt on the least contestable facts. In France, with both elements, anything dealing with the political history of 1939–45 incites the kind of spirited passions that do not die quickly.

But the same is true of all events which call up all the feelings and interests of an age: Who was "neutral" in Paris in 1793? In our own time, who can be totally neutral in the face of revolutionary events?

Living and acting without these prejudices is inconceivable; life is only a series of choices, and we become more confused as these choices become less obvious. But none of us makes his choices solely from such prejudices; we also choose among individuals and actions and among details concerning these individuals and actions, and we are constantly confronted with the logic and sequence of events and consequences which make up the web of history. There is no one who can truly be classified as being in the mediocre middle of morality, but only those who have not yet encountered the events that will reveal their true nature. Likewise, there are no true "neutrals," but only those who do not understand. Experience is a very secret heritage and difficult to communicate, which perhaps explains the understanding and clarity of thought that occurs among adversaries who have participated in the same drama.

So we cannot expect to find witnesses without "bias," but this bias, when it is candid and in good faith, is only one of a number of causes for involuntary error, and it is sufficiently overcome by the same general precautions taken against these causes in their entirety. Prejudices arising from something less than good faith can easily fall into the category of direct falsehood and are all the more amenable to identification because they are obvious and systematic.

The pervasive element of bias will always affect interpretation, of course, and it is almost impossible to dislodge. But, conversely, a total absence of emotional "involvement" amounts to almost unbelievable incomprehension. There is a very narrow line between bias and incomprehension, and this narrowness is one of the most basic problems of humanity and history.

22

Classification of Information

Given a body of data, one of the first steps in the elimination of every type of error, voluntary or involuntary, organized or random, would be a properly executed classification of the information.

This classification should be of primary importance to anyone seeking a valid knowledge of a society, living or dead, since his goal is more than simple possession of a document; he must also construct some sort of "decoding" system. It is thus essential to avoid adopting, except as a supplementary aid, the usual abstract classifications—alphabetical, for example. One should, rather, attempt to devise a form more concretely related to the nature of the entity he is examining. In my own case, I have had occasion to create systems of social investigation—almost from nothing—for human groups between which no bonds of any sort existed: stable societies of peasants or African nomads on one hand, and an unstable society which was created by an event and dissolved when that event concluded.

In both instances, the challenge was to devise methods of data compilation and verification which could be adapted to a widely varying array of social conditions.

The first groups could be classified as archaic societies, but still living, accessible, and the product of a slow and solid growth from deep roots. The other, the concentration camp "society," was complex and formless, and had existed during a brief present, with no past and no future.

Concerning the latter, it was impossible to utilize "internal structures" as a basis of classification, and I was forced to resort to more conspicuous and exterior criteria, such as physical location and time spans. In studying these prisons I proceeded cell by cell; for the convoys, I went from one rail car to another; for the camps, it was a block-by-block, barrack-by-barrack, bed-by-bed process. This abundance of detail was absolutely necessary; it seemed to be the only possible way of establishing the integrity of my investigation and of imposing some form of control over the testimony—not over its good faith or lack of it (I had other tests for that), but over the reliability of my witnesses' memories, and, going a step further, it would serve as a measure of memory in general.

Memory is an imperfect instrument, and we should not demand more than it can provide. When it has recorded a brief scene or even an episode which may have been noteworthy, but still isolated, we should allow a large margin of error. But when the reconstruction of a prolonged condition is involved, we can achieve surprisingly accurate results, especially when there are enough witnesses.

This invariably direct relationship between the reliability of memory and the duration of its subject was so strong that I could foresee which of the various stages in the deportation might be completely reconstructed, and I could even estimate the number of witnesses necessary for such a reconstruction. Whenever an event, or "stage," was relatively brief, the number of errors was accordingly high, but with a great deal of patience, cross-checking, and a careful evaluation of the "specificity" of each bit of testimony, it was possible to limit the degree of inaccuracy. The following example will illustrate this procedure.

So far as I know, there exist only two complete and authentic lists, prepared by the German authorities, covering convoys of deported Frenchwomen. As soon as I left Ravensbrück I attempted—primarily through interviews, but also with scattered fragments of documents—to reconstruct the composition and progress of other convoys. This procedure began along the lines I have just described, with a delineation of each step of captivity followed by each segment of a convoy (resistance activities, arrest, and imprisonment in Paris or the provinces, regrouping at Fresnes, Romainville, or Compiègne, the journey by rail from France to Germany, distribution among the various blocks or cells at the destination, departures in work Kommandos, etc.). At each stage, more or less homogeneous groupings were formed and then broken up.

The stage of shortest duration provides a representative example, that is, the journey from Paris to Ravensbrück, which usually lasted from four to seven days. During my inquiry conducted some eight years later, I learned among other things (from a dozen witnesses who related the complete history of their captivity) that a certain convoy was made up of five or six railroad cars. In each of these cars there were two or three prisoners who, for one reason or another, attracted the attention of their seventy comrades and were thus definite markers for a particular group. With these milestones, every witness I questioned could be identified with one of the rail cars, and then followed, step by step, until the liberation.

For this very brief portion of the drama, my witnesses gave me a widely varied collection of names: some told of three, some mentioned a dozen or so, a rare few could recall more than twenty of their comrades. All of this covered a group which stayed together probably a week at the most and included seventy women.

By consulting a dozen survivors from each of the other groups, I managed to gather sufficient information to reconstruct the prisoner lists, and as I totaled the numbers I noticed that in almost every case the sum was larger than the group that had actually been in the rail car. One expects to encounter errors but, in lists such as these, errors of omission rather than addition.

I believe, however, that these errors were not conscious fabrications but simply the result of mistaken impressions; it was as if the imperfect camera of memory had taken multiple exposures.

These prisoners, forced to share the few square yards of their rolling prison for as much as a week, had for the most part been strangers to one another when the train left France. In these conditions, the presence of a few former cellmates obviously became very important to them. In addition, they encountered for the first time a certain number of newcomers with very noticeable personalities, and the errors I could isolate invariably related to these special characters. This seems logical enough; the impressions my witnesses associated with the departure of their train became confused with their feelings on being quarantined; these perceptions were abstract, intellectual, and passive in a way, while the first re-encounter with a Resistance comrade was personal, concrete, detached from the general confusion, and easily placed in time.

Identifying the errors and arriving at an acceptable list of names was a task requiring only time and the patience to arrange the information in tabular form. In one column I listed the names given by a group of a dozen witnesses (eighty-five, for example), then aligned twelve other columns, each corresponding to an interview; occurrences of names were marked accordingly for the twelve informants.

An example of the results of this process was Mme. Ab., an informant who gave me twelve names, including that of a young woman who spoke German and served as interpreter during the journey and who, for that reason alone, was conspicuous within her group. But not one of the other eleven informants for this transport could remember the young interpreter—rather strange, since she was said to have had a very forceful personality and had been arrested as part of a large Resistance group. I also noticed that Mme. Ab. had given me a half-dozen other names, either cellmates or Resistance comrades, which had gone unmentioned by my other eleven witnesses. A partial error by Mme. Ab. later became apparent: she had actually made the trip in the company of these half-dozen comrades, but not in the same car as the interpreter; identification of Mme. Ab.'s car was relatively easy. Her mistake was all the more understandable because the convoy, like all the others, was quarantined as soon as it arrived at Ravensbrück, and the overcrowded conditions in the quarantine block were an uncannily faithful reproduction of the circumstances of their journey by train. Eight days after their arrival, Mme. Ab. left in one direction and the young interpreter in another. So far as I know, they never saw each other again.

I could list numerous similar instances, caused by almost identical circumstances and equally correctable with the device I have described—a mechanism which provided a sort of collective profile of that uncertain ray of light the human mind can always cast upon its past. But there were also an equally large number of faultless memories—cases where each new witness provided confirmation of another.

What did we who endured the world of the concentration camps know about it? Little, actually, except that its dimensions went beyond what man can ordinarily comprehend, that its administrative machinery was riddled with weakness and duplicity, and that its records were carefully and selectively destroyed—the most secret first (meaning, of course, the most illuminating and incriminating).

The gates of the last German camp finally opened, and this "other world" passed from the real to become part of the intangibles of history. But it would return, as naked as its own dead.

This world's first appearances as "history" were certainly not the least distorted: during the war crimes trials I attended in 1946 and 1947, I made the striking discovery that both witnesses and defendants, using the same esoteric language, were at first understood only among themselves, excluding their judges and the public. The witnesses, finally brought back to the reality of prior experience, later learned to "translate" what they had to say, and the gaps seemed to close, little by little. Perhaps the truth was there somewhere.

This abominable universe seemed totally incoherent by itself—more terrifying than Dante's visions, more nonsensical than a child's game of cards. At first, the odds were more or less equal as to which fate a deportee might suffer, and whether he would follow a route to freedom or death depended on a very fickle destiny: in one group, the chances were one in five that one would survive; in another there were the same odds that one would be killed. Out of all this we would see only confused "averages."

In this world of uncertainty and darkness, as insanely horrifying as the worst nightmare, mental landmarks of space and time were missing then and, to a large degree, have still not been found. Lives were risked in the simple process of recording events, but these details were almost lost in the vast *terra incognita* of an incongruous and obscure universe.

I still believe that a day will come when the documents on the deportation will emerge from the mildew of cellars and strongboxes scattered around the world. The gaps and errors will be there, as will the evil intentions and intentional falsifications. History should then have enough of the interwoven threads of a sieve to sift out the worst contradictions and errors. But it would also be necessary to use everything available from personal testimony, even while making every possible effort to retrieve the documents which were not destroyed. Only at the confluence of all the personal interviews and these critically scrutinized "documents" can we find the complete resurrection of a tangled history.

APPENDICES

1

Gas Chambers in the Western Camps

By 1953, when I had finished my own investigation into the history of a convoy of Frenchwomen, I could not have imagined that the existence of a gas chamber at Ravensbrück would ever be disputed. In that regard, I must admit being quite disturbed later when I read the study by Olga Wormser-Migot.[1]

If such errors as hers could be made by a person who, although she did not live through the deportation, had access to reliable information (and I can vouch for her intellectual honesty), what might be done by some of the lesser "subcontractors" of history?

The author devoted many long years to an investigation of the concentration-camp system and to the necessary but thankless task of lobbying for corrective legislation, applying to both civilian and military sectors of German society, for which I (and others) must be eternally grateful. Her efforts to illuminate the laws and administrative documents of Nazi Germany seem very valuable, so far as I can judge. On the whole, unfortunately, she seems to have been overwhelmed by the enormous mass of data, the confusion of which led to errors and false conclusions.

Disregarding for a moment some of the unfortunate generalities (that the term "gas chamber" became "one of the leitmotifs of the heroic epic of the deportation"), we should examine some of her assertions concerning gas chambers in the Western camps (p. 541):

Concerning Mauthausen, we have established that a "convoy of no return" left for Hartheim despite the availability of a small gas chamber at Mauthausen (the existence of which

---

[1] *Le Système Concentrationnaire Nazi* (Presses Universitaires de France, 1968).

*has been denied by many prisoners, contrary to postwar con-
tentions by the camp's SS).* . . .

*Why all these trips from Mauthausen to Hartheim and
from Ravensbrück to Jugendlager (Mittwerda or Uckermarck) if there were gas chambers at Mauthausen and
Ravensbrück?*

*Beginning in 1934, there was extensive correspondence be-
tween the SA and the SS on the necessity of establishing edu-
cational institutions for "spiritual growth" at Uckermarck.
The location of these "institutes" seems rather odd: on the
Ravensbrück death lists reported in May 1945 by Marie-
Claude Vaillant-Couturier (copied from those made up by a
Czech prisoner who worked in the camp offices), the words
"Uckermarck" and "Jugendlager" were invariably synony-
mous with death. Was all of this a simple coincidence, or was
it that instead of "re-education" camps at Uckermarck they
had decided, as of 1934, that "spiritual growth" was to be
accomplished by destruction of the body?* . . .

*Out of 3,000 prisoners in February 1945, twenty-five deaths
per day were counted.*[2] *According to Mme. Sturm, an Austrian prisoner who was in the camp from 1939 to 1945, the
gas chamber—"a small concrete-block room, 16m. x 11m."—
was built in 1943 when Suhren arrived at Ravensbrück. It
was in the main camp, adjoining the crematorium.* . . .

*Her deposition, however, is riddled by improbabilities and
contradictions:* "One day when I went to look for something
in the part of the building which had not been converted into
a gas chamber . . . I found a gypsy woman who had managed to escape from a gas-chamber convoy. She told me that
those convoys to 'Uckermarck' were actually intended for the
gas chamber." *What gas chamber? Hiding in the room next
to the gas chamber after escaping from a group destined for
that same gas chamber would seem rather strange, as would
the ease with which an ordinary prisoner was allowed to get
so near that "secret" installation by fetching "something"
from the adjoining room.*

According to Wormser-Migot, there was also some dis-
agreement as to the location of the gas chamber. Vaillant-
Couturier placed it behind the main camp wall, next to the
cremation ovens, and noted that prisoners leaving the Revier
went directly to the gas chamber without passing through
Uckermarck. Wormser-Migot cites another witness, however,
who stated that *prisoners were selected at roll calls and left
for a gas chamber situated not far from the Jugendlager.*

The author continues: *The same witness (Irene Ottelard)*

---

[2] *Trial of Suhren and Pflaum, February 23, 1950.*

*also recounts the killings by the "white powder" or the injec-
tions by "Sister Vera." Ottelard, and others, did not suffer
either of these fates because of some of Sister Vera's whims,
that is, to spare someone who could sing well or sew a nice
dress.*

*It seems inconceivable that they would take aged and ill
prisoners from the Revier and blocks of the main camp to
be sent to the Jugendlager, so that then these same women
could be "selected" for a gas chamber back in the camp they
had just left—and all this while others were being sent directly
to the same gas chamber. One might rather believe that the
gas chamber was adjacent to the Jugendlager, from which a
prisoner was not supposed to return.*

*This same witness—after asserting that they were constantly
required to go out for roll calls and "selections" for Jugendlager—says that she was never present at these selections because she was always "in bed." Another contradiction by a
witness, or an inconsistency of the system?*

*During courtroom questioning concerning the gas cham-
bers, a number of witnesses responded to the effect that "I
heard about it but I did not see it." When witness Sophie
Z., a German political prisoner, declares "I have heard that
some Jews were gassed," it is obvious that a willing or unconscious confusion has arisen between the tales of Auschwitz
and the reality of Ravensbrück. When the presiding judge
asked the witness why she mentioned only the Jews, she responded: "Because the prisoners themselves said that only the
Jews were gassed."*

*Mme. Koehler, a defense witness at Suhren's trial, was as-
tonished at the contradictions and imprecision in prisoners'
accounts concerning the gas chamber: "Some witnesses
claimed that the gas chamber was located near the 'decanta-
tion' plant;[3] Mme. S. says it was near the crematorium;
others, that it was next to the new laundry house. No one
seems to have seen it, least of all those former prisoners I
have interviewed."*

*Marie-Claude Vaillant-Couturier says she saw it near the
crematorium, behind the kitchen. To this, witness Koehler
adds: "So say some prisoners working in the Kommandos,*

[3] *This was the water-filtering facility in which the body of a
dead infant had been found by a prisoner "specialist" who had
come from Oranienburg. From this arose the myth that newborn
children were thrown into the water, and perhaps it was the source
of another myth, that this facility was converted into a gas chamber in the minds of the prisoners.*

*who could see part of what was happening in the camp but
by no means everything."*

Violette Lecoq testified at the Suhren-Pflaum trial: "A
transport was made up at Block 10—thirty women designated
for the gas chamber. At the last moment they could round
up only twenty-nine, so an SS made me get on the truck. I
was fully clothed; the other women were naked. The truck
went around Block 10, then down the Lagerstrasse, arriving
at the camp gate. We then left for the Jugendlager." Violette
Lecoq returned because she was not naked—they took her to
be a supervisor.

This would imply, of course, that the gas chamber was near
the Jugendlager. Can we imagine that they would take naked
women up to the Jugendlager just to bring them back to a
gas chamber supposedly located in the main camp? Camouflage? But such a double transfer would only double the risk
of attracting the other prisoners' attention.

At his trial, Suhren took a rather peculiar position regarding the gas chamber . . . not disputing that it existed, but
denying any responsibility for the construction of it or for
supplying its victims. He seemed to have been unaware of its
location. But Suhren's testimony does not establish that a gas
chamber definitely existed; in fact, his entire defense was
based on his assertion that he was no longer at Ravensbrück
as of February 1945, the date when the gas chamber went
into use.

We should note finally that the statements on the Ravensbrück gas chamber place it in time as beginning in February
1945, the date of the arrival of the evacuees from Auschwitz,
and the date when the Ravensbrück prisoners learned that
there had been gas chambers at Auschwitz.

Some clarifications concerning the Mauthausen camp will be
found in the following appendix by Serge Choumoff, a
former prisoner there. As for Ravensbrück, here are, in summary, some facts pertinent to Olga Wormser-Migot's observations.

Concerning the "convoys of no return," known at Ravensbrück as transports noirs, my comrades employed in the
Revier in 1943 and 1944 knew at the time that those groups
were leaving for Linz—the site of Hartheim castle and its gas
chamber—and their accounts were confirmed by SS Dr. Treite.
(See p. 132.) This was not the only destination for such transports: Grete Buber-Neumann, who worked in one of the administrative offices and saw the first transport noir depart during the second half of 1942, knew its destination all too well—
the ominous installation for special gassings at Bernburg. The

last of the transports of no return left Ravensbrück for Linz-Hartheim in November 1944—one month *before* the opening of Jugendlager, one month *before* on-the-spot exterminations began at Ravensbrück.

The author speaks of Uckermarck, Jugendlager, and Mittwerda as if they were three different detention sites. We have already seen how Uckermarck evolved from a camp for German juvenile delinquents into a supplementary concentration camp known as Jugendlager. Its existence became known at Ravensbrück only during the last weeks of 1944, and, in sum, the words Uckermarck and Jugendlager stood for the same place—and a very real place at that. Thousands of women were sent to Jugendlager-Uckermarck; most of them died, a few score survived, and at least two of these (who have been officers in our association of Resistance prisoners) are still very accessible for consultation on the subject.

On the other hand, the word "Mittwerda" signified a totally fictitious location. No one ever saw such a camp, and no one ever saw a survivor among those whose names had been placed on the "Mittwerda" lists.

It is quite unlikely (and almost unbelievable) that an exchange of letters in 1934 concerning Uckermarck and referring to so-called "spiritual growth" could have had anything to do with planned exterminations at that location. It was in fact some seven years later that the real extermination measures became a matter of policy in Germany—first for the Russian war prisoners, then for Jewish civilians and, almost at the same time, for those whom the SS had deemed "biologically inferior." But these measures did not become effective at Ravensbrück until sometime later (early 1942) and even then had repercussions only through the transports noirs.

And what about the "contradictions" concerning the location of the gas chamber? All of the witnesses in a position to know have recalled it as being alongside the cremation ovens as part of an enclosure connected to the main camp wall, behind the kitchens, and thus only a few yards away from direct observation by many prisoners. (There were a great many prisoners who never actually saw it, but these were obviously not the ones to be consulted for eyewitness testimony.) Outside of execution times, it was in a location where almost any prisoner might be sent on some errand or another. Thus the story of the gypsy who escaped from a gas convoy is probably true, or at least not unbelievable. But, according to what I was told at the time, she was recaptured and executed in the gas chamber twenty-fours later.

As for the Jugendlager, all of the many witnesses who went there have said specifically that this "little camp" was situated in exactly the opposite direction, about one kilometer from the main camp, beyond the workshops known as the "industrial park." The women selected for Jugendlager generally went on foot, across the industrial park, while those destined for the crematorium left in trucks, through the main gate. Movement between Jugendlager and the crematorium was by truck, and never through the main camp; even the many bodies of those who died "natural" deaths at Jugendlager were taken out by the exterior route.

As I have pointed out earlier, roll calls at Jugendlager were daylong affairs, and they were obligatory, since they were used as a means of murder. But Irene Ottelard remained "in bed," and for a simple reason: Jugendlager had a so-called infirmary and the services of a "nurse." This was Vera Salveguart, and the sick in this "hospital" did not participate in the roll calls. "Sister Vera" was supposed to account for a certain number of deaths each day and chose according to her own whims the "patients" she would force to swallow the famous white powder.

The disappearance of 170–80 women every night—first to Jugendlager only, then sometimes to the Revier in the main camp, sometimes to Jugendlager, sometimes to the tubercular block—was continuously reported from the very first occurrence by the prisoner-nurses and prisoner-clerks to their comrades, and this ominous information had immediate repercussions throughout the camp.

One only had to listen to know the destination of the women who were forcibly taken away, half-naked, in February and March of 1945, or at least when they left from the main camp: the gas chamber and the cremation ovens were separated from the camp by nothing more than a wall, and the same trucks made the trips back and forth. Invariably, their names were entered on the lists entitled "Mittwerda." I later checked these lists not only with eyewitnesses from Ravensbrück but against civilian national registries; the result was the same: no one returned from "Mittwerda."

Inconsistencies in the reported movements among the main camp, the Jugendlager, and the crematorium site can at least partially be attributed to the fact that the gas chamber was not available continuously. There was room for 150 (according to Schwarzhuber), and the women were killed 170 at a time (according to the prisoner-clerks); the building then had to be ventilated by strong blasts of air before the victims could be removed. The Jugendlager, on the other hand, could accommodate thousands of prisoners—up to 6,000.

The author has found it "peculiar" that Commandant Suhren confirmed the existence of a gas chamber while de-

ying responsibility. Surely Suhren did not even imagine that
someone might deny that a gas chamber existed at Ravensbrück, else he would have done so himself; he believed quite
rightly that the surviving prisoners would know about it, and
he also knew that it had been confirmed immediately by all
of his collaborators, some of whom had described it in detail
and told precisely how the victims were gassed. (See the testimony by Dr. Treite and Deputy Commandant Schwarzhuber,
pp. 131–32 and 148–50—the type of testimony essential to
any historical study of the concentration camps.) And what
of his contention that he was no longer in command at the
time of the exterminations by gas? Had he in his "confession"
perhaps revised the date when these exterminations began?
Did he persuade his collaborators to go along with such an
alteration? Should we date Schwarzhuber's reported conversation with him in January instead of February? I think not,
and I believe Schwarzhuber's testimony to be reliable from
beginning to end.

Regarding the so-called "discovery" by Western prisoners
of the existence of gas chambers in the East (in February
1945, on information from evacuees from Auschwitz), even
a casual reading of certain testimony sufficiently shows that
this was not an isolated occurrence and that there was a constant circulation (interrupted only by the Russian advance)
among the camps in Germany and those in Poland. As soon
as I arrived at Ravensbrück in late 1943 I encountered Czech
prisoners from Auschwitz in my own block. And arriving
from Auschwitz on August 1, 1944, were all the survivors
of a convoy of 230 Frenchwomen who had been deported
on January 24, 1943, including Marie-Claude Vaillant-
Couturier and Hélène Solomon-Langevin, both well-known to
all the French deportees and mentioned by Olga Wormser-
Migot (whose reading of some testimony seems very casual
indeed) in another book:[4] *Marie-Claude Vaillant-Couturier,
Nuremberg trial v. VI, p. 21ff.: reporter-photographer. Arrested February 9, 1942. Interned at Santé and Romainville.
Deported on January 24, 1943, with the first convoy of female
political prisoners, to Auschwitz. (The convoy included
Danielle Casanova, Païe Politzer, Hélène Solomon-Langevin,
Laure Cattet, etc. Of 230 women, forty-nine returned.) Transferred to Ravensbrück on August 1, 1944, liberated by the
Russians on April 29, 1945. Remained at the camp to aid
the sick and in other aspects of the repatriation process. Repatriated June 25, 1945.*

[4] *Tragédie de la déportation*, Hachette, 1954, p. 54n. I have included an excerpt of Vaillant-Couturier's Nuremberg testimony on
pp. 156–57.

2

The Mauthausen Concentration Camp

(A letter by Serge Choumoff,
a former prisoner and author of
a book on that camp. *Le Monde*, June 7, 1969.)

*Olga Wormser-Migot's book and some of the comment about
it have raised questions which cannot pass without some attempt at response. The author asserts that "there were no gas
chambers in the Western camps" and that this means of extermination existed only in those camps located in what is
now called Eastern Europe (East Germany excepted)—camps
which for the most part received from all countries those
Jewish prisoners destined for the "final solution" to the Jewish
question.*

*One of the Western camps she uses as an example is
Mauthausen, the "mother" camp for all those located on Austrian territory, including Gusen and Ebensee. Since I was a
"resident" of these Austrian camps for some twenty-five
months, I shall limit my own comment to that part of the
system.*

*The primary bases for her contention are contradictions and
inconsistencies among Mauthausen prisoners' accounts concerning the gas chamber, and her acceptance of certain testimony as casting serious doubt that such a facility ever existed
at all—and all this without citations of specific items of testimony. The author thus appears to take the role of arbiter
among the Mauthausen survivors. In reality, there was never
any debate among the prisoners as to whether a gas chamber
existed, and there has been no testimony denying that existence, which might explain the lack of citations.*

*The author does take note of the deathbed confession by
Franz Ziereis, the commandant of Mauthausen, that there was
indeed a gas chamber there. (His statement was given in May
1945 in the presence of a group of prisoners and two American Army officers, and was included as evidence at the Nuremberg trials, ref. 3870-PS.) But she states flatly, "It seems
that [Ziereis], willfully or otherwise, created the myth of a
gas chamber at Mauthausen." Wormser-Migot ignores an im-*

portant historical study of Mauthausen (de Bouard in the Revue d'histoire de la Deuxième Guerre Mondiale, July 1954) *and seems totally unaware of the physical evidence of the gas chamber which can still be viewed by any visitor to the remains of the camp. Her observations on the Hartheim castle —the former asylum and "euthanasia" center—are little more than references to a seemingly tenuous and episodic relationship between the euthanasia program and the concentration-camp system, while Hartheim had in fact been an integral part of Mauthausen since at least 1942 as a site for exterminations, the facilities for which included a gas chamber. Nor was Hartheim reserved for Mauthausen prisoners: many civilian and war detainees from Germany perished there as well. Thus, contrary to Wormser-Migot's implications, we have a very tangible relationship between the process of "euthanasia" and the operations of the concentration camps.*

In the same vein, it should also be noted that we knew of a railroad car outfitted as a rolling gas chamber—this again from Ziereis' confession, in which this piece of equipment was described in detail.

And so, according to the SS who ran the camp (and confirming the unanimous testimony of the prisoners who were able to learn such things), the Mauthausen camp, in effect, had three gas chambers: one "portable," one at the main camp, and the installation at Hartheim castle. What can one think, then, of the author's statement leading into her secondary argument: "We have attempted to demonstrate in our primary argument that there was no gas chamber at Mauthausen"? Why even attempt such a thing?

One can only be astonished in the face of such willingness to deny historical evidence with only the support of alleged testimonial confusion between "gas chamber" and "cremation ovens" among certain witnesses, and an "unconscious desire for a re-evaluation of the evils perpetrated in regard to the deported Jews." As for the last-mentioned factor, the following phrase tops everything: "The term gas chamber has become one of the leitmotifs of the heroic epic of the deportation—for the Jews with good reason; for the non-Jews in the name of a highly complicated process by which the psychologist and psychoanalyst are expected to support the conclusions of the historian."

In the "Western" camps the final weeks of the war were particularly dramatic and dangerous. At Mauthausen they attempted a final, systematic liquidation near the end of April 1945; some 1,300 were gassed at Mauthausen itself and another 1,500 at Gusen (where I was at the time), and this we knew without seeing official documents ordering the execu-

tions or understanding what the exact reasons might have been.

The plans for total liquidation at Ebensee and Gusen had already necessitated certain preparations at Mauthausen which were quite visible to all prisoners. Ziereis said (and it was confirmed by a representative of the International Red Cross): "On orders from Reichsführer Himmler" the complete extermination of prisoners at Mauthausen and Gusen was to be carried out. But Wormser-Migot does her utmost to establish that there was no such order: "The emptying of the camps was not ordered by Himmler himself. . . ." The author also tries to separate the deadly liquidation of the concentration-camp system from the "normal" workings of the system itself: "The emptying of the camps in the face of the Allied advances was not part of the structure of the system but only signified its collapse. . . ."

The final mass slaughters in the Western camps affected the entire inmate population of those camps, that is, principally non-Jews. In this regard, we have the following assertion by Wormser-Migot: "None of the SS leaders . . . or camp commanders admitted during their trials or in their memoirs to having personally participated in the crimes against the non-Jews in the concentration camps. . . ." One can only be astounded at such a statement, and for our purposes here I shall cite only Ziereis' own words: "I personally took part in all of the executions. . . ."

I must also call attention to the author's standards concerning historical records, by which she defines "firsthand" to be only information originating from official Nazi sources before May 8, 1945. Given all the available accounts and documents, regardless of origin, it is precisely these which give the historian his primary duties: to sift and collate his information, make interpretations if necessary, cross-check with other sources, separate the real from the fanciful and evaluate trial testimony, investigations, and historical documents from every possible source. In these circumstances, it should be unthinkable to regard, and often reject, as "secondhand" the Allied documents, trial confessions and other personal accounts, and even such physical proof as the Mauthausen gas chamber itself, simply because of arbitrary chronology. If we are concerned about the sanctioned methods currently applying to the study of contemporary history, we should raise a serious protest here: the Wormser-Migot book was written as a dissertation for a State doctorate.

3

The Dachau Gas Chamber

Information on the gas chamber at Dachau is based on a first-hand document—a report drawn up on May 25, 1945, by Captain Albert Fribourg, a chemical engineer and member of the French Army liaison unit with the American Sixth Army Group. The report was the result of two missions by Fribourg: the first to Dachau itself, shortly after the liberation (April 29) of the oldest of the German concentration camps. The second was on May 17 to the Ludwigsburg camp, where Fribourg was able to question Dr. Schuster, the man allegedly responsible for the extermination installations at Dachau and Auschwitz.

The first mission was carried out under difficult physical conditions: "There were at least a thousand naked, decaying bodies, men and women, in and around the building." His other observations were equally graphic.

Concealed by a curtain of trees behind the SS office building, the extermination facilities consisted of four cremation ovens, basement boilers, and a so-called "shower room" (marked by the proper inscription *"Brausebad"*) measuring 26′ × 20′ × 6.5′ and with a capacity of 100 persons.[1] The room could be hermetically sealed: there was a glass-sealed observation tube instead of windows, and two airtight metal doors; the walls were of closely jointed and polished fireproof brick. Near the observation tube, to the left, was a metal box with two buttons, green and red; to the right was a panel with four lights—pink, orange, white, and red. To the right of the door was another lighted panel, this time with three colors—red, orange, pink. Two sets of pipes, maneuverable

[1] Not to be confused with the real shower facility located in the main part of the camp; with a capacity of 500, it had two non-airtight wooden doors, a dozen windows, and a normal water system.

from the outside with four handwheels, went into the room from above. One set opened into the "shower room" through two grilled openings, and Fribourg noted that an electric ventilator was part of this system. The second system, all insulated, went across the roof and included a device which seemed to be a steam or hot-water humidifier. Buried low in one of the walls were two funnels slanted toward the floor of the room. The interior opening was covered by a grill, and access from the outside was regulated by a movable valve.[2]

In the same building were four small rooms officially designated for "disinfection of clothing"; here were the cylindrical containers of Zyklon pellets. In each room, electric air conditioners regulated the temperature (75°) and the humidity.

According to seven prisoners who were reportedly well acquainted with the operation of the gas chamber and were questioned by Captain Fribourg, the installation had been built late in the history of the camp and was used for newly arrived prisoners. The presence of the thousand nude bodies was further proof of its recent utilization.[3]

In conclusion, there can be no doubt that:

1. A gas chamber was installed at Dachau by the SS during the last days of their power.
2. Deaths by gas were only the smallest fraction of the Dachau death total.

[2] As Captain Fribourg noted in 1972: "This is important, since the Zyklon pellets were probably dropped from the outside through these funnels."

[3] Dr. Broszat, of the Institute of Contemporary History in Munich, was definitely in error when he said in a letter published in *Die Zeit* (August 19, 1960) that (1) the Dachau gas chamber was not still in service when the camp was liberated, (2) that there was no Brausebad (shower room) sign.

Dr. Krausnick, another associate of the Institute, has said (October 4, 1967) that gas chambers built toward the end of the war in various camps in Germany, including Dachau, were either considered as not being "in service" or had been relatively lightly used compared with those in the Eastern extermination camps.

Captain Fribourg noted in 1972 that "by all evidence the gas chambers located in the immediate vicinity of the cremation ovens were built to be used as such. I believe one can say without risk of error that only the rapid Allied advance prevented them from being used even more."

4

Buchenwald

The book by Eugen Kogon,[1] originally in German, remains one of the most important and carefully documented studies of the Nazi concentration-camp system. The author, a prisoner of the system for seven years, was arrested in Vienna on March 12, 1938, because of his fealty to the Austrian dynasty and his unconcealed hostility to the principles of Nazism, all of which placed him near the top of the Gestapo blacklist when Austria was invaded.[2]

French deportees at Buchenwald remembered Kogon as a loyal man, completely trustworthy, willing to help others, very intelligent, and often cheerful, despite a certain moodiness and nervous tension, which his friends attributed to the many narrow escapes from death during his long and painful captivity. He gives only the slightest attention to himself in his book, and one feels that his goal was to achieve the strictest, most anonymous objectivity possible. But despite the intentional unobtrusiveness of the narrator, his character is quite apparent: sincerity, a nobility of feeling, and a lack of political sectarianism (although he is devoutly religious—a Catholic—and an ardent German patriot, which might seem surprising in light of his strong opposition to the *Anschluss*). Still, Kogon has been both an Austrian monarchist and an authentic German patriot, and it is this devotion to Germany which made his objective account of its crimes so painful.

But the real value of Kogon's book lies not just in the character of the author but in his exceptional position as an observer of Buchenwald and, by extension, of the concentration-camp system as a whole; his seven years of captivity were ample opportunity for him to experience all of its contradictions and absurdities. At first he was simply a wretched and

[1] Eugen Kogon, *The Theory and Practice of Hell*, op. cit.

[2] But it might have been that the direct cause of Kogon's arrest was some Nazi officer's desire to take over his excellent library.

lowly prisoner, then an "old hand" with all the craftiness born of experience. With this status, according to the "rules" operative in all the camps, he moved into a relatively high position in the Buchenwald hierarchy: for many months he was secretary to the SS doctor and prisoner-boss of Block 50. These jobs gave him access to hundreds of confidential documents and provided abundant opportunity to gather the most precise information, not only on what actually occurred in the camp but on the "theories" which determined the course of events, that is, the orders and memoranda which directed, among other things, the rates of industrial production and human extermination.

A principal reason for the excellence of the book's information was that the final collation of documentation was conducted by Eugen Kogon himself, at Buchenwald, between April 16, 1945 (five days after the first American armored troops had arrived), and the beginning of May, under the direction of an intelligence team from the Psychological Warfare Division, and verified by a group of knowledgeable and reliable fellow prisoners.

The facts and circumstances of the Buchenwald story were thus starkly present and accessible—there in full force for everyone to recall. The camp archives were still available for verification, as were the prisoners who had been responsible for maintaining them (to explain when and how a given document had been written, altered, or removed). And finally, neither Kogon nor his informants had yet been resubjected to the rigors of "ordinary" life, where political prejudices and personal considerations might have, ironically, been detrimental to the truth of the Buchenwald experience. No matter what might be discovered and written about in the future, Kogon's efforts will, for all these reasons, remain an exceptionally valuable examination of this abominable and bizarre world.

In a brief summary, Kogon presents what in his opinion conceived and nurtured the Nazi concentration camps: first (with the goal of creating the mythical superrace), the coordinated effort to eliminate all elements considered "impure"; second, the financial advantages of resurrecting the ancient and discredited institution of slavery; then, "satisfaction" for the SS overlords; and finally, the large-scale use of prisoners for scientific "experiments."

There is an account of the early history of the system: from 1933 to 1936 there were a few camps, all controlled by the SA, which, except for Dachau, usually held fewer than 1,000 prisoners at a time. *There was scarcely a form of perversion and sadism which the SA failed to practice. These, however,*

*were always acts of individual bestiality. The system had not
yet reached the stage of mass organization.*

The SS began taking complete control of the camps in
1936: Dachau expanded, Buchenwald came into being (summer, 1937), then Sachsenhausen, Gross Rosen, Flossenburg,
Neuengamme, Ravensbrück, Mauthausen. Appearing after
1939 were Auschwitz, Lublin, Maïdaneck, Riga, Natzweiler,
Bergen-Belsen, etc. Kogon notes in passing what he calls the
"curve" of inmate conditions which applied to every camp:
*far below the "normal" level in the initial camp phase; rela-
tively stable in the ensuing years; near-disastrous in the first
six months of the war; relative improvement during the war
years, partly because of the increasing importance of manpower in war production; outright disintegration in the final
four to eight months.*

Kogon estimates that between eight and ten million persons
were interned in these camps during the twelve years of Nazi
rule, but he believes that the total number in the camps at
any given time was rarely more than one million. These
martyrs were taken from those elements of society which the
Nazis had decided should be eliminated, but the prisoners had
to be "classified" and marked for the extermination to be
methodical. The regime's political enemies wore a red triangle
on the left arm, major criminals a green triangle, the Jehovah's Witnesses (who considered Hitler the Antichrist), a
violet triangle. Wearing a black triangle were the "asocial"
elements, a broad category covering vagrants, pickpockets,
and other petty criminals, or those who might have been late
for work a few times. Jews wore a yellow triangle, sometimes
superimposed with a slanted, different-colored triangle (signifying "political," "criminal," etc.), to form the Star of
David. These markings were found in all the camps. Buchenwald had, in addition, a brown triangle for the gypsies (they
wore the black of "asocial" at Ravensbrück), a pink triangle
for proven or supposed homosexuals, and a seemingly endless
series of various other signs: a black-bordered triangle for the
so-called "race defilers," a black circle for a political prisoner
assigned to a disciplinary company, red and white circles for
those accused of trying to escape (who also wore an armband
with the word *"Blöd"*—idiot.) On top of all this, their standards for assigning these insignia were totally absurd.

Kogon then deals with the physical outfitting of the camps,
with their total lack of hygiene, water shortages (especially
severe at Buchenwald), and the hierarchies of guards and
prisoners. He describes the conditions of arrival at the camps,
the prisoners' daily routine, their work, punishments, and food

rations; each of these subjects provides precise, intelligently observed, and significant facts, all of which must be studied for a thorough understanding of the grotesque and sinister world of the "SS State."

Regarding the food situation, I should note Kogon's revealing citation of an exchange of letters involving Dr. Schiedlausky (who wreaked his havoc at Ravensbrück before becoming medical officer at Buchenwald, and whose 1947 trial at Hamburg I followed with keen interest); in one letter Schiedlausky states: *The field office of the Todt Organization* [the Nazi construction organization] *reports that post-mortems reveal a state of chronic starvation. They are unable to account for this, since the prisoners received supplementary rations for heavy manual workers. Their letter hints at the possibility of irregularities. . . . I discussed the situation with the officer concerned here, SS Major Barnewald. He states that . . . in the unlikely event of irregularities, they cannot be placed at our door.* Kogon then adds, *. . . there was, of course, honor among thieves. "In the unlikely event of any irregularities" indeed! Those who know about Barnewald and Schiedlausky can only smile bitterly.* If other witnesses like Kogon had not survived—that is, if the "master plan" of the camps had been successful—it is only with this kind of document that the story of Buchenwald could have been told.

After some revealing details on the profitable sidelines and copious embezzlements by the SS, Kogon continues his analysis of the camp's daily life: "recreation," such as it was, and "sanitation and health," an equally sorry state of affairs, and all very much like conditions in the other camps, with the few inevitable exceptions attributable to the whimsy and invention of a camp's commandant.

The author's chapters on the "scientific experiments" and the "special places of execution" would no doubt be the most difficult to document today, even with all the resources of archives and the confessions of some criminals, simply because so many of the witnesses disappeared. Among Kogon's "special places" (including some used for purposes other than execution) were the cremation ovens; the gas chambers in some camps; the spot at Buchenwald where "Detail 99" bludgeoned and machine-gunned thousands of prisoners; the hideous "bunkers" for solitary confinement and torture; the Buchenwald theater, used for torture and execution by day and cinema by night; the brothels in several of the camps; the "Little Camps" and tent camps where, as at Ravensbrück, the operative principle seemed to be execution by deprivation.

Kogon's examination of the medical "experiments" deserves special attention because the crimes themselves were among the worst committed by the Nazi regime, and because the author's status at Buchenwald put him in a uniquely advantageous position for having access to information.

A central theme of Kogon's work—and of the concentration-camp system—was the rationale for the Nazi crimes: reprisals and liquidations involving the millions of "inferior" race and other "undesirables." His subjects are widely varied: the destiny of the Jews in the camps;[3] the special fate reserved for the Poles; liquidation of Russian prisoners of war; the NN transports; executions of parachutists and secret Allied agents; special transports to outside gas chambers; extermination of tuberculars, invalids, and pregnant women; the especially cruel treatment of homosexuals; the suffering of the Jehovah's Witnesses and other "undesirable" sects; the treatment of children and adolescents.

Every page reflects thousands of crimes, but I do not believe that all of them should be viewed with the same strength of condemnation. The executions of secret agents, the parachutists, and the NN,[4] the persecution of the religious opposition—these, unfortunately, must be judged in light of the painful but obvious conclusion that no group is completely innocent. But the deliberate, scientific, massive slaughter of defenseless people—the millions whose only crime was to have

[3] Since the evacuation of the Eastern extermination camps was begun in January 1945, the survivors of such places as Auschwitz, Lublin, and Treblinka had to be sought out at Buchenwald, Ravensbrück, Sachsenhausen, or Mauthausen. Through this process Kogon gathered the terrifying depositions—from which he includes lengthy verbatim sections—from Jews who narrowly escaped death.

[4] The letters NN, the abbreviation for *"Nacht und Nebel"* (Night and Fog), marked a category of prisoner found in all the camps. The main thing we know is that, without exception, it caused a worsening of a prisoner's situation and corresponded with a higher decision that he would not survive but simply disappear into the "Night and Fog." Such poetic labels were one of the special affectations of Himmler's gangs. Here is what Kogon has to say about "Operation Whitecap" and "Operation Zephyr": These were *names for the roundups of Frenchmen to be sent to the German concentration camps. The state in which these men sometimes arrived can scarcely be pictured. In the summer of 1943, hundreds of Frenchmen, scantily dressed or completely naked, were unloaded at the Weimar railroad station, together with their dead, from cars into which they had been herded since Compiègne. They were then marched to Buchenwald in a group that included high government officials, professors, officers (especially of the French police), and engineers* (p. 189).

been born Jewish or Polish; the calculated annihilation of millions of Russian prisoners; the coldly conceived, coldly ordered, and coldly executed murders of children of "impure" race, pregnant women, the sick and the aged—all of these, even in view of humanity's criminal past and scarcely better present, remain a horribly special case. The originality of this massive machine of murder arises from one of its basic premises—a hatred that was based more on race than on politics or religion. All of the human slaughter latent in Hitlerian ideology became all too apparent during the course of its evolution. When we finally come to the last weeks of the war, when we see the frightening co-ordination (possibly accidental) that presided over the final exterminations, it seems that these "patriots" wanted to make it impossible for their fatherland to be reconciled with the rest of humanity. From the most insignificant noncom up to Hitler himself, the attitude seemed to be "since we are going to be destroyed, Germany should be destroyed with us." Psychiatrists tell us that a pathological hatred of others actually conceals feelings of self-abhorrence; in much the same way, the collective neurosis known as "racism" becomes, in the final analysis, a camouflage to hide a hatred of everything human.

The constant underground struggle between the SS and anti-Fascist forces in the camps is the serious and controversial subject of one chapter. Every camp had some form of secret prisoner organization, but the one at Buchenwald was exceptionally efficient. It has been established that the Buchenwald underground was originally a creation of the German Communist party and was augmented, little by little, by Communists of other nationalities, largely in proportion with military developments on the outside. The concentration camps, like a good tape recorder, reflected all the movements of the war: inhabited first by German Communists, then by Austrian anti-Nazis, who were soon crossbred with Czechs and Poles, then with the Dutch, Belgians, French, Russians, Greeks, and Yugoslavs. . . .

The first antagonists in this underground struggle were the "politicals" (German Communists) and the criminal convicts, to whom the SS tended to be partial because of a natural identification with an element they most closely resembled, and out of hatred for the politicals. In the end, the extraordinary discipline of the party put them on top, giving them control over many of the camp's interior operations: the offices where lists for transport and execution were made up, disposition of sick prisoners, surveillance and policing within the blocks, etc.

Even if one can make material sense out of these muted but bitter confrontations among the Communists, other political parties, common criminals, and the SS, I have doubts about the possibility of truly objective conclusions. This situation, I'm afraid, poses a moral problem in which everyone—no matter what he may say—brings his prejudices; that is, does one have to dirty his hands and compromise with the crime in order to save lives and values that might otherwise be lost? Or should one struggle uncompromisingly to avoid contamination by the shame of a shameful enemy? (What good is there in destroying an enemy if, in the process, we take on his hated characteristics?) This conflict is much more theoretical than real, or, more precisely, it is a reality only to an observer. The participant himself is already too deeply involved on one side or another when he blindly passes the crossroads where, to conform with the rules set by psychologists and philosophers, he was supposed to make his choice.

Kogon details the facts of the underground situation with sincerity and precision, and he puts some well-placed blame on the underground leaders for some of their actions (in particular, their selection of political enemies for extermination). And their positive actions were more often based on self-preservation rather than altruism, but the camp as a whole often benefited.

It was during the last days of Buchenwald that the secret prisoner organizations demonstrated their greatest power. Combining a concerted and general resistance with cleverly devised acts of individual intimidation (in which Kogon himself was a central figure), they were indispensable in saving 21,000 prisoners, *while a remnant of the 26,000 men who had been shipped out of Buchenwald during the final weeks were starving and suffocating in fifty railroad cars on the outskirts of the Dachau camp. . . .* (p. 257)

In his last three chapters ("The Psychology of the SS," "The Psychology of the Prisoners," "The German People and the Concentration Camps—After 1945"), Kogon presents the fruits of his observations and judgments; all are extremely valuable, but they do not exhaust the issues. But as a German, he is in a better position than foreign enemies to make such judgments about the monsters born in his homeland—the SS, the Gestapo, the Nazi political corps. Of the SS, Kogon notes that *they never doubted what their leaders told them; it was pleasant and often even convenient to believe. Doubt would have been treason, whereas their slogan said that their "honor was loyalty." They remained true to themselves.*

But, as was noted in an earlier citation of Kogon (p. 178), they were also expected to show a degree of "independence" and, in the absence of orders, to know "what had to be done." Does this independence account for the hideous slaughters of March–April 1945, when almost as many prisoners were killed as during the entire previous history of the camps? This proportion does not actually apply for the camps as a whole because of the millions who died during the long-term racial exterminations, but for the "non-racial" camps the numbers are striking (Buchenwald: 13,056 during the first four months of 1945, compared with 20,406 for the eight preceding years). I am certain that if we knew all the comparable figures for Ravensbrück, Bergen-Belsen, Mauthausen, Sachsenhausen, Dachau (where liberations came later and where underground organizations were less efficient than at Buchenwald, if they existed at all), the ratio would be even more startling.

Kogon's observations on the psychology of the prisoners would, understandably, apply even more to the German inmates than to the foreigners: *The prisoner was full of resentment toward the outside world. He had a sense of having been abandoned.* And more true for men than for women: while some male prisoners aided their comrades for the highest motives, others did so as they became hardened to the necessity of the task, and many became cruel to the point of sadism, largely because of repressed sexual desires. In the women's camps, only the most selfish in character became so hardened, while for many the incredible personal suffering only increased their concern for the needs of others. And finally, some of Kogon's observations seem more applicable to Buchenwald than to Auschwitz: *There is one psychological puzzle in the attitude of the prisoners toward the SS that is very hard to explain. . . . With a few altogether insignificant exceptions, the prisoners, no matter in what form they were led to execution, whether singly, in groups, or in masses, never fought back.* In my view, this phenomenon can be attributed to the crushing deterioration of nerve and spirit among the prisoners, and it was difficult to explain at Buchenwald because it was less apparent there than in the true extermination camps. This is an oversimplification, but a full book would be necessary for an exploration of the nuances of this situation.

I should also mention Kogon's observations on the particularly bad position of the French prisoners in the camps. As he says in one of his earlier chapters (p. 189): *By virtue of their temperament and their generally smaller physical resistance, the French suffered more from the hardships of camp life than other groups. Their marked individualism and usually high intellectuality involved them in many avoidable difficulties with which their fellow prisoners then often showed*

*little patience. A number of Frenchmen managed to establish
excellent connections in the camps. But by and large they were
badly off. It proved impossible to unify their ranks in order
to make them more capable of resistance, to increase their
value to the prisoners, for politically they were incredibly divided. Only the minority group of French Communists had
close contact with the camp underground at Buchenwald.*

Temperament? Marked individualism? High intellectuality?
Politically divided? Indeed so, but one might also cite a tradition of being well fed and a custom of non-brutal social
relationships. And perhaps their national Red Cross was less
than it should have been. Whatever the case, the French were,
because of both their virtues and their faults, physically and
psychologically "unsuited" for the concentration camps. Of
this there is no doubt.

In his concluding chapter, Kogon deals with the delicate
questions of Allied miscalculations after the war and of some
of the injustices perpetrated on the German people. It is possible for a foreigner to cheat justice on the issue of Germany's
over-all responsibility: while an observer might know of the
crimes committed by some Germans, he is often unaware of
the suffering and humiliation inflicted on other Germans, usually innocent, in "atonement" for these same crimes. The position of the latter was opposite in principle but still analogous
to that of other embittered Germans who considered themselves unjustly persecuted and feigned total disbelief when told
of Nazi crimes, especially the crimes committed in the concentration camps. So in these two positions the foreigner and
the bitter German found their moral comfort, but at the sac-
rifice of both spiritual values and the "realistic" chances of
avoiding similar catastrophes in the future.

THE BUCHENWALD GAS CHAMBER

(Details provided by Prof. A. S. Balachowsky,
member of the Institut de France, Director of
the Laboratory of General and Applied Entomology.
Letter dated November 11, 1971.)

I would like to confirm for you that no gas chamber
as such existed at Buchenwald, but that the SS leadership had planned to construct one around the beginning
of 1945.

For this purpose they had closed off an area near the
SS barracks, and construction of a building began in January. The camp underground knew about these develop-

ments and, accordingly, put into operation a regular system of sabotage which involved not only a slowdown of construction, but tearing down during the night or the next day what had been built the day before. So by March 1945 the construction of a gas chamber had become a dead issue.

This sabotage resulted in the deaths of a large number of prisoners. Besides the deaths, the Kommandos responsible for the construction endured the constant surveillance of the SS with their trained dogs, which mauled any worker who stopped to rest, even for a minute. But none of this prevented the work slowdown which effectively killed the project. This abortive construction effort was also hampered by the effect of the Allied bombings on the movement of materials.

The purpose of this projected gas chamber was the massive elimination of prisoners already at Buchenwald and of other Kommandos arriving in a state of complete physical deterioration. But from January through April, this extermination was carried out in Block 61, and the death figures were carefully recorded in the SS "minutes." These records were recovered when the camp was liberated and played a part in the Nuremberg trials. The numbers totaled as follows:

January	6,677
February	5,614
March	5,479
April	915

The figure is so low for April only because on the eleventh, at 4 P.M., the camp was liberated by Patton's army.

The executions in Block 61 were by injection. Every morning, a large number of syringes, needles in place, were laid out on a table, each filled with a concentrated phenol solution. With the help of a Kapo, an SS orderly took each prisoner and gave an injection to the heart, resulting in instant death.

The bodies could not be burned in the cremation ovens, which by then were barely functioning because of a lack of fuel—also caused by the Allied bombardments. So the bodies were thrown into huge pits near the camp, and the SS were dreadfully afraid of a disease outbreak from such a situation.

Such is the information I can give you, and I submit it as an eyewitness.

5

Former SS in Algeria

(An account by Nelly F., arrested in Algiers on
February 27, 1957, acquitted by a military
tribunal on July 25 after five months of detention.)

It was 3:15 in the morning when a squad from the 1st Foreign
Parachute Regiment came to search my home. They were
hoping to find a Moslem friend suspected (so I learned later)
of having worked with Ben M'Hidi. They were disappointed,
and so I was taken away. After a long and circuitous trip
with many stops (for other arrests?), the convoy arrived at
the Villa Sésini.[1]

The interrogation began with this gentle preamble: "We're
not sweet children of Mary here. Not the nice blue berets,
mind you, but those nasty green berets. It's five in the morning, and we want to have your friend in our hands by six.
And don't bother to look for help. To hell with chaplains and
lawyers around here! You won't see any at Sésini!"

The "normal" questioning was over in five minutes, and
then they took me to the torture room. This procedure was
not something reserved for me alone: it was applied systematically, and I learned from my subsequent cellmates that
they had all suffered torture and special forms of interrogation, many of them in the apartments where they were arrested.

After the torture, they made me go three days without food.
At mealtimes they took my only cellmate somewhere else to
be fed so that she could not sneak me any food. This cellmate
was Hamida, a young Moslem woman who did not remain
long at Sésini.

The man in charge of our cell was also an executioner,
a German legionnaire and a rather backward brute. He
worked under the direct orders of a group of Frenchmen—
two officers of the 1st REP and three PJ policemen (who
wore the uniforms of parachute corps officers, but whom the
soldiers did not salute).

[1] The former German consulate in Algiers.

Eight days after my arrest they took me out of the cell for another interrogation. When we arrived at the appointed place they took away my hood (they always put a hood over our heads when we left the cells), and I noticed another prisoner whom I already knew (Denise, a Frenchwoman, like me listed as a "Christian"). Her terrible appearance frightened me, and I could tell that I did the same for her.

This was also the first time I was able to get some idea of the physical arrangement of our surroundings. There was only one cell between mine and the infirmary, and this cell had been occupied for God knows how long by a Moslem boy who had gone mad. We were in the basement, and there was an air vent opening to the outside about six feet up. A corridor led from the infirmary and the cells to the area where the ordinary legionnaire-soldiers were quartered. Officers quarters and offices were located on the floor above. There were other cells elsewhere, where most of the prisoners were kept, but they never gave me a "tour" of that section.

A few days after my arrest I received a visit from a man we came to call the "oilman," simply because he talked about Algerian petroleum resources at every opportunity. He was a fat little fellow, always ready with a laugh; he was not really so bad on his own, but he always seemed to be present at the torture sessions. At any rate, he told me "there are people in Paris[2] interested in your welfare, but it won't do you any good, and it might be very harmful; our general doesn't like that sort of thing."

Also during these first days, someone came to my cell and asked if I would like to see "the doctor." I refused because the idea of a "doctor" in league with these executioners was totally inconceivable.

But finally the wounds caused by the ropes they had tied me with became infected, and one leg began to swell. So when I was asked a second time if I would like to see a doctor, I consented. This must have been around the beginning of the third week.

The infirmary was another world; the courtesy alone was marvelously impressive. There was one German male nurse who was older than the others; this was Karl, a former SS. There were also another German and another Frenchman, but it was Karl who set the tone. He was obviously respected by the others because of his personality and because he was an "old warrior."

When one entered the infirmary, Karl would give a good

[2] Author's note: I was one of the "people in Paris."

heel-clicking, stiff-necked German salute. He spoke to us politely, and we felt we were returning to the normal world.

I had been impressed first of all by the politeness of the situation and by the tactfulness. Karl said, for example: "I'm a ladies' man, but a sick person is something sacred, not just a woman." For women who had received breast and genital injuries from our torturers' electrodes, getting medical treatment was another atrocious torture, especially for the Moslem women.

Thereafter, he asked no questions, and the moral support he provided was not in assuring us we were "right," but in simply avoiding any allusions to the reasons for our being in prison. He would go about the duties of a nurse, talking about one thing or another—sometimes about himself.

Karl managed it so that the treatments lasted as long as possible; now and then, our guards would protest from the other side of the door, but Karl paid little attention.

My comrades also received regular treatments at the infirmary. (We were usually taken there in pairs.) Hamida had been alone in the cell for several days before I was brought in, and so we became a constant pair on the infirmary trips—and there were many movements back and forth. Besides Hamida, there was a woman I shall call N., who was no longer able to use her hands. (She had been tortured at the Maison-Carrée instead of the Villa Sésini; her assailants were from the "nice" blue berets—Lieutenant J. and Lieutenant C., who were said to have killed Audin.) There were also Mme. S., Fatima, Zaïa (who was acquitted a few months later), and an actress (Mme. D.)—these women were all Moslem. Then there was Colette, a poet and ardent Communist.

During three long periods every day, this situation gradually created an atmosphere that was almost familial. Whenever one showed up at the infirmary, Karl had something waiting: fruit, biscuits, eggs. . . . I can still see him warming some chocolate for us on his hotplate: "This reminds me of my mother," he said. "She always gave us chocolate on Sundays. . . ." Bit by bit, he told us his story.

Karl was fifteen or sixteen years old when he was recruited into an SS regiment. He was soon sent to the Russian front, where he was taken prisoner. For the first twenty-five days he was made to stay on his knees in a cell where there was no room to stand up; there were periodic "visits" for beatings. He was then sent to Siberia and became so seriously ill that he could see no reason for even trying to stay alive. But he finally came under the care of a Russian woman doctor, who changed his mind in that regard. And here in Algeria, doing the job of a nurse, watching over his chocolate, he said in his rather strange accent, "I would like to do the same thing for you."

After he was released he returned to Germany, only to find his home destroyed and his family dead. He signed on with the French Foreign Legion and did a tour of duty in Indochina. When his time was up he found that he knew nothing but war, and re-enlisted. And such was his long road to Algeria.

Karl never talked about anything that might have military significance, and he never criticized his superiors. I know of only one occasion when Karl lost his composure: this was when they brought Fatima to the infirmary.

She was very attractive; perhaps that was why her torturers worked without stopping for an entire night, performing, among other things, insertions of electrodes in her vagina. Captain F. brought her in himself, with a great deal of manly posturings (as a matter of custom, it was the soldier-executioner-torturer who escorted the prisoners). F. told her something like "things were overdone a bit with you. You'll be taken to the infirmary." He even made sure that the ventilator was opened and the bedpan cleaned (a chore that was often overlooked). Fatima was so ashamed that for a while she could not talk about what had happened, even to the other women.

When Karl saw her, he blew up. I remember one thing he said: "They kept telling us that we, the Germans, were the bastards. And we believed them. Now 'they' are more bastard than us. . . ."

Karl's solicitude extended to all the prisoners who came under his care. He would give up his day off if the more seriously ill needed attention. I also learned that he used his own funds to get the little things he gave us to eat and to buy medicines which were not normally allotted to his infirmary.

Among the soldiers' favorite expressions were how "horny" they were and how they were "going to go raise some hell." One day Karl said he too planned to raise some hell. The next day I asked him how it went. "I stayed here," he said. "Those fellows were all drunk, and somebody had to protect you women."

Karl's attitude toward the prisoners in my group, and I think toward all the prisoners, was not impulsive or subject to ups and downs, but was constant and considered. And I think Karl's example led some of the younger and more impressionable legionnaires to exhibit their better instincts.

Whatever the cause, there were other legionnaires, also German (a majority of those in the Sésini detachment and, I

think, in the 1st REP were German), who showed a degree
of pity, kindness, and even understanding.

As for the regular French military units, their attitudes toward prisoners could have been determined by political opinions. But there was no such situation in the Legion; they didn't
give a damn about a "French Algeria." A legionnaire did the
duty of a soldier, but a soldier without a cause.

When I was taken to be questioned for the last time they
did not make me wear a hood, and while passing through
the guardhouse I was surprised by the words and gestures of
encouragement from some of the soldiers. There were other
examples: while it often happened that the officer in charge
"forgot" to feed us for twenty-four hours or more (he was
always complaining about his workload, which was primarily
the torturing of prisoners), there were usually anonymous
hands slipping us something under the door or through the
air vent—a chocolate bar, a piece of fruit, a lighted ciga-
rette. . . .

The torture, the beatings, the abuse—all were the work of
a small team of executioners, usually a half-dozen in all. The
other officers and soldiers did not add to our troubles, although they were probably free to do so. I did not witness
a single spontaneous act of brutality by the soldiers during
the four weeks I was kept at Sésini; it was the torture gang,
small though it was, that made Villa Sésini a den of horror.

Plan of Ravensbrück

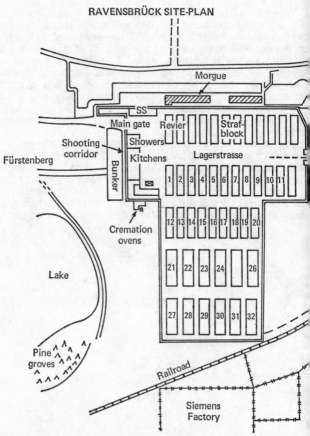

RAVENSBRÜCK SITE-PLAN

Morgue

SS

Main gate

Revier

Straf-block

Shooting corridor

Showers

Kitchens

Lagerstrasse

Fürstenberg

Bunker

1 2 3 4 5 6 7 8 9 10 11

Cremation ovens

12 13 14 15 16 17 18 19 20

Lake

21 22 23 24 26

27 28 29 30 31 32

Pine groves

Railroad

Siemens Factory

The unnumbered blocks were used as warehouses;
the ones I was able to enter were full of unused old
clothing.

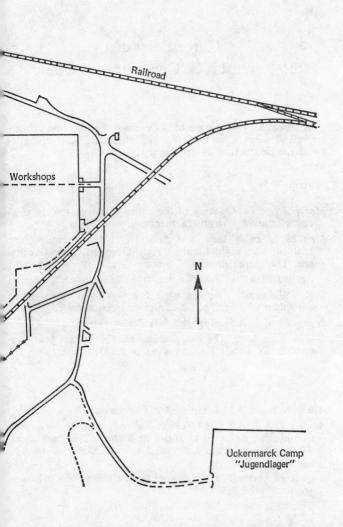

Chronology of
the Ravensbrück Concentration Camp

This chronology was assembled by cross-checking the prisoners' clandestine notes with the bits of information that survived the destruction of the camp records.

1939

March 23 or 24: Opening of the camp with a few score prisoners brought in from Lichtenburg.

May 18 (possibly May 29): Arrival of a larger group from Lichtenburg: Eight hundred sixty Germans, seven Austrians. There are "politicals" among them.

Arrival of a "religious" group from Mohringen.

June 29–August: Four hundred forty gypsy women arrive with their children. None of the children survived.

September 23: Arrival of the first Polish prisoners.

End of December: The last prisoner number of the year (according to Wanda Kiedrzynska) is 2,583.

1940

April: Number 3,114 is recorded (Armando).

August 2: Number 4,203 (Grete Buber-Neumann, a German Communist, delivered to Hitler by Stalin). There are about 4,000 women in the camp, and the death rate is four to eight a month.

August 23: Arrival of a transport from Cracow; the prisoners are numbered 4,308 to 4,433.

The total number of dead in 1940 was eighty-four.

1941

anuary: There are 550 gypsies in the camp.

April 5: Prisoner number 5,929 is registered (Hermina Salvini, an Austrian). There are about 4,500 women in the camp.

August: Number 6,723 (Adamska) is recorded.

September: Number 7,722 (Helena Dziedzicka, a Polish woman, part of a political transport with prisoners numbered 7,521–7,935).

December: Five Polish women are sent to Auschwitz for execution. An SS doctor circulates in the camp for a massive "selection" of sick and old prisoners who are to be sent later, in small groups, to Buch and Bernburg . . . to be killed.

1942

anuary: Number 9,543 (Hilda Synkova, a Czech political). Some Russian and Polish prisoners are executed.

ebruary: Nine hundred Jewish women leave for an unknown destination. They have been told that they are being sent to a munitions factory, but there is no such factory mentioned in all the mass of paperwork in the camp offices. Their fate is unknown, but one can assume (with horribly obvious good reason) that they died at Auschwitz.

ebruary 3 through March: Ten small transports leave for Berlin-Buch and Bernburg. The prisoners sent to Bernburg were to be gassed; those at Berlin-Buch were to be executed. How did the prisoners at Ravensbrück know all this? I am not completely sure, but one should not dismiss the possibility that the information came from the SS themselves, since they worked side by side, every day, with German political prisoners in all of the various camp service units.

March 24 or 26 and April 3: Two transports of 1,000 women are sent to be the first inmates of a "women's camp" at Auschwitz. The transports are made up primarily of Germans with "green triangles and black triangles"— criminal convicts, "asocials," and some gypsies. It is quite likely that some of these women were used as "police" at Auschwitz.

End of March: A transport of 800–900 women, mostly Jewish, leaves for Maïdaneck (Lublin). We know that they were executed.

April: Number 10,000 is recorded. There are about 5,500 women in the camp.

August: Number 13,055 (Odette Zelbstein from Saarbrücken). Two hundred women from the Strafblock and 180 "racials" are sent to Auschwitz.

Seventy-five Polish students are taken away for Dr. Gebhardt's medical experiments.

During the autumn: Six hundred women are sent to Auschwitz.

November: Number 14,843 (Claire Van den Boom, Belgian).

December: Eighty German Christian fundamentalists who have refused to work for the war effort are flogged; thirty-five die.

The *official* death toll for 1942, copied at the Revier by Zdenka Nedvedova, includes twenty-six for May, ten in June, nineteen in July, nine in August, nineteen in September, nineteen in October, fifteen in November, and twenty-eight in December.

1943

In 1943 and 1944 the Revier nurses counted sixty small transports of the so-called "insane" sent to the gas chambers at Linz; so we can arbitrarily accept a figure in the neighborhood of thirty for each year.

The *official* mortality for 1943: ten dead in January, twenty in February, thirty in March, thirty-nine in April, thirty in May, forty-three in June, thirty-two in July, forty in August, thirty-five in September, forty-seven in October, fifty-four in November, and eighty in December, for a total of 460.

March: The first labor transport is sent out.

April 29: Number 19,244.

A crematorium with two ovens is put into service. Until this date, bodies were cremated at Fürstenberg. (A third oven will be built at the end of 1944.)

July: Prisoner number 21,649 is registered.

August: Number 22,068 (Zdenka Nedvedova).

ptember: Number 22,476. During the month 150 Frenchwomen leave for Neubrandenburg.

ctober 31: Number 24,588 (my own).

1944

Beginning with January 1944 I have set up a chronological
ble in a somewhat different form—more precise than the
rlier chronology but with gaps nonetheless.

Column (1) gives the time period, month by month.

In column (2) I have entered the prisoner-numbers reg-
ered for that month (except for a few instances, I was un-
le to determine whether a given number should correspond
ith the beginning, middle, or end of a month); in any case,
e figure gives an idea of the total number of prisoners reg-
ered as entering the camp as of that month.

Column (3) is the actual population of the camp as offi-
ally recorded at roll calls. The difference between (2) and
) corresponds with the total of dead, released, or sent out
the various transports (execution or labor transports to
her locations).

In column (4) are the *official* death figures as recorded
the Revier, which are different from those recorded by the
litical bureau (column [5]). This difference, in column
), is very important in that it corresponds with the number
"executions" in the strictest, and individual, sense of the
rd.

Column (7) contains the information I was able to gather
the exterminations (the mass executions) carried out for
asons of illness or old age. Column (8) includes miscel-
eous information.

1944

1	2	3	4	5	6	7	8
January		17,300	116	120	4	Major *transport noir* leaves for Maïdaneck (Lublin): 800-1,000 victims. Transport composed of sick and all women over sixty years.	
February	27,887	18,362	57	68	11		
March	30,206	20,460	57	59	2		
April	38,818	24,720	90	91	1		
May		28,078	151	192	41		
June	42,158	30,849	84	153	69		Transports to Neubrandenburg, Hanover, Limes, Bartensleben.
July		34,041	85	89	4		
August	57,455	39,258	94	106	12		August 2-30: 14,000 Poles arrive from Auschwitz (including on August 24 a group of Franciscan nuns).
September	69,222	41,802	111	116	5		Warsaw evacuees arrive, housed in military tent. September 2: transport to Leipzig. October 2: transport to Zwodau.
October	78,230	35,260	185	192	7		
November	82,299	34,608	272	289	22	Final *transport noir* to Linz: 120 victims	
December	91,748	43,733	727	811	84	December 5-10: Auschwitz evacuees placed in Jugendlager, which will hereafter serve as a "relief" facility for Ravensbrück exterminations.	

1	2	3	4	5	6	7	8
January	?	45,733	1,221	?	?	Beginning January: "pink card" prisoners leave for Jugendlager. January 15: poisonings in Block 10 of main Revier: twelve of eighteen dead. January 28: 1,800 Poles leave for Jugendlager.	January 12: Deputy Commander Schwarzhuber arrives from Auschwitz. End January: Dr. Winkelmann arrives.
February	?	46,473	1,514	?	?	Beginning February: selection in the blocks by Winkelmann. Extermination by poison, starvation and shooting. Commander Suhren finds this too slow (according to Schwarzhuber) and orders gas chamber built.	
March	?	37,699	1,123	?	?	Gas chamber intended for 150 victims at a time is receiving women in groups of 170-80. Two "gassings" on Easter Sunday. The "Mittwerda" lists have 3,660 names.	
Beginning April	108,400	11,000	?	?	?	Mid-April: another 6,000 women to Jugendlager.	April 3: 300 Frenchwomen liberated by Swiss Red Cross.
April 23					12		Remaining French survivors liberated by Swedish Red Cross. April 30: Russian Army arrives.
End April	123,000				50		

INDEX